MAN BEFORE GOD

Thomas Merton on Social Responsibility

MAN BEFORE GOD

✳

THOMAS MERTON ON SOCIAL RESPONSIBILITY

FREDERIC JOSEPH KELLY, S.J.

DOUBLEDAY & COMPANY, INC., GARDEN CITY, NEW YORK 1974

Library of Congress Cataloging in Publication Data

Kelly, Frederic Joseph, 1922–
Man before God: Thomas Merton on Social Responsibility

   Includes bibliographical references.
   1. Merton, Thomas, 1915–1968.
BX4705.M542K44   282′.092′4 [B]
ISBN 0-385-09399-3
Library of Congress Catalog Card Number 73–10970

Grateful acknowledgement is made to the publishers, authors and copyright owners of works quoted in this book for permission to reprint excerpted materials. Excerpts from works by Thomas Merton: Foreword to *The Mysticism of the Cloud of Unknowing* by William Johnston (Copyright ©1967 by Desclée & Cie); *The Sign of Jonas* (Copyright © 1953 by The Abbey of Gethsemani, Inc.); *Conjectures of a Guilty Bystander* (Copyright © 1966 by Doubleday & Company, Inc.); "The White Pebble" in *Where I Found Christ*, edited by John A. O'Brien (Copyright © 1950 by Doubleday & Company, Inc.); *Seasons of Celebration* (Copyright © 1965 by Farrar, Straus & Giroux); *The Living Bread* (Copyright © 1956 by Farrar, Straus & Cudahy); *Seeds of Destruction* (Copyright © 1964 by Farrar, Straus & Giroux); *The New Man* (Copyright © 1961 by Farrar, Straus & Cudahy); *Disputed Questions* (Copyright © 1960 by Farrar, Straus & Cudahy); *The Secular Journal of Thomas Merton* (Copyright © 1959 by Madonna House); Preface to *In Search of a Yogi* by Dom Denys Rutledge (Copyright © 1962 by Farrar, Straus & Company); *No Man Is an Island* (Copyright © 1955 by Harcourt, Brace); *A Thomas Merton Reader*, edited by Thomas McDonnell (Copyright © 1962 by Harcourt, Brace & World); Introduction to *God Is My Life* by Shirley Burden (Copyright © 1960 by Reynal and Company); Preface to *No More Strangers* by Philip Berrigan (Copyright © 1965 by The Abbey of Gethsemani, Inc.); *A Penny a Copy*, edited by Thomas C. Cornell and James H. Forest (Copyright © 1968 by The Macmillan Company); Introduction to *Silence in Heaven* (Copyright © 1956 by Studio Publications in association with Thomas Y. Crowell); "Is the World a Problem?" *Commonweal*, LXXXIV (Copyright © 1966); "A Buyer's Market for Love?" *Ave Maria*, CIV (Copyright © 1966) and "Nonviolence Does Not—Cannot—Mean Passivity," CVIII (Copyright © 1968); "Letter to the Editor," *The Center Magazine*, IV (Copyright © 1968), reprinted with permission from *The Center Magazine*, a publication of the Center for the Study of Democratic Institutions in Santa Barbara, California; *Bread in the Wilderness* (Copyright © 1953 by Gethsemani, Inc.); *Breakthrough to Peace* (Copyright © 1962 by New Directions Publishing Corporation), *The Behaviour of Titans, New Seeds of Contemplation, Raids on the Unspeakable, Zen and the Birds of Appetite* (Copyright © 1961, 1961, 1966, 1968 by The Abbey of Gethsemani, Inc.), reprinted

by permission of New Directions Publishing Corporation; Introduction to
The Prison Meditations of Father Delp by Alfred Delp (Copyright ©
1963 by The Abbey of Gethsemani, Inc.); *Opening the Bible*, "Concerning the Collection in the Bellarmine College Library" in *The Thomas
Merton Study Center*, I, "War and the Crisis of Language" in *Thomas
Merton on Peace*, "A Catch of Anti-Letters" in *Voyages*, II, "Camus:
Journals of the Plague Years" in *The Sewanee Review*, LXXV (Copyright © 1970, 1963, 1969, 1968, 1967 by The Trustees of the Merton Legacy Trust). Excerpts from works of other authors: "Monastic Life
and the Secular City" by Thomas Landess, *The Sewanee Review*, LXXVII
(Copyright © 1969); "Is the Church Obsolete?: The Crisis of Religion in
a Secular Age" by William Robert Miller, *The American Scholar*, XXXVI
(Copyright © 1967 by the United Chapters of Phi Beta Kappa);
"Thomas Merton" by Patrick Hart, *The Lamp*, LXIX (Copyright ©
1971).

The author gratefully acknowledges the kind permission granted by The
Trustees of the Merton Legacy Trust to quote from certain specified
unpublished materials written by Thomas Merton.

To the monks of Gethsemani
spread throughout the world
in memory of our brother

Louis
with fraternal affection
in Christ

Contents

Biographical Data on Thomas Merton

1915   January 31, born at Prades, France; son of Owen Merton, artist (New Zealand) and Ruth Jenkins, artist (U.S.A.); baptized an Anglican.

1916   Moved to U.S.A. Lived at Flushing and Douglaston, Long Island.

1921   Death of his mother.

1922   Went to Bermuda with father; attended elementary school.

1923   Returned to Douglaston; lived with grandparents.

1925   Went to France with father; residence at St. Antonin.

1926   Entered Lycée Ingres, Montauban, France.

1928   Went to England.

1929   Entered Oakham School, Ruthland, England.

1931   Death of his father.

1932   At Oakham acquired higher certificate and scholarship to Clare College, Cambridge.

1933   Visit to Italy, summer in the U.S.A., entered Cambridge in the fall; studied modern languages (French and Italian).

1934   Gained second in modern language tripos, part one, Cambridge. Moved to New York.

1935   February, entered Columbia University.

1937   At Columbia, editor of 1937 *Yearbook*, art editor of *Jester*.

1938   January, graduated from Columbia, B.A. Began work on M.A. thesis.

1938   November 16, baptized a Catholic; Edward Rice, godfather.

1939   January, graduated from Columbia, M.A. September, teaching in Columbia University Extension.

1940   Spring, vacation in Cuba.

1940–41   Fall, started teaching English at St. Bonaventure University, Olean, New York.

1941   December 10, entered Abbey of Gethsemani, Trappist, Kentucky.

1944   March 19, simple vows.

1947   March 19, solemn vows.

1948 December 21, ordained subdeacon.

1949 March 19, ordained deacon.

1949 May 26, ordained priest.

1951 May, appointed master of the scholastics at Gethsemani.

1951 June 23, received American citizenship.

1955–65 Master of novices, Gethsemani.

1963 Awarded Medal for Excellence, Columbia University.

1964 Honorary LL.D., University of Kentucky.

1965 August 15, permitted to retire to hermitage at Gethsemani.

1968 September, departure for the Orient.

1968 December 10, died at Bangkok, Thailand, twenty-seven years after entering the Abbey of Gethsemani.

Foreword

In a recent period of only a few days, three letters
came to me from readers seeking information and light
about Thomas Merton. One letter came from a young
woman studying in Liberia, another from a teacher in
California and the third from a Protestant minister in
Washington. The three letters coming so close together
was doubtlessly a coincidence—all referred to a column
I had written some years ago on Thomas Merton—but
deeper than this was their being part of a pattern of
interest in this gifted and committed man, a pattern
that has been sustained by so many people since his
death in December 1968. It would be inaccurate to call
this interest a renewal or resurgence and leave it at that,
because those terms suggest that Thomas Merton's importance had declined but now, thanks to a lucky carom
that bounces authors between fame and obscurity, he
was again well known. But what is happening with
Thomas Merton is entirely different: it is an awareness
that is spreading to an even larger audience of citizens,
to those who may have "heard about" Merton when he
lived but were content to leave him on the margin of
their thought. This widening awareness has a depth of
feeling that is not likely to be washed away when a new
tide of cultic interest comes along. Those who are now
finding Thomas Merton have been looking for him with

considerably more than casual effort, and they are not
likely to let go of him casually, either.

While reading through this valuable and carefully
researched book by Frederic Kelly, a Jesuit priest who
has a long background not only in teaching the works
of corporal mercy and rescue but in practicing them
also, I kept thinking of my correspondents in Liberia,
California and Washington. How useful and enlightening
these chapters will be to them, adding to their own
knowledge of Thomas Merton the deft insights of Father
Kelly. Among these insights, perhaps the most solidly
based is the author's insistence that Thomas Merton,
however creative, independent and original he may have
been, was still struggling to make sense of the same
problems that hound the rest of us. Thomas Merton lived
in a monastery but he never used this physical isolation
as an excuse for moral or social apartness. On this large
point it is refreshing to see Father Kelly reporting that
Thomas Merton deliberately avoided Harvey Cox's *The
Secular City* when it was "must reading" in the mid-
1960s, preferring to wait ten years to read it, to see if it
could be held up by forces other than the popularity
lists. Merton, Father Kelly makes clear, wanted to share
the agony of the world's problems but he wanted also
to avoid joining step in what might prove to be a march
to quick-fix solutions. We are indebted to Father Kelly
for telling us not only what Thomas Merton chose not
to read for his current information but for informing us
what he wisely did read: among other sources, *I. F.
Stone's Weekly*. As for Merton's suspicions about the fad
value of *The Secular City*, they appear to have been
confirmed by Cox's later books, volumes that suggest
his trip through the secular city was mostly sightseeing,
one-stop at that.

At a time when the mysteries of the spiritual life are being explained in the public press by the likes of Chuck Colson and Rennie Davis—both say they have been re-born—Father Kelly's exposition of Thomas Merton pays homage not just to an authentic man of religion but develops the theme of what Merton believed authentic religion should be in man. Father Kelly provides the kind of introductory discussion needed by those who may be new to Merton, but he also offers the kind of rich documentary detail that will satisfy those who want to add still more shadings to what they have already read of Merton. It is a difficult dialectic but Father Kelly is a careful researcher and a clear writer. Thomas Merton should be served in no other way.

Colman McCarthy
Washington, D.C.

Introduction

Thomas Merton (1915–68) was a promising poet
and writer during his college and post-collegiate years,
but, on his own admission, he was a disorganized personality searching for meaning in life. After a rather
sudden conversion to Catholicism while he was a student
at Columbia University, he entered a Trappist monastery
in 1941, seeking to isolate himself completely from society
in the hope of finding God in solitude and prayer. He
did, however, under monastic obedience, continue his
writing from within the monastery. For close to twenty-
seven years he maintained this isolation despite the fact
that publication of his autobiography, *The Seven Storey
Mountain* (1948), brought him great literary prominence.
His early monastic writings were on strictly religious and
monastic themes, aside from his first six volumes of poetry,
published between 1944 and 1957. Though he remained
a strictly cloistered monk until just before his sudden
death in 1968, from about 1958 on his writings disclose
a vastly expanded social consciousness, and a much
broader awareness of man's place and function in the
world. The general context of his life shifted so that he
became publicly concerned about social problems and
the impact of social change on man's relationship to God
and to his neighbor. From the vertical, other-worldly devotion of his earlier works, Merton shifted his emphasis

to a direct, horizontal, deeply engaged, often militant concern for the critical situation of man in the world. Despite his physical isolation from society in the monastery, he was in fact not withdrawn but deeply involved in the world of his fellowmen. The reasons behind this new emphasis in Merton's life will be investigated in the course of this study of his teachings about the social dimensions of all men before God in the world of politics and economics, of social and cultural change.

This study will expose the development of Merton's concept of man's place in the world as shown through his many writings on a great variety of social topics. The investigation will bring out the implications of Merton's thought for modern life and action in a technological age. By exposing Merton's thought on the function of religion in human life and the process of the transferral of Merton's concerns from religious ones to contemporary secular problems, an insight can be gained into his concept of what the social dimensions of contemporary religious man should be.

The religio-social problems about which he was writing in the last ten years of his life covered a wide spectrum: the threat of nuclear annihilation; war and peace; violence and the nonviolent alternative for social change; race and racism; modern trends toward dehumanization through technology and urbanization; the mistreatment of minority groups; Marxism and the threat of collectivism; the unity of mankind and the need for reconciliation; ecology and the threat to environment from modern technology; renewal within the Christian Church; ecumenism and the dialogue of world religious philosophers; oriental spirituality; secularism and the process of secularization. Merton's thought on these subjects, his understanding of who man really is and what man should do in confrontation with these problems, is a valuable contribution to the understanding of contemporary religious man.

It is of interest to note the expansion of the roster of models that he used, the persons he deeply admired, those who might be considered his heroes. In his earlier years his models were taken mostly from the calendar of the saints: St. Bernard, St. Augustine, St. John of the Cross, St. Thérèse of Jesus and the monastic saints of the early Middle Ages, such as St. Anselm, among others. Though he continued his devotion to these prototypes, in his later years his admiration was also evident for those who might be considered secular saints because of their social involvement, such as Mohandas K. Gandhi and Dr. Martin Luther King. He greatly admired several modern literary figures such as Boris Pasternak, William Faulkner and Albert Camus, as well as several Latin American poets, because of their deep religious understanding.

That Merton came to look upon himself as something of a social critic is evident from the topics that he chose for consideration in the 1960s. The development of his social criticism and the peculiar contribution which he made to the social criticism of the turbulent era of the 1960s will be considered in the course of this study. The implications for the life of contemporary religious man which this investigation will develop will be drawn mainly from Merton's social commentaries.

From the analysis of Merton's writings, certain principles of life for religious man will become evident, basically man's need for true self-identity as a foundation for his freedom of action in social life. The recognition of who he is as a person before God and his fellowmen is essential to living a full human life. This study will be expository in the sense that Merton will be allowed to speak for himself. His ideas on religious man will be presented from primary sources, from his own statements in his various writings. The chronological development of his ideas is important in this study and will be emphasized to show the development of his social consciousness. Attention will be paid to the literary sources which Merton himself used for the development of his own ideas on social change and on the approach religious man should use in attempting to control and direct it.

This exposition of Merton's thought will be developed in five chapters. Firstly, Thomas Merton, the man and his writings, will be considered. Secondly, the emergence of Thomas Merton as a social critic will be presented. Thirdly, the notion of religious man in the writings of Thomas Merton will be analyzed and some principles of social action will be derived. In the fourth chapter, the focus of this study is narrowed to the social dimension of religious man. Fifthly, the specific social concerns of a truly religious person as presented in the writings of Thomas Merton are analyzed and exposed for study. In the concluding chapter a critical evaluation of Merton's specific contribution to the contemporary understanding of the situation of man before God and his relationship to his fellowmen is presented.

The primary sources of this investigation are the fifty published books of Merton, including his twelve volumes of poetry. Merton also wrote over 250 articles in a great variety of journals. Over sixty of these journals are major periodicals of political, religious or literary opinion. Seven of his books on social questions are actually compilations of articles published previously in these periodicals. He also wrote a large number of forewords, introductions and prefaces to books or collected works of others. His many book reviews are a valuable source of information about his social ideas. Besides these primary sources, many secondary sources such as reviews and commentaries on Merton's work were consulted, as well as the two biographical sketches so far published, *A Hidden Wholeness* (1970) by John Howard Griffin and *The Man in the Sycamore Tree* (1970) by Edward Rice.

Another source of valuable information about Merton was a visit to the Abbey of Gethsemani which the author made in May 1971 to research further primary materials. Though the author never had an opportunity to meet Merton personally, it was during that extended visit of ten days that the author was able to have long interviews with about twelve of the monks of Gethsemani who had lived for many years with Merton and had known him well. Another visit was made in September 1971 to a small Trappist monastery in Oxford, North Carolina, to interview three monks who were close friends of Merton. The information gained in these interviews provided valuable insights into Merton's character and development. It is well to note that though Thomas Merton wrote under his secular name, he was known to his confreres by his name in religion, Father Louis.

Several of the writings of Merton used in this study are still unpublished. Permission has been granted by the Trustees of the Merton Legacy Trust, which controls the copyright on these unpublished materials, to use certain specified documents. The author expresses his gratitude to the Trustees of the Merton Legacy Trust for this permission.

For the convenience of the reader, the important dates in the life of Merton are also listed.

Since this is a work derived from primary sources, the author in no way claims that the ideas expressed in

this study are all his own. By far, the substance of
this work is Merton's thought expressed either in direct
quotations or in paraphrase. The author's function was
to thematize, within a limited scope, the general outlines
of Merton's thought of man's place before God and its
social implications. Those readers who might wish further
explicit documentation for the sources of the statements
made in this study are referred to the author's previously
published work, *The Social Dimension of Religious Man
in the Writings of Thomas Merton,* University Microfilms,
Ann Arbor, Michigan, 1972.

I

THOMAS MERTON—
THE MAN AND HIS WRITINGS

In his later years, Thomas Merton was to reject and disavow *The Seven Storey Mountain*, which had brought him literary fame in 1948. He said, "The man who wrote that book is dead."[1] Many of his early readers never knew that in the 1960s Thomas Merton wrote about many of the themes which were barely hinted at in his autobiography: war and peace, pacifism, the threat of totalitarianism, race and racism, human poverty and dehumanization.

To appreciate this many-faceted, complex man as a preliminary to interpreting his social commentaries, various aspects of his life will be considered: Thomas Merton as poet, as artist, as a writer and man of letters, as a monk-priest, as spiritual director, as hermit, as contemplative, and finally, as a social critic. His poetic and artistic bent colored all of his writings in a variety of ways, as did his monastic vocation, but it was the contemplative mode, with which he approached his writings, that will be of deepest interest in this study.

* * *

Thomas Merton considered himself a poet to the end of his life, and volumes of his poems were published with great regularity. Since he had been a lonely child, he was forced to use his imagination to penetrate the externals of things. Early attempts at verse were not too successful and he claimed he was never able to write good verse before he became a Catholic. Though he won a prize at Columbia University for some verse that he "ground out" in the spring of 1939, he considered *Our Lady of Cobre*, written in Cuba during his trip there in 1940, to be his first real poem. His interest in Latin America, and Spanish and Portuguese poetry, would remain throughout his life, as was indicated by his many translations of Latin American poetry as a mode of making it better known in North America and through his constant encouragement of Latin American poets. It is of interest to note that when he packed his literary effects at St. Bonaventure University before his departure for Gethsemani in 1941, he destroyed one half-completed and three completed novels, but he sent all his poems, a carbon copy of *Journal of My Escape From the Nazis* (later published as *My Argument with the Gestapo*) and a journal he had been writing, to his former teacher and friend Mark Van Doren.

Though his first poem published as a Trappist appeared in *The New Yorker* in 1942, it was not until 1944 that James Laughlin of New Directions published *Thirty Poems of Thomas Merton*, hailed as "the major literary event of the past decade," a truly "epochal event," in the words of the enthusiastic reviewer, Sister Julie.[2] It was the beginning of a continued collaboration with Laughlin, who published eleven volumes of Merton's poetry over a period of twenty-five years, the last volume being published posthumously in 1969. Merton's development as a poet with a social conscience can be seen from the themes he selected over the years: standard religious themes at first, salted with many world-rejecting views in the early volumes of the 1940s and 1950s, to more mordant, conventional poetry in the early 1960s (*The Behaviour of Titans* and *Emblems of a Season of Fury*), into the social criticism contained in the anti-poetry of the late 1960s (*Cables to the Ace* and *The Geography of Lograire*).

The Sign of Jonas records his struggles with himself over his writing of poetry in the monastery. Thinking that such literary "distractions" were interfering with the contemplation he should have been seeking, for deeply ascetical reasons he resolved at the time of his ordination to the diaconate, March 20, 1949, to "stop trying to be a poet."[3] This he did, even though "there is something in my nature that gets the keenest and sharpest pleasure out of achievement, out of work finished and printed and distributed and read."[4] However, this resolution faded over the years, as was evidenced by the appearance of *The Strange Islands* in 1957.

Among the many reasons why Merton was so attracted to St. John of the Cross and was able to develop a lifelong affinity for the Spanish mystic was that St. John was primarily a poet, and Merton deeply appreciated his three greatest poems, poems that contained the doctrine which later filled John's three great books on mystical prayer. He looked upon St. John of the Cross as the greatest poet and greatest contemplative, as well as one of his favorite saints.

The influence of William Blake on Merton was lifelong, from the time he discovered Blake at the age of sixteen. His master's thesis at Columbia University was on "Nature and Art in William Blake." A critic said in 1956, "Merton followed Blake in adopting Blake's prophetic role in writing poetry so that at least a third of all Merton's poetry is a crying in the wilderness to a doomed world."[5]

In the 1960s, Thomas Merton occasionally used his poetry as a supplementary mode of communicating his ideas on social criticism and protest. *The Behaviour of Titans* (1961) had meditations on the Prometheus and Atlas myths, which afforded Merton the chance to "shoot poetic darts at some contemporary false gods."[6] In his "Message to Poets" meeting in Mexico City in 1964, he encouraged young Latin American poets to maintain their artistic integrity and independence in the face of the blandishments of commercialism and cultural conformity. He was of the opinion that "only poets are still sure of their prophetic sense that the world lies."[7] In an article commemorating the one hundredth anniversary of the birth of the Nicaraguan poet Ruben Dario, Merton called for poets to exercise this prophetic role, to put forth a new view of the world against the power types and technocrats and to hold out to the suffering of the world hope in God and mankind.

Merton used his poetic talent in collaboration with C. Alexander Peloquin to advance the cause of racial justice. Four of his "freedom songs" were set to music by Peloquin at the time of Dr. Martin Luther King's assassination and became part of the repertoire of the civil rights movement. One of Merton's poetic tributes to the late Dr. King was recorded by the Ebenezer Baptist Choir in Atlanta, and may well be one of the classics of the era of civil rights, in the opinion of Mrs. Coretta King.

The business of the poet, Merton wrote in a review article, is to reach the intimate, the ontological sources of life which cannot be apprehended in themselves by any concept, but which, once intuited, can be made accessible to all in symbolic and imaginative celebration.[8] He himself delighted in celebrating these sources of life in much of his poetry. A poem for him was an expression of an inner poetic experience, but the experience was far more important than the poem itself. When asked by a student at Brescia College in 1965 how he wrote poetry, he responded that he just wrote it. He would get an idea and put it down, and add to it, and take away what was useless, and try to end up with some kind of a poem. On the impulse of the moment, he could occasionally write excellent poetry without revision, as evidenced by *An Elegy for a Monastery Barn* and *Night Flowering Cactus*.

In a 1961 interview with a literary editor, Merton insisted that good religious poetry must present a challenge and be disturbing to the reader. He was outspoken against most Catholic poets, who, in his opinion, were content to write comforting and sweet-sounding verse. A true religious poet is able to point the way to God, and actually himself enter into the kingdom of the Lord, instead of merely telling people of the wonderful words and music he has heard coming from within the King's palace.

Merton confessed in 1966 that he had the opportunity to read only a few contemporary United States' poets, but he went on to say that though some had unquestionable maturity and excellence, few really say anything. "In the midst of technological and scientific virtuosity we find ourselves (many of us anyway) in a spiritual stupor. My own work is, in its way, a protest against this."[9] The anti-poems which were published in *Cables* and *Lograire* at the end of his life are examples of this protest. When he first held a printed copy of *Cables* in his hand he said, "At last I've said what I really wanted to say."[10] One of his fellow monks observed, "His anti-poetry was really Joycean. *Lograire* is Louis' *Finnegan's Wake*."

That Merton mellowed with the passing years is evident from his last volume of anti-poetry, *The Geography of Lograire*. In spite of the many sardonic descriptions of the technological world, it is also the most humorous of his poetry. The poems are filled with compassion for the world, and the bitterness therein is directed, not against the world, but against the dehumanizing institutions of the world.

A critical judgment of Thomas Merton's poetry is beyond the scope of this study, but one citation gives a lead to what future generations might think of Merton's place in the twentieth-century world of poetry. William Robert Miller, a Protestant lay theologian who has written on nonviolence, said:

> After the death of Bach, there were few composers who wrote sacred music and still fewer of any status who devoted much of their time to it. Except for Gerard Manley Hopkins and perhaps Thomas Merton, very little Christian religious poetry of serious literary quality has been written since before the French Revolution.[11]

* * *

Since Thomas Merton was the elder of two sons born into a family of artists, it is not surprising that an active interest in art and artists would be encouraged and cultivated from his earliest years. His father, Owen Merton, was a New Zealand painter who worked mostly in watercolors in various parts of the world and had several exhibits of his work. As Merton said, "My parents . . .

were in the world and not of it . . . because they were artists. The integrity of an artist lifts a man above the level of the world without delivering him from it."[12] His early recollections of his American mother, who died of cancer when he was very young, centered around her great ambition for perfection: "perfection in art, in interior decoration . . . in raising children."[13] In a short sketch of his ancestral background, he attributed part of his artistic temperament to "the Welsh in me that counts, that is what does the strange things, and writes the books, and drives me into the woods. Thank God for the Welsh in me and for those . . . Celts."[14]

Merton recalled some early attempts at drawing at the age of five, and great enthusiasm for books on medieval church architecture at the age of ten. During his grand tour of the European continent at the age of eighteen, a deep enthusiasm for Byzantine mosaics led him to visit the churches of Rome, which brought on the first formal interest in religion and induced him to read the New Testament for the first time. He appreciated the influence of his godfather, Tom, in guiding his literary taste and leading him to a deeper appreciation of art. Jacques Maritain's *Art and Scholasticism* was one of the source books he read with great interest while doing his master of arts thesis on "Nature and Art in William Blake" at Columbia University and he quoted it extensively. He relied on the same book for the article on "Art and Morality," which he wrote for the *New Catholic Encyclopedia* in 1966.

That Merton considered himself an artist is evident, not only from the sketches and calligraphies which he produced, but also from a variety of comments he made about himself. Ten pages of some of his cartoons and sketches from his Columbia University days are to be seen in Edward Rice's book *The Man in the Sycamore Tree*. He also gave many lectures at Gethsemani on art, sacred and secular, and wrote many critical articles on the same subject. In 1949 he complained about the difficulties of monastic life, stating, "It's not much fun trying to live a spiritual life with the equipment of an artist."[15] He referred to his own background as an artist in an article about his conversion to the Catholic Church: "I knew something of the life of an artist and intellectual because my father was an artist, and I was brought up, for better or for worse, as an intellectual."[16] In 1967 he excused himself before a perceptive critic of his social commentaries because he did, on occasion, preach too much and did deal in metaphors instead of concrete facts, with this statement: "It is the weakness of an artist, perhaps pardonable, because all artists are peculiar anyway."[17]

Merton was attracted to Zen art because, among other reasons, there is no artistic reflection. The work of art "springs out of emptiness and is transferred in a flash, by a few brush strokes, to paper." It is not a "representation of" anything, but rather it is the subject itself, existing as light, as art, in a drawing which has, so to speak, "drawn itself." It is a concretized intuition.[18] It was these free, concretized intuitions, capable of standing by themselves, which Merton was attempting to produce in his drawings.

One of the aspects of Zen art which attracted Merton is that the "artist," the "genius as hero," completely vanishes from the scene. There is no self-display because the "true self" that functions in Zen experience is empty, invisible and incapable of being displayed. However, there is considerable self-revelation of "Merton as artist" in a statement he made in the "Notes" which accompanied the public exhibition of his works.

In a world cluttered and programmed with an infinity of practical signs and consequential digits referring to business, law, government and war, one who makes such nondescript marks as these is conscious of a special vocation to be inconsequent, to be outside the sequence and to remain firmly alien to the program. In effect, these writings are decidedly hopeful in their own way in so far as they stand outside all processes of production, marketing, consumption and destruction.[19]

Merton emphasized the freedom and peace which these "graffiti" attempt to convey. These marks "desire nothing but their constitutional freedom from polemic, from apologetic, from program."[20] And ideally one who views these works should be "basically a peaceable man and content to accept life as it is, tolerating its unexpected manifestations, and not interpreting everything unfamiliar as a personal threat."[21]

Another aspect of Merton's artistry which should be noted was the late flowering of his professional competence as a photographer. The development of this new talent has already been described in great detail by his photographer-journalist friend J. H. Griffin. The title of Griffin's book is taken from Merton's poem Hagia Sophia, in which Merton said that "there is in all things an invisible fecundity, a dimmed light, a meek namelessness, a hidden wholeness. This mysterious Unity and Integrity is Wisdom, the Mother of all, Natura naturans. There is in all things an invisible sweetness and purity, a silence that is a fountain of action and of joy. It rises up in wordless gentleness and flows out of me from the unseen roots of all created being."[22]

In 1960 he collaborated with Shirley Burden in a contemplative photographic study of the Abbey of Gethsemani and wrote an introduction which highlighted the spiritual aspects of photography, seeing through this medium the abbey not so much as a sociological phenomenon but as a religious mystery. But it was not until he became a hermit in August 1965 that he had the leisure and the opportunity to develop his own talent as contemplative photographer.

He had learned much in photographic technique from such photographer friends as Shirley Burden, Edward Rice, Eugene Meatyard and especially John Howard Griffin, and used his camera as a contemplative instrument to the end of his life. His *Asian Journal* (1973) contains many of his truly artistic photographic studies. His camera work broadened the Renaissance dimension of the man. It was the photography of spirituality. In his nondocumentary work, Merton's focus was primarily on nature, and his pictures blend into a psalm of sorts, to stir the soul in a way comparable to the last of his fifty books. His life at the hermitage gave him more of the critical distance and perspective which are so necessary for a contemplative, as mass society becomes at once more totally organized and more mindlessly violent, so that he could concentrate on the microcosm of a flower, rocks or gnarled wood. In his pictures, as in his poems, he favored the sharp focus of detail and precision over the wide-angle lens of generality.

Though he had said in a statement about painting that "nothing resembles reality less than a photograph,"[23] he was later able to appreciate the Zen potential in a contemplative picture. One expert commentator said that his serious works were truly meditations. He did not seek to capture or to possess, and certainly not to arrange the objects he photographed. He lent his vision and his lenses to them in a real way, but he allowed the objects to remain true to themselves and reveal themselves. Much of the hidden Merton comes through his contemplative photographic studies, revealing the inner qualities of toughness, sensitivity, love of nature, silence and solitude.[24]

* * *

It is, of course, as a writer that Merton is best known to the general public. His autobiography, *The Seven Storey Mountain* (1948), was on the best-seller list in the New York *Times* for eighteen months and was so widely read that he soon became a major Catholic literary figure. Three volumes of poetry had appeared before this, as well as three translations of French books on monastic topics, but it was *The Seven Storey Mountain* that established the literary image which plagued him for the rest of his career.

The superiors at Gethsemani encouraged his writing from the very beginning of his religious life. He was assigned to do translations from French (three of which were published without mention of his name), write vocational booklets and a martyrology of Cistercian saints. Though he complained about "the writer who had followed him into the monastery,"[25] everybody calmly told him writing was his vocation. He had brought all the instincts of a writer with him into the monastery, and confessed that one activity was born in him and in his blood, "I mean writing."[26]

These instincts first became evident at the French *lycée* in Montauban, where he experimented with writing novels at the age of ten to eleven. By the age of thirteen he had the first notions of making writing his career. He continued to train himself throughout his student days in France and England by writing for school publications. In 1931 his first effort to see print appeared in the *Oakhamian*, a school magazine. He was editor of the *Columbia Yearbook* in 1937, as is evident from the number of pictures of himself spread throughout the book, as well as art editor of *Jester*. He wrote an unpublished autobiographical novel, *The Labyrinth*, during a summer at Olean, New York, in 1938, and two and a half other novels, all of which he destroyed when he was "leaving the world."

The fifty books published after his entrance into the monastery include three autobiographical items, two biographies published over his objections, six theological works, thirteen popular works on religion and devotion, ten volumes of commentary on social questions, plus one which he edited and to which he contributed both the Introduction and a major article, twelve volumes of poetry, plus one "macaronic" novel. There are also seventeen monastery publications of varying lengths designed to explain Trappist life and stimulate vocations. A 118-page book, *Thomas Merton: A Bibliography*, was compiled by Frank Dell'Isola in 1956. It includes, among many other items, a list of the foreign translations, forty-nine up to 1956, in eight European languages, as well as English, to which should now be added several Asiatic language editions, notably three in Japanese. One reason, among others, for the rapid dissemination of his major works in foreign languages is the existence of Trappist and Benedictine monasteries throughout the world. More than

250 articles were written for a variety of periodicals. Over sixty of these are major journals of political, religious or literary opinion which are easily available; others are small, obscure, "little magazines," usually of literary appeal, which had a limited circulation. Merton cultivated a penchant for writing for out-of-the-way "little magazines." Among his effects at Gethsemani is a marked copy of an article, "Big Little Magazines," about the popularity of these small magazines of limited appeal, their popularity among the "literati" and the number of prominent authors who started their rise to literary fame in this type of publication. He himself helped launch many first issues of these magazines by contributing an article, a poem, a drawing. He edited his own little magazine of verse and short commentary, *Monk's Pond*, at Gethsemani for just one year as an experiment (1967–68), and greatly enjoyed his new role as literary editor, as his editorial comments attest. In addition to all this writing, Merton carried on an enormous personal correspondence. Sometimes as many as one hundred letters a week would arrive for him at Gethsemani in the late 1960s.

The Sign of Jonas is the best source for the detailed story of "The Trials of Brother Louis as Monk-Writer." Spread throughout the book are many references to his struggles with his own conscience over his hyphenated identity, his troubles with slow and picayune censors, his lack of time for writing (one and one half to two hours a day at the most), his worries over the literary perfection of his work and his ambivalent attitude toward literary fame. Though he confessed that he preferred spreading manure in the field to working at his typewriter, he finally admitted that his lamentations over his writing had been foolish and confessed that it was impossible to stop writing altogether. In obedience to his abbot, who "shaped my whole monastic destiny by deciding I should write books,"[27] he finally resolved his inner conflict with "that shadow"[28] and settled down to compile what ultimately amounted to a "pillar of print" as a *Time* magazine obituary described his literary production.[29]

One intermediate stage of the resolution of his inner conflict between his life as a contemplative and as a writer was described in his article "Poetry and the Contemplative Life." This led to a considerable flurry of controversy, especially in Catholic magazines for the next several years, whetted considerably by a very critical review by Dom Aelred Graham, "Thomas Merton, a Modern Man in Reverse." Eleven years later, Merton published "Poetry and Contemplation: A Reappraisal" after the original controversy had long subsided. Two unpublished parts of the original manuscript of *The Seven Storey Mountain* appeared in 1950 and helped illuminate the hidden dynamics of Merton's inner conflict, and its resolution under obedience.

According to one statement of Merton, *The Seven Storey Mountain* was actually written between 1944 and 1946,[30] so that it reflected the ideas of a man who had been in religion only two to four years, barely out of the novitiate. But Merton spent three years "toning it down" because the censors were concerned about his scandalizing "the nuns in Irish convents . . . and young girls in boarding school."[31] In another place he stated, "In 1946 I wrote *The Seven Storey Mountain*."[32] When it was published in 1948 it became a literary sensation: 353,000 hardcover copies had been printed by 1963. By 1968, 600,000 hardcover copies had been sold in the United States, plus innumerable paperback copies. Published in both Ireland and England in 1949 under the title *Elected Silence*, it appeared in Danish, Dutch, German, Italian and

Spanish translation in 1950, in French in 1951, Portuguese, 1952, and Japanese, 1964. It found a surprisingly receptive audience in the uneasy, searching post-World War II years, a book suffused with spiritual zeal, perhaps the last great flowering of Catholic romanticism. In his autobiography, Merton wrote briefly in several places about topics of social concern which would later occupy him more fully: poverty, racial justice, peace and war, technological dehumanization, rejection of "worldly values," totalitarianism and ecumenical understanding. The literary editor of the autobiography described it as "a perfect book for someone who might no longer have any formal expression of religion yet knew something in life was missing."[33]

Over the years, Merton strove to correct the false public image of a monk which *The Seven Storey Mountain* helped to create. He admitted that it changed his life once he became "an author." How much, he did not know. As an author in a monastery, he felt like "a duck in a chicken coop."[34] He tried to adapt himself by forgetting that he was an author, and treated his autobiography as if it were the work of someone else. This was neither completely reasonable nor possible, yet it helped to prevent him from taking himself too seriously.

He later realized that to belong to God he had to belong to himself. He could not belong to people. In order to be remembered or even wanted, he had to be a person that nobody knew. "They can have Thomas Merton. He's dead. Father Louis—he's half-dead too. . . . I shall not even reflect on who I am and I shall not say my identity is nobody's business, because that implies a truculence I don't intend."[35] In a conference on prayer in 1951, he reflected that many promising authors have been ruined by premature success which drove them to overwork them-

selves in order to make money and renew over and over
again the image they have created in the public mind.
That reflection may well have a kernel of self-revelation in
it, since he often complained that his writing kept him
from the isolation and solitude which his growth in contemplation required.

He realized that his writings from 1957 on, which
turned more and more to questions of social concern, rep-
resented perhaps a successful attempt to escape the limitations that he had inevitably created for himself in his
autobiography, a refusal to be content with the artificial
public image that the book had created.

By far the best source of information about the mature
attitude of Merton toward *The Seven Storey Mountain*
is a rare, published interview of October 1967. The in-
terviewer suggested that they had to get *The Seven
Storey Mountain* out of the way first, and use that as a
point of departure. Merton's revealing reply:

> Yes, I'll accept *The Seven Storey Mountain* as a
> point of departure, and I'll be glad if we can de-
> part from it and keep moving. I left the book be-
> hind many years ago. Certainly, it was a book I
> had to write, and it says a great deal of what I
> have to say; but if I had to write it over again,
> it would be handled in a very different way,
> and in a different idiom. It is a youthful book,
> too simple, in many ways, too crude. Everything
> is laid out in black and white. I had been in the
> monastery only about five years when I wrote
> it. I still did not understand the real problems
> of monastic life, or even of the Christian life
> either. I was still dealing in the crude theology
> I had learned as a novice: a clean-cut division

between the natural and the supernatural, God and the world, sacred and secular, with boundary lines that were supposed to be quite evident. Since those days I have acquired a little experience, I think, and have read a few things, tried to help other people with their problems—life is not as simple as it once looked in *The Seven Storey Mountain.* Unfortunately, the book was a best seller, and has become a kind of edifying legend or something. That is a dreadful fate. I am doing my best to live it down. But that apparently is not a matter of much interest to anyone. The legend is stronger than I am. Nevertheless, I rebel against it and maintain my basic human right *not* to be turned into a Catholic myth for children in parochial schools.[36]

By definition, when an author writes an autobiography, a spiritual and a secular journal, he is forced to much self-concern and introspection. After Merton unburdened himself in *The Seven Storey Mountain, The Sign of Jonas* and *The Secular Journal of Thomas Merton* and left them behind, he talked less and less about himself and his writing became more obviously free of self-consciousness. His basic honesty and more balanced opinion of himself was evident when he disowned the "naïve essence," "intolerable defects," "callow opinions" and "youthful sarcasms" of these early autobiographical works.[37] He continued, without a doubt, to express his opinions, to give his views, sometimes vehemently, and to publish his insights, but with less notable self-concern, because the focus of his interests was broadening in the 1950s. From internal, domestic, spiritual, in-house problems of the Catholic Church, he enlarged his horizons to include more universally pressing problems. Changes in the world, in the Catholic Church, in the monastery and development within Merton himself forced him to shift the emphasis of his writing to more truly universal concerns. A glance at his bibliography will show that the number of "theological" and "spiritual" books declined after 1957, while all eleven volumes of his social commentaries have been published since 1960. The themes and ideas to which he gave poetic expression from 1961 on show a marked emphasis on social questions. His great friend and mentor in philosophical studies, Father Daniel Walsh, points out that the publication of *The New Man* (1961) was, in Merton's mind, a turning point in his career as a writer and thinker.

Among his effects at Gethsemani is a hand-drawn scale of evaluation of his books, done by Merton. On the vertical margin are the calibrations: best, better, good, fair, poor, bad, awful; on the horizontal margin the titles of his books are written in chronological sequence, from *Thirty Poems* (1944) to *Mystics and Zen Masters* (1967). Of the thirty books evaluated, his own judgment was: awful, one; bad, one; poor, three; fair, five; good, six; better, fourteen. Of the ten books in the categories from awful to fair, all but one (a volume of poetry) would be categorized as "spiritual" or "devotional" books.

There are many aspects of Merton's life and writings that merit detailed study. For example, he could be considered a spiritual writer, theologian, philosopher, Church historian, art and literary critic, book reviewer. Among his many other forms of writing, one genre Merton used was the "book review," of which he published over sixty. They were often the "board from which he dove into a topic which interested him" or "the Scripture text on which he launched his sermon."[38] The wide variety of the books he reviewed gives some idea of the broad range of his reading interests.

The paradox of Merton's hyphenated career as contemplative-writer remained with him, and was never fully resolved, but it ceased to bother him. His father in religion, St. Bernard, had resolved the contradiction in his own vocation, withdrawing from the world to become a more perfect instrument of the power and wisdom of God in the world. Merton would be able to do the same.

Reflecting on the futility of literary cares and preoccupations in the face of death, he realized that "my chief care, which is central to me, my work as a writer" was admittedly something which kept his "self" in view and hampered him, "still I do not feel very guilty about it." He put himself in the hands of God with the hope that "the love of God will free me." The important thing for Merton was simply "turning to Him daily and often, preferring His will and His mystery to everything that is evidently and tangibly 'mine.'"[39]

His expanding social conscience as a writer can be judged from the way he worked his life into another dimension in which the thoughts and emotions of the past counted for less and less. His experiences of the past became less and less *his* experiences, and were more and more woven into the great pattern of the whole experience of man, and even something beyond all experience. "I am less and less aware of myself simply as an individual who is a monk and a writer, and who, as a monk and writer, sees this or writes that. It is my task to see and speak for many, even when I seem to be speaking only for myself."[40]

By the early 1960s, he had finally given up trying to adapt to a "writing career" that was a "stupid fiction." He knew that he had to stop trying to adjust himself to the fact the night would come and the work of writing would end. It was in the present that he must give to others whatever he had to give without reflecting on death. "It is not a matter of adjustment or peace. It is a matter of truth, and patience and humility. Stop trying to 'adjust.' To what? To the general fiction?"[41]

When writing with apologies to an unbeliever, he admitted that he was not entitled to speak in anybody's name but his own. "I am quite sure that what I want to say will not be endorsed by many of the clergy, and it certainly is not the official teaching of the Catholic Church. On the other hand, I take my faith seriously and am not a priest for nothing. I am a Believer, though not the aggressive kind."[42] Still, he definitely spoke as a Christian and identified himself with other "Believers"— Catholic and Protestant—reserving the right to disagree with them and even to scandalize them a little.

One of the most revealing sources of information about Merton the writer is his "First and Last Thoughts: An Author's Preface," written in 1962 for an edited selection of his writings. He had learned from experience that controversy over speculative questions was not only a waste of time but seriously misleading, because an author was all too apt to follow the echo of his slogans into a realm of illusion and unreality. He tried to avoid writing simply as a propagandist for a particular cause or limited program. He denied that he was merely a spokesman for a contemplative monastic movement, much less was he purely and simply a "spiritual writer." He admitted that the books and articles of the period of the most recent transition, 1957–62, which contained the beginnings of his social commentaries, seemed to be at that time the most significant for him.

He looked upon his writing talent as a gift from God,

as a sign of the divine mercy, which he must give back to God by sharing it with others. While he agreed that monastic life was a life of hardship and sacrifice, he said:

> I would say that for me most of the hardship has come in connection with writing. . . . I am a writer, I was born one, and will probably die as one. Disconcerting, disedifying as it is, this seems to be my lot and my vocation. It is what God has given me in order that I might give it back to Him. In religious terms, this is simply a matter of accepting life, and everything in life as a gift, and clinging to none of it, as far as you are able. You give some of it to others if you can. Yet one should be able to share things with others without bothering too much about how they like it, either, or how they accept it. . . . Let me accept what is mine and give them all their share, and go my way.[43]

In this same context of gifts, he was grateful to God for three major ones: "First, my Catholic faith; second, my monastic vocation; thirdly, the calling to be a writer and share my beliefs with others."[44]

In the last decade of his life, Merton had learned to accept the totally paradoxical aspects of his life without apology, as a source of acknowledged insecurity, and as a sign of God's mercy to him. He was free at last from personal literary worries. His attitude toward his own works was well expressed:

> My unspoken (or spoken) protests have kept me from clinging to what was already done with. When a thought is done with, let go of it.

When something has been written, publish it,
and go on to something else. You may say the
same thing again, someday, on a deeper level.
No one need have a compulsion to be utterly
and perfectly "original" in every work he writes.
All that matters is that the old be recovered on
a new plane and be, itself, a new reality. This
too gets away from you. So let it get away.[45]

His isolation in the monastery was both a loss and a
gain to him as a writer. He considered his isolation as
sufficient proof that he could not possibly be a member
of the "Catholic Establishment." As were other writers
and theologians, he was merely trying to formulate a few
basic questions without getting into any controversies.
Toward the end of his life, in 1967, he said:

I think the main trouble (from the point of view
of the Catholic Establishment) is that I don't
follow the current fashions. I don't conform. I
have a few tastes and ideas of my own, and if I
want to go in the opposite direction to everybody else, I am likely to do it, without asking
permission. . . . I don't get too excited about
climbing on every bandwagon, because where I
am the bandwagons never come around. I am
too far off the state highway.[46]

In reference to the "problems" of the world, and the relation he should have to the world itself, he looked upon
himself as a voice,

a voice of a self-questioning human person who,
like all his brothers, struggles to cope with tur-

bulent, mysterious, demanding, exciting, frustrating, confused existence in which almost
nothing is really predictable, in which most definitions, explanations and justifications become
incredible even before they are uttered, in which
people suffer together and are sometimes utterly
beautiful, at other times impossibly pathetic.
. . . I am, in other words, a man of the modern
world. In fact, I *am* the world just as you are.
Where am I going to look for the world first of
all if not in myself?[47]

The Zen quality of his writing in later years is beauti-
fully expressed in the Japanese edition of *The Seven
Storey Mountain* (1964). "Therefore, most honorable
reader, it is not as an author that I would speak to you,
not as a storyteller, not as a philosopher, not as a friend
only: I speak to you, in some way, as your own self. Who
can tell what this may mean? I myself do not know. But
if you listen, things will be said that are perhaps not
written in this book. And this will be due not to me, but
to One who lives and speaks in both."[48]

One of his last statements on his social commentaries
was made in 1968. He asserted that his writings had attempted to formulate reflections on the modern world
and its problems with the peculiar perspective which a
life "out of the world" gives a monastic observer. He
never claimed that that perspective was the only true one
or that he had better answers than anyone else. He did
not think that he had implicitly judged others or asserted that he, as a monk, knew more than they. "I feel
myself involved in the same problems and I need to work
out the problems of the world with other men because
they are also my problems."[49]

A high school girl wrote to Merton asking, "How can a Catholic writer have the greatest possible influence on his public?" In a personal reply, Merton distinguished various types of "publics" and dismissed most of the types as being of no interest to him. The public he was interested in were the people who really needed to read him, for whom he had to have something important to say. "A writer must want to say it to the men of his time, perhaps even to others later. But it must be a bit desperate if it is going to get out at all. And if it is desperate, it will be opposed. Hence no writer who has anything important to say can avoid being opposed and criticized. Thus a writer who wants to reach, or help rather than influence people, must suffer for the truth of his witness and for love of the people he is reaching. Otherwise his communion with them is shallow and without life. The real writer lives in deep communion with his readers, because they share in common sufferings and desires and needs that are urgent."[50]

How did the public respond to Merton? In the upsurge of general interest in all books of a religious nature in the late 1940s and through the next decade, they purchased his books in vast numbers. Critical reviews of his books and poetry considered him among the leading Catholic authors, and foreign language translations insured an international influence. Eugene Exman, for twenty-five years head of the Harper & Row religious book department, considered the religious books of this period to be better written, better edited and profitable ventures for the big trade houses. He listed Thomas Merton, Bishop Sheen, Fulton Oursler and Henry Morton Robinson as the most popular.

In 1949, Merton was awarded the Golden Book Award by the Catholic Writers Guild of America for *The Seven*

Storey Mountain, as the "best non-fiction book by a Catholic writer." The same guild gave the St. Francis de Sales award to Merton for *The Ascent to Truth* in 1951. On June 5, 1963, the University of Kentucky at Lexington conferred on Thomas Merton the honorary degree Doctor of Literature. Since he was not allowed to attend the ceremony, a singular exception was made by the university to allow the degree to be conferred *in absentia*. No mention will be made of the fact that Merton was voted "best writer at Columbia" in 1937, as Merton recalled with wry humor, because the selection was "rigged" by campus politicians.

On the advice of friends, Merton started in 1963 to take measures to insure the future influence of his literary legacy. The Thomas Merton Collection was formally inaugurated as part of the Bellarmine College Library at Louisville, Kentucky, on November 10, 1963, later to be housed in a special Merton Study Room dedicated November 8, 1964. After consultation with lawyer friends, Thomas Merton indicated his desire that his manuscripts, tapes, drawings, photographs and kindred items, not otherwise disposed of, should be bequeathed to the Merton Legacy Trust. Three friends of long-standing were designated as trustees to protect the copyrights for the Abbey of Gethsemani, to insure the integrity of his literary heritage and to supervise any publication of the vast collection of unpublished material. The collection has grown to include over three thousand items, two thousand of which are in manuscript form, including also the bulk of his correspondence, still to be edited. One of the first responsibilities of the trustees of the legacy after the death of Merton in 1968 was the selection of his old friend and collaborator John Howard Griffin to write his biography, the publication of which is anticipated in the

near future. On October 16, 1967, the academic blueprint
for the future growth of Bellarmine College called for
the establishment of a Thomas Merton Studies Center, of
national and even international dimensions, for the study
of his work and influence in the broad fields of humanism,
spirituality and social questions. It is hoped that in due
course the studies center will sponsor various forms of
publications relating to the work of Merton and his influence.

When Merton entered the Cistercian Order of the Strict
Observance, commonly known as the Trappists, at the
Abbey of Gethsemani in Kentucky as a candidate for the
choir, he started to live as a monk, a *monachus*, one who
lives alone, not in the sense of being totally isolated from
all human companionship, but as a person in a small
community of men with similar ideals of isolation "from
the world," who devote themselves to penance, solitude
and prayer, a cenobitic form of monasticism. Since the
monks have to support themselves, they do so by the labor
of their own hands, usually in a rural setting. It will be of
interest to study the development of Merton's concept of
himself as a monk, a study which will reveal the development of his social consciousness, both in its breadth and
depth.

His choice of vocation was well described in his autobiography. His early life in France enabled him "to drink
from the fountains of the Middle Ages," which still retained many monastic flavors. With his father he visited
many ruins of ancient monasteries, and developed an interest in monastic architecture. He became conscious of
the "Church" as an all-pervading reality, so that he was
"always at least virtually conscious of the Church."[51]

A visit to the Trappist monastery near Rome in 1933
induced the fleeting thought "I should like to become a

Trappist monk."[52] A more effective desire for a religious vocation came after his conversion to the Catholic faith, formulated in September 1939: "I am going to become a priest . . . I ought to enter a monastery and become a priest."[53]

His lifelong friend Dan Walsh was very influential in helping him direct his early desires for the priesthood toward the Abbey of Gethsemani. Merton was first attracted to the Franciscans, but it was decided that his was not a Franciscan vocation. He did, however, teach English at the Franciscan University of St. Bonaventure for three semesters just prior to World War II and it was there that he decided that God was calling him to a more strictly contemplative life among the Trappist Fathers. One might speculate: did Merton have any attraction toward the Society of Jesus? Shortly after deciding to become a priest, he read "a little green book" about the Jesuits and visited the Jesuit Church of St. Francis Xavier on Sixteenth Street in New York City. At benediction there his desire for the priesthood was strengthened. He had known something about Jesuit life from reading the life of the Jesuit poet Gerard Manley Hopkins, but was not too interested in joining the Society of Jesus because "Dan Walsh didn't know any Jesuits."[54] At Walsh's suggestion, Merton made a retreat at Gethsemani in Holy Week, 1941, which confirmed his desire to become a Trappist monk. His actual mode of confirming the direction of his priestly vocation was reminiscent of St. Augustine's "*tolle, lege.*" While at St. Bonaventure, after his retreat, he opened the Scriptures at random and put his finger on the page: "*Ecce, eris tacens* [Behold, thou shalt be silent]" (Luke 1:20). Silence meant Trappist for Merton.

Merton entered Gethsemani on December 10, 1941, at

the age of twenty-seven, just twenty-seven years to the day before his death in Bangkok. Within the monastery community, he found that the life of a monk, like that of every Christian, was signed with the sign of Jonas because he was living more consciously by the power of Christ's resurrection. Merton felt like Jonas himself, because "I find myself traveling towards my destiny in the belly of a paradox."[55] The paradoxes of his life were not singular, but many, as he worked out his monastic vocation.

St. Benedict had introduced the vow of stability into the monastic rule, knowing that the limitations of the monk himself, plus the limitations of the community he lived in, formed a part of God's plan for the sanctification both of individuals and communities. By making a vow of stability, the monk renounces the vain hope of wandering off to find "a perfect community." Neither Gethsemani nor Merton were perfect in a variety of ways, but he persevered as a member of the community until his death on December 10, 1968, despite desires for a more perfect opportunity for contemplation which persisted well into the 1960s. One of the monks of Gethsemani who knew Merton well said, "It was a good thing the Abbot kept him in. If Louis were allowed to do one-tenth of the things he wanted, he would have been going in all directions at once!" As early as 1953 he realized that not only had Abbot Frederic Dunne, his spiritual father, "made" him a writer but had disposed his life, under Divine Providence, in a way that he had a greater opportunity to become a contemplative at Gethsemani. A monk, in the eyes of the abbot, had to be a real monk, a man of prayer and a man of God. He could not abide activism and a secular spirit being masked under a cowl.

Merton's search for God at Gethsemani implied a life

of penance and austerity, labor and poverty, as well as prayer, and he lived the full life of penance and labor at Gethsemani. True, the external austerities of life at Gethsemani were mitigated somewhat during his life there, some of the mitigations being partially due to his researches and studies, as well as to the positions he held in the monastery. But these mitigations were in the direction of freedom, not ease of life, freedom for the monk from a multitude of "devotions" and "practices" and above all "macerations." After all, the reason a man becomes a monk and withdraws from the world is primarily to find, not suffering, but joy and freedom, freedom from all the cares and burdens of worldly business and ambition. A monk desires this freedom not for its own sake but for the sake of union with God by contemplation.

Underlying the Cistercian insistence on manual labor, aside from the very practical reason of self-support, was a powerful insistence on "social consciousness." Just as the poverty and labor of the early Cistercians had an explicit reference to the social situation in which they lived and developed their social concern, so too Merton's own manual labor at Gethsemani was a means of identifying with the laboring poor. He always enjoyed his opportunities for outside manual work, particularly in the woods of the monastery, and kept some of it in his daily schedule as much as he could. In this respect, he was by no means an "ivory tower intellectual."

But in reality there is only one reason for a monk's existence: not farming, not chanting the psalms, not building beautiful monasteries, not wearing a certain kind of costume, not fasting, not manual labor, not reading, not meditation, not vigils in the night, but only God. And that means: love. For God is love. If the monk loves Him, he possesses Him. Everything else about the monastic life is only a means to an end. To possess God is to be "in God" and as with all other Christians the monk is "in God" only by being "in Christ." Being "in Christ" implied for Merton being concerned about all men as brothers in Christ and loved in Christ.

After many attempts in his earlier books and articles to "explain" the monastic vocation by emphasizing "withdrawal from the world," Merton realized the futility of trying to explain what is essentially a part of the mystery of God's love and mercy. A transition in his attitude about explaining his existence as a monk can be detected about 1955, when he started to plumb the mystery of silence and solitude more deeply. Though Merton talked much about monastic vocation and silence, he admitted that he could not explain it satisfactorily to himself, much less to others, but as a contemplative he was better able to understand it.

In another attempt to describe his situation as a monk, Merton shifted his terminology to try to highlight the existential "feel" of the monastic vocation, rather than provide explanations or definitions. His words presupposed some actual experience of having found God to some degree in contemplation.

> The monastic vocation is a spiritual charism . . .
> a call to hope . . . a call to an eschatological
> battle between light and darkness. . . . The
> very essence of monasticism is hidden in the
> existential darkness of life itself. . . . For God
> is to be found in the abyss of our own poverty—
> not in a horrible night, nor in a tragic immola-
> tion, but simply in the ordinary uninteresting
> actuality of our own everyday life.[56]

Merton experienced difficulty in trying to justify his own experience as a monk. In a part of the original essay that was not printed in the final edition of his *Seasons of Celebration* (1965) he said:

> the monastic life is wholly centered upon the tremendous existential silence of God which no-body has ever been able to explain, and which is, nevertheless, the heart of all that is real. . . . The monk cannot enter fully into this silence unless he renounces the vain attempt to explain or justify his own existence. The monk is essentially and before all a man of silence and soli-tude. . . . The monk's vocation is always a call to sink deep roots in the silence of God. . . . The monk is one who, alone and poor, yet rich in a love that is wide enough to embrace the world, feels within himself the silence of God expanding into a tremendous smile.[57]

Possibly Merton realized that this effort did not bring across accurately enough the "feel" of the mystery of the monk finding God, and himself, in the mystery of God's silence.

In reference to the monk as a preserver of the past, Merton stated that the monk does not, in fact, exist to preserve anything, be it even contemplation or religion itself. His function is not to keep alive in the world the memory of God. God depends on no one to live and act in the world. On the contrary, the function of the monk in our time is "to keep himself alive by contact with God."[58]

A monastic life that attempts to achieve contact with

God may sound very romantic. Merton dispelled that illusion.

> It is not. It is terribly prosaic. We spend much, often too much time, struggling to reconcile what cannot, what need not be reconciled. Perhaps we must confess that some of us came here with a kind of secret romantic enthusiasm in our hearts and that we are angry because it is all shot. . . . Meanwhile the water moves, the leaves move, things grow in silence, life reaches out all around us. The silence of God embraces us, consoles us, answers our questions (once we have the sense to stop asking).[59]

From 1956 on, Merton began to reflect on himself vis-à-vis the world from his monastic isolation, and began to consider himself a "guilty bystander." His *Conjectures of a Guilty Bystander* was published in 1966. His transition into a social critic was almost complete at that time.

Merton's studies of early monastic history led him in the direction of an ever more real freedom for the monk. He was concerned about a certain "ghetto mentality" that is liable to creep into monastic life, with an emphasis on unhealthy restrictions of real freedom. When a monastery turns in on itself, interpreting interpretations of interpretations of the rule, it becomes a ghetto.

> There is nothing of the ghetto mentality in St. Benedict. That is the wonderful thing about the Rule and the Saint: the freshness, the liberty of spirit, the sanity, the broadness, the healthiness of early Benedictine life. . . . St. Benedict never said a monk must *never* go out, *never* receive a

letter, *never* have a visitor, *never* talk to anyone, *never* have any news. He meant that a monk should distinguish what is useless or harmful from what is useful and salutary, and *in all things* glorify God.[60]

One can feel Merton's horizons expanding when he reads:

> Monasticism is often understood as "Christianity for the few," as an affirmation of sacred life in a sacred realm, the little, holy, self-contained, world-denying world of the monastic enclosure. Is this good? Perhaps, but it is terribly limited. . . . A monasticism that simply affirms the religious and cultural values (of the past), even on the highest "spiritual" level, has had its day. . . . It will "do" of course, but at the risk of evasion from the realities of our present situation, and the abdication of present responsibilities of God's word in the world.[61]

Mulling over Dilthey's statement "The monk is the true philosopher," Merton agreed, with reservations and distinctions, allowing that the problem of being a monk cannot be resolved merely by fidelity to a religious ideal. He introduced another dimension, fidelity to the inscrutable demands of God's love,

> a demand for which there is or can be no purely rational justification. Certainly no ideology will suffice to account for monastic solitude, the flight from the world for prayer and loneliness. All attempts to reduce this to an ideology can only undermine the monastic vocation in the world.

> A seeming ideology is perhaps necessary for be-
> ginners. But one becomes a monk precisely when
> he renounces the attempt to explain his vocation
> in terms of ideology.[62]

Merton embraced with enthusiasm the studies of Father Paul Evdokimov, the Greek Orthodox theologian,
writing on the Desert Fathers and the radical traditions
of both Eastern and Western monasticism. Evdokimov's
view of the Church and the world was summarized by
Merton: "Since the world presents a lying vision, the
unworldliness of the monk must be not only nonconformist, but provocatively so. The monk is in revolt
against the false claims of the world. This has to be
properly understood, yet the principle is true."[63] For
Merton, the literature of the Desert Fathers shows the
spiritual radiation of men who are outside history, men
who have taken history to themselves and transcended it,
who render it transparent, thus showing its inner and
secret dimensions. The monastic life, then, is not a mere
refusal of history. But for this understanding of history
to mature, there must be true sanctity, and truly monastic
sanctity.

The influence of his studies in oriental religions, which
expanded Merton's mental horizons tremendously, can be
detected in his formulation of the "search" of the monk
in the following terms:

> The monk—and the Yogi—do not seek a spiritual
> technique for its own sake. The monk seeks to
> transcend himself, to attain an inner and spir-
> itual unity, a purity of heart and of mind that
> will enable him to be enlightened by the Spirit
> of God and will bring him eventually to union

with God. Language that attempts to express this must necessarily be symbolic. It may prove baffling to those who are not moved to seek such things for themselves. Yet however cryptic the language of these professionals may remain, the striving for enlightenment, for liberation, for salvation, for union with God remains an empirical fact. Yogi and Christian contemplatives both exist, and there is every reason why they should compare notes. When we see them doing so, and when we observe that they are able to agree on a great number of things, including the rarity of saints and "true yogis," we cannot help but be grateful, interested and even impressed.[64]

The monk is, like it or not, by reason of his humanity, a man of and in the world of his fellowmen. Most monks, historically, have been laymen, not clerics, and the monk will attain greater self-understanding by identifying himself with his fellow laymen. So "a monk comes to realize that he is only required to be himself, and not to justify his existence. He is not an ethereal, unworldly being, nor yet a glorified canon appointed to chant the office. He can discover the true meaning of his vocation by drawing closer to the simplicity and labor of the layman which is his traditional lot."[65]

After Vatican Council II, which brought the Church into a new historical age, Merton adapted himself quite readily and eagerly to the new spirit of "openness to the world" and "dialogue with the world." This led to new efforts to understand the demands of a dialectic between "openness and dialogue" and "solitude and contemplation." The Cistercian tradition had emphasized "separation from the world"; the Benedictine tradition was ori-

ented to "dialogue with the world." Both are necessary
for modern monks. Separation, because the monk is essentially one who lives "alone," in a radical way cut off
from the agitation and confusion of the "world"; dialogue,
because the Church today is more than ever conscious of
her mission to bring Christ to a world that is agitated,
confused and near the point of desperation. For the modern monk, neither a "turning to the world" that would entirely destroy monastic solitude nor a "flight from the
world" that would leave him totally estranged from his
contemporaries can be allowed.

In view of the proposed renewal of canonical legisla-
tion in reference to monks after Vatican II, Merton insisted that to preserve the distinct Cistercian charism it
is necessary that Cistercian life should be entirely centered upon living, meditating and celebrating the Christian mysteries. Hence the need for a certain disengage-
ment, a freedom, a leisure without which such a continual
reflection would not be possible. Thus the chief obligation
for such a monk is to preserve for himself a certain dimension of awareness which cannot be authentic without a
certain depth of silence and interior solitude. A monastic
renewal that does not in some way envisage this dimension of spiritual understanding and direct experience of
the things of God will hardly be worth undertaking. Nor
should canonical definitions of monastic life give the impression that a monk has to be a special kind of a person,
a gnostic, a mystic or a prophet. The monastic vocation is
an ascetic charism, a special gift which is supposed not
only to make the monk holy, and by his holiness of life to
constitute him as a silent sign of Christ living and praying
in the Church, but to enable him to "taste and see that
the Lord is sweet" and to experience in his inmost being

the full reality of God's mercy to man and to his infallible promises to his Church.

What attitude should a monk have to the problems of the world? In an article written four years after he had been "silenced" because of his active engagement in the early days of the present peace movement, Merton made these reflections: the true approach of the monk is not to be sought in devising some explicit or implicit answer to any specific problem. The monk is not a man of answers, nor should he be concerned with either an optimistic or pessimistic attitude toward these questions, no matter how crucial they may seem. His life is an expression of eschatological hope and joy, of the presence of the Lord in His creation which He has redeemed and which, by the power of His Spirit, He will transform, a life of complete openness to the Spirit and hence openness to all that is blessed by God, whether in "the world" or out of it. So, without proposing this or that "answer" to the problems of social injustice, war, racism, technology, automation, etc., the monk will be all the more open, in compassion and love, to his brother in the world, because he is liberated, by his vocation, from the false answers dictated by the world itself. This openness is illusory unless it is paid for by obedience to the Spirit and to the word of the cross. While he does not provide answers, the monk does provide a service through contemplation, that is, listening in silence, questioning, humble and courageous exposure of what the world forgets about itself—both good and evil. Like the Staretz, Zossima, in Dostoevski's *The Brothers Karamazov,* the monk identifies himself with the sinful and suffering world in order to call down God's blessings upon it.

Someone may ask, "What does a monk do?" The question really intends, "What does a monk produce?" That is the trap. It assumes that to make life meaningful, the monk has to produce, to be on the market with some respectable product or service, or project some institutional image which the world could approve. But monastic life is not a matter of production, or of projecting an image, or getting results. Results are not bad; they are just secondary. What matters above all is that a monk be someone, not do something. By simply being himself, a monk, he gives positive witness to the presence of Christ in the world, a witness not so much ascetical as eschatological; a witness that is not so much a denial of the flesh as an affirmation of the Word made flesh, taking all things to himself in order to fulfill them and transform them in himself.

This witness of the monk should be a sign of freedom, a sign of truth, a witness to the inner liberty of the sons of God with which Christ has come to endow mankind, showing that the happiness of a Christian does not depend on the promises of this world. The monk gives this witness not by preaching but simply by living and incarnating in his daily life the full meaning of what he believes, namely, the Gospel of Christ, which teaches him to live in direct dependence on the bounty of God and to share that bounty with all men in a life of simple, honest work, study and prayer.

What sort of a person should a monk be? In a compilation of his twenty-one major essays on monastic renewal, published in a variety of journals between 1964–68, Merton gave many of his final observations on this question, in the process revealing in many ways what sort of a person "Brother Louis, the monk" really was. Though only God knows how closely in his own life Merton attained to the ideal he portrayed for the monk, he at least held this ideal out for himself and others. It is interesting to note that among the few items which Merton carried in his baggage on his oriental trip in 1968 were the relics of eight saints, which might give some indication of the religious models he held out for himself. He had with him relics of: St. Thomas of Canterbury, St. Thérèse of Jesus, St. John of the Cross, St. Charbel (a Lebanese hermit recently canonized), the Venerable St. Bede, St. Romuald, St. Peter Damian, St. Nicolas of Flue. A monk is definable not in terms of what he accomplishes exteriorly in quantity, but partially at least by what he is and by the tone and quality of his life. Since the actions and works of a monk are quite commonplace and even trivial, to describe his ordinary life is apparently to describe nothing at all. Hence, the fatal tendency to dramatize the monk's life with a description of his special costumes and decor, a unique behavior, a ritual solemnity and obsequiousness. This is an attachment to feudal anachronism, and such masks make the monk a museum piece. These cultural accretions have nothing to do with the basic monastic charism. Merton refused to paint a portrait of the modern monk along the lines of the work he did, his external mode of behavior or even his "praying for the world."

The monk is precisely a man who has no specific task. He is liberated from the routines and servitudes of ordinary, organized human activity, from what is merely partial and fragmentary in a given culture, in order to be free. Free for what? Free to see, free to praise, free to understand, free to love. This ideal is easy to describe, but much more difficult to realize. His freedom is supposed to enable the monk to face reality in all its naked, disconcerting, possibly drab and disappointing factuality, without excuses, without useless explanations, without subterfuges. His being called "out of the world" makes a monk free of its fictions, its myths, its rationalizations, its routine demands, its deceptive promises, its organized tyrannies. If the monk merely substitutes other myths, routines and tyrannies, even more petty than those of the world, the more he is to be pitied.

To the extent that he breaks through the limitations and the inevitable artificiality of normal social life, the monk is a "marginal man." The monk seeks to be free from what William Faulkner called "the same frantic steeple-chase towards nothing" which is the essence of worldliness everywhere. This freedom helps in the cultivation of a certain quality of life, a level of awareness, a depth of consciousness, an area of transcendence and adoration which is not usually possible in an active secular existence. Paraphrasing Lévi-Strauss, Merton said the monastic life should deliver the individual and the charismatic community from the massive automatic functioning of a social machine that leaves nothing to peculiar talent, to chance or to grace, so that the monk may "dip into the ocean of unexploited forces which surrounds a well-organized society, and draw from it a personal provision"[66] of grace and vision.

By being continually awake, alert, alive and sensitive to areas of experience usually not opened up in the midst of "worldly routines," the monk can more easily attain a certain perspective, an authentic understanding of God's presence in the world and God's intentions for man. The need for a certain distance from the world does not make a monk love the world less, nor does it imply that he never have any contact with the outside world. His mode of life should enable him to concentrate more on the quality of life and its mystery, and thus escape in some measure the tyranny of quantity.

The renunciation of the world is not a denunciation

nor a denigration, not a precipitous flight, a resentful withdrawal, but a "vacation" in the original sense of "emptying." The monk discards the useless and tedious baggage of vain concerns and devotes himself to the one thing necessary, the quest for meaning and for love, for his own identity in the peace of Christ. This deep desire for God, seeking the actual experience of union with God, draws a monk *to a totally new way of being in the world* which enables the monk to discover by personal experience and to verify existentially the inner meaning and value of human life on earth. Thus the monk pushes the very frontiers of human experience and attempts to go beyond, to find out what transcends the ordinary experiential level. Since all men are somehow sustained by the deep mystery of silence, of the incomprehensibility of God's will and God's love, the monk feels himself called to a more intimate communication with that mystery. This intimate communication leads the monk to explore the hidden meaning of the mystery of Christ in the world of our time, which presupposes on the part of the monk some understanding of the modern world, and of himself as a modern man.

What then is required of a monk is not a cold and perhaps stultified "unworldliness" which may at bottom be no better than egoism, but a Christlike selflessness and purity of heart which can take upon itself the sins and conflicts of the world and "baptize" them by his own repentance.

Interestingly enough, ministerial priesthood is not mentioned, because traditionally the greater number of monks have not been priests. Yet, Merton had also been ordained a priest. What further dimensions and self-understanding did the priesthood add to his life?

It is not to be imagined that the priesthood is something

essential to the monastic state as such. On the contrary, one can be a monk without being a priest. In early monasticism, only one or two of the monks in each monastery were ordained priests, to serve the needs of the monks themselves, not for apostolic ministry outside the monastery. In the course of history, the proportion of priests in the monasteries increased, so that a division of the monks into two grades was introduced. Choir monks were priests, designated to chant the long choral office, while the lay brothers did the more menial tasks for the support of the entire monastic community. In the Trappist discipline, though the priests also had a share in the manual work of the community, the distinction between choir and lay brothers was maintained. Such was the situation when Merton entered Gethsemani in 1941. In present-day Gethsemani many of these distinctions have faded. The two novitiates have been merged since January 1, 1963: type of dress, order of the day, offices within the community are more common to all, except for those offices which canonically require priesthood. The number of priests in proportion to simple monks is steadily decreasing. Merton himself had a part in this process of leveling the distinction between grades. Would Thomas Merton have entered as a candidate for ordination today? "If Louis were to enter today, I doubt if he would have become a priest. He probably would have remained a simple monk," observed one of his fellow monks.

As a choir novice, Merton was set on a course of training and studies that led as a matter of course to the priesthood. After his simple vows in March 1944 he had formal courses in philosophy and theology to attend, as well as his other duties in the monastery, to prepare himself for the subdiaconate in December 1948, diaconate in March 1949 and priesthood on May 26, 1949. The priesthood was a canonical requirement for the various administrative positions he was ultimately appointed to: lecturer in theology to the choir scholastics, 1949–51; master of students (an office newly created at that time, because of the increased number of scholastic candidates in the early 1950s) and theology teacher, 1951–55; and master of the choir novices for ten years, 1955–65. He was relieved of all these duties when he was allowed to become a hermit at Gethsemani in August 1965 and began his "life free from care."

During his years as a priest at Gethsemani his priestly ministry was directed entirely to the needs of the community, which included a large number of priests. His ministry was largely confined to teaching, spiritual direction and hearing confessions, and to conferences on monastic formation and asceticism, plus a variety of other topics, for the scholastics and novices. From about 1960 on, he gave Sunday afternoon conferences which were open to the entire community, attendance at which was optional, though the greater number of the community did attend. Prior to his Asian trip (September–December 1968) he never left the monastery for any public priestly ministry. Only once, in 1968, just before he left for Asia, did he have occasion to say a private Mass in the home of a friend, in English, and he came away thrilled with the possibilities that such a liturgy opened up for the more intimate participation of the faithful. He did on occasion hear confessions in the guest house, directed a retreat for some of *The Catholic Worker* staff in February 1962 and for a group of the peace movement, which included the two Berrigan brothers, in November 1964. During his hermit years (August 1965 to September 1968) he also gave a few conferences to groups of contemplative nuns who came to Gethsemani.

On his way to the Orient, he gave a few spiritual conferences to religious in New Mexico and California, and conducted a retreat for contemplative nuns in Anchorage, Alaska. He also gave a few spiritual conferences to religious in India before his death. The Trappist custom required that the Sunday sermon be delivered in the chapter room, and Merton took his turn for these, but they were not public. Homilies at the Sunday community Mass at Gethsemani, to which the public was admitted, were not introduced at Gethsemani until 1965, but by that time Merton was a hermit, and not assigned to preach. The homily he preached at the first Mass of Father Dan Walsh at the Carmel in Louisville in May 1967 was a rare exception by way of ministry outside his monastery, but it can hardly be considered public.

So, by and large, Merton was a monastic priest all his priestly life, and his active ministry was confined to the community at Gethsemani. Even there he preferred not to officiate in the monastic church once concelebrated Masses became the standard practice in the mid-1960s, though he would attend and concelebrate on Sundays after he became a hermit. Otherwise, his daily Mass was in private, preferably in Latin. On one occasion while still a deacon he fainted in the sanctuary during the community Mass; subsequently he was reluctant to perform specific duties in the sanctuary.

What did Merton have to say about the monastic priesthood, and his own priesthood, in particular? Surprisingly very little, in proportion to the tremendous volume of his writing. He had said in 1953, "As far as I know, nothing special has been written about what the priesthood means in a contemplative monastery."[67]

One very good index of his real lack of interest in developing this idea is the list of topics of conferences which

Merton gave at Gethsemani from 1962 on, when the custom of recording his conferences began. The Merton Studies Center has on file 196 tapes, each with four tracks, containing talks given to the novices, and later to the community, from April 1962 to September 1968. About twenty-five of the tracks are empty, leaving a total of about 759 conferences, most of them twenty-five minutes in length, others fifty-five minutes. Of these, 605 were given by Merton himself; interspersed with these are sixty-five by Father John Eudes Bamberger, fifty-nine by Dan Walsh and thirty by assorted guest speakers to the novices. Of the 605 Merton conferences, not one treats explicitly of the priesthood.

Another index is the twenty-four volumes of *Collected Essays*, published and unpublished, at the Merton Studies Center. They contain no essay on the priesthood. Among the unpublished courses he taught to the scholastics and novices on monastic history, the early fathers of the Church, asceticism and mysticism, etc., there are only four conferences with reference to the priesthood: "Maturity and the Priesthood," from his *Monastic Orientations*; "Mary, the Mother of the Priest"; "Priestly Models," on twelve monastic priests; one miscellaneous conference, "St. Pius X on the Priesthood." In his retreat talks before religious profession and major or minor orders, he did no doubt speak explicitly on the monastic priesthood, but the notes for these talks are unpublished. Nor did he himself write anything special on the subject. In his published material on the monastic priesthood, Merton said very little that was in substance new or original. Two chapters in *The Sign of Jonas* reflect his pious excitement and internal struggles about writing, either prior to his own ordination to the priesthood or immediately afterward. These chapters contain by far most of what Merton had to say on the monastic priesthood. The last explicit reference which Merton made to the monastic priesthood was in the context of the identity problem facing monastic priests. No doubt this same identity problem had also been Merton's down the years, though he never published anything on his own personal thoughts about it.

The priesthood inevitably brought an expansion of his social horizons. Since a priest is ordained not for himself alone, Merton realized that he now belonged to all men. The two most characteristic aspects of divine charity in the heart of the priest are gratitude to God and the increased realization of God's mercy to men, exercised through the priest. In Merton's mind, it is useless and illusory to look for some spectacular and extraordinary way of serving God, when all ordinary service is transfigured by love for God. The priesthood, for Merton, made charity for all men the easiest thing in the world.

At the Mass, Merton was both deepest in solitude, yet at the same time, he could mean most to the universe. As he said in *The Sign of Jonas* (1953), "This is really the only moment at which I can give anything to the rest of men."[68] Merton realized that the priestly character impressed on him at ordination made him, without ceasing to be himself, another Christ. As a priest, it was his task to help supernaturalize the world, so that through him the glory of God could seep into creation until things were saturated in a prayer of praise. The function of the priest is to be another Christ, in a far more particular sense than the ordinary Christian or the monk, to keep alive in the world the sacramental presence and action of the risen Savior.

The only other passage in which Merton referred to his priesthood at any length was written in 1950, for a collection of "conversion stories." In the context of the

Mystical Christ, the "whole Christ," he reflected on his baptism and his priesthood. He described the steps of his conversion, climaxing in the priesthood. "However great may be the grace of monastic profession, it still falls far short of the priesthood."[69] The effect of his priestly power was described as "a torrent of interior suffering which has only one function, to break you wide open and let everybody in the world into your heart." The absolute imperiousness of Christ's love in the heart of the priest leads to a deeper realization of the demand that "you love one another as I have loved you."[70]

Merton also wrote a book on the Eucharist, *The Living Bread* (1956), in which the ministerial priesthood was presupposed and in the background throughout, though there were no explicit references to the priesthood in general, or to his own priesthood. The entire book was written at the request of the leaders of the new movement, The Daily and Perpetual Adoration of the Most Blessed Sacrament of the Eucharist Among Priests of the Secular Clergy, canonically erected in Rome. Two chapters of this were published in *Convivium*, the annual publication of the Sacerdotal Union of Perpetual Daily Adoration. Then, too, Merton wrote a review of *The Divine Milieu* by Pierre Teilhard de Chardin in 1961, which was never published. In it he stressed the concern of Teilhard, as a priest, as one sent by Christ with a mission to love the world as Christ loved it, and therefore to seek and find all the good that is hidden there, for the recovery of which Christ died. In Merton's opinion Teilhard can only be understood in these priestly and eucharistic perspectives.

Toward the end of his life, Merton confessed that he had never for a moment thought of changing the definitive decisions he had taken in the course of his life: to be a Christian, to be a monk, to be a priest. Two months before his ordination, he wrote on the morning of March 14, 1949, "The priest cannot legitimately put himself first in any way whatsoever. Christ is always first. A priest does not exist merely for his own sanctification, but for the sacrifice of Christ and for the Gospel, for the people and for the world. . . . He has the whole Church on his conscience, and gives up his will in order to become an instrument for the salvation of the world and for the pure glory of God."[71] That statement was written in the morning. By the afternoon of the same day he had another insight into the monastic priesthood, and wrote rather bitterly, "I took up the *Spiritual Directory* to read the chapter on 'employments' because in point of fact that is what the priesthood means in a Trappist monastery: employments, jobs, business."[72] Does this lone, cynical statement destroy the value of the idealistic view in which Merton held the monastic priesthood? Hardly. It was more likely a complaint against the system which Merton wrote down and promptly forgot. But the fact remains that he published very little about his own concept of the function of a priest in a contemplative monastery, and said little about his own priesthood other than rather standard pious clichés. "Priesthood turned out to be a crisis in Louis' life—many of his problems came from his priesthood. If he had to do it again, no priesthood, simple monk," stated one of his fellow monks at Gethsemani.

* * *

The general public knew Merton best as a "spiritual writer," others were aware of his poetry, some also knew him as something of a "social critic." But within the monastery, he was best known as a teacher and lecturer, and later as a spiritual director. Most in the monastery were not aware of his great literary activity, nor were they particularly concerned about it. It was not until 1964 that mimeographed copies of his recent writings were given general circulation within the monastery and by then he was writing much on monastic renewal, which would have been of natural interest to the monks. Copies of his books, as they were published, might find their way to the library stacks, but no fuss was made over them, most of the monks being totally unaware of the number of books which he published. From 1950 on, he was lecturer in monastic spirituality and history, scripture and patristics in the choir scholasticate. During the years 1950–55, the series of six volumes of *Monastic Orientations* (unpublished) was compiled, which were intended to provide a general background for monastic and liturgical life, highlighting the intellectual and patristic foundations of monastic spirituality.

In 1952 the extraordinary influx of candidates for Gethsemani peaked when the community numbered 279. It is wrongly stated that this unusual growth started suddenly after World War II. Actually it began in the late 1930s. Merton himself was in part responsible through his writings for this great increase in vocations, not only to Trappist foundations, but to other contemplative monasteries as well. There were seventy members in the community when he entered in 1941, but this number continued to grow through 1952. The monastery was originally designed to house just about seventy, so old buildings had to be renovated, new buildings raised and new monastic foundations undertaken in other parts of the country. The reconstruction and renovation of the monastery lasted from the early 1950s until September 1967, when the renovated church was finally completed. Sprinkled through his journals and books are frequent references to the noise and confusion which this reconstruction entailed. Two new foundations were made under Abbot Frederic Dunne (1935–48): Conyers, Georgia, (1944) and Huntsville, Utah, (1948). Abbot James Fox (1948–68) arranged the foundation of Mepkin, South Carolina, (1949), Piffard, New York, (1951) and Vina, California, (1955). A failing Trappist community in Chile was "adopted" by Gethsemani in 1966. Another foundation was planned in Norway (the Bishop of Oslo is a Trappist) in 1965, but the project was aborted.

To insure the continued intellectual and spiritual formation of the choir scholastics after their novitiate, the scholasticate was reorganized in May 1951. A new position was created in the administration of the community, the master of scholastics (*Magister Spiritus*), and Merton was assigned to this position. With this arrangement, his work as spiritual director was formally begun. During his years as master of scholastics, there was an average of forty scholastics under his direction. His assignment as teacher continued, but he now had a more intimate, personal relationship with the young monk-scholastics. This was the area in which his real influence at Gethsemani was to be felt. As one of the monks observed, in reference to this appointment, "Louis was a Spiritual Director first; writing was strictly secondary."

From the early 1950s on, Merton desired more opportunities for solitude to deepen his contemplation. The sheer mass of numbers within the confines of the enclosure at Gethsemani made physical solitude very difficult to achieve. He began to think more and more of ways to become a "hermit" at Gethsemani. Finally, in 1955, he received permission from the abbot to arrange a small hermitage at the foot of the fire tower in the monastery woods, some distance from the actual monastery. Because of his duties in the community, it would require commuting by jeep, and Merton was notoriously inept with machines. Three days after he received the permission to begin a hermitage, the master of choir novices at Gethsemani was elected abbot at Piffard, New York, vacating his position at Gethsemani. Merton volunteered to be master of choir novices, and the abbot appointed him, on condition that he promise "not to make them all hermits."[73] Merton agreed, and the urge for his own hermitage faded, for a while.

His involvement in the spiritual formation of the community now deepened. He was required to give four conferences a week, usually thirty-five minutes in length (11:30 A.M.–12:05 P.M.), which the scholastics under temporary vows also attended. Actually, there was a series of four topics running concurrently in these conferences: monastic history, monastic spirituality and asceticism, the rule and observances, and liberal arts topics, such as poetry, art, world literature, religious themes in literature. Many of his conferences ultimately became the basis of articles for journals, book reviews, etc., and were later compiled into books.

But it was in private spiritual direction that Merton spent most of his time, other than very regular attendance at the choral office. Until well into the 1960s, the choral office at Gethsemani consisted of: the daily office, the little office of the Blessed Virgin Mary every day, the office of the dead on ferial days, the total of which required eight hours regularly. On major feast days, there was the full pontifical liturgy to attend in the monastic church. In addition to this, there were the common meditations in the church for all, thirty minutes in the morning, fifteen minutes in the evening. If Merton missed the

choral recitation of compline due to prolonged spiritual
direction in private, he would always make it up privately
in the chapel at night.

It is easy to see why writing was secondary. He would
interview each of the novices privately for one hour
weekly, longer if necessary, with a regularly posted list of
appointments. His door "was always open" to anyone of
the community who sought additional direction, novices,
scholastics and professed of final vows. Some idea of the
time spent on personal direction can be perceived from
the fact that from 1956–59, for instance, there were
twenty-eight choir novices at Gethsemani. That meant
that at least twenty-eight hours a week went to spiritual
direction of novices alone. As one of the monks said, "One
never had the impression that he was in any way rushed,
or that Merton was disinterested. He was a good listener,
and gave each one as much time as he wanted for direction."

Until 1963, Merton would regularly attend the two-
hour morning working period outside with the novices.
The two-hour working period in the afternoon was re-
served for writing. "After 1963, both working periods
were delegated to the Undermaster," said one of the
monks at the monastery. In connection with his duties of
spiritual formation, he also had a personal interview with
the abbot each week for one hour. He was also the personal confessor for Abbot James Fox for seventeen years.
Thus Merton could say in 1965, "As Master of Novices I
am supposed to guide and instruct the new ones who
have just entered. I have them for three years, give them
classes and so on. This takes most of my time."[74]

During most of his years as spiritual director of the
scholastics and later as master of choir novices, he had
little direct contact with the formation of the lay

brothers. But when the novitiates were merged on January 1, 1963, he also had charge of the brothers' formation. By that time the number of novices had dwindled considerably. During Merton's time as master of novices, only one out of five choir candidates persevered. When the new abbot took office, January 1, 1968, there were about 125 monks in the community. From 1962 on, tapes of Merton's conferences were played for the brothers in the kitchen during the early morning food preparation. A glance at the twenty-five-page list of conference tapes, preserved at the Merton Studies Center, will indicate the vast range of topics he covered. Besides spiritual formation, the brothers were also exposed to a rather full liberal arts course.

A series of Sunday afternoon conferences, usually one and one half hours in length, was optional for anyone in the community, but was generally well attended. One of his fellow priests recalled that "because of an innate modesty and a general reluctance to preach or address his fellow priests, Louis rarely spoke of prayer since it might reveal too much of his own prayer life, which he kept strictly private. However, with the election of the new Abbot on January 1, 1968, at the request of Abbot Flavian Burns, he did speak more frequently about prayer at these Sunday conferences until his departure for Asia in September."

Very little is published as yet about Thomas Merton as spiritual director. The best sketch to date is by his fellow monk and collaborator Father John Eudes Bamberger, who was both physician and psychiatrist in the Gethsemani community.

> The chief impression that Father Louis made on
> his fellow monks was that he was a true brother.

In our Community he surely was one of the best loved of people. His whole manner was open and outgoing and so constantly enthusiastic that he quickly formed community. Many of us as young monks came to feel that he was a friend and spiritual father. Behind his criticism, his directness and his independence, there was a great deal of obvious integrity and human affection. He was moved by an immense élan for all that pertained to the contemplative and monastic life. Though he continually stressed solitude, silence and meditation, yet he did so in an atmosphere of human warmth and wholesome insistence on the demands of good relations with the brethren. In spite of his steady complaints about being too busy with writing, direction and teaching, it was evident that he enjoyed all three. His conferences were always very thoroughly worked out in advance and invariably full of enthusiastic interest in his topic. He led discussions brilliantly, and with an easy firmness kept things right on the subject at hand. He was always much appreciated for these conferences which continued for eighteen years, regularly.[75]

Interviews with many of the monks at Gethsemani produced these observations about Merton as spiritual director.

He had a charism for spiritual direction without personal and emotional involvement . . . he was always adaptable . . . never pried . . . his conferences always showed excellent order and organization. . . . As Spiritual Director, he didn't have answers, he would help the individual find answers. . . . Louis didn't "push" mysticism and contemplation. . . . He met you on the level where you were. . . . He didn't try to sell the novices on St. John of the Cross. . . . He always respected persons . . . no probing into private affairs. . . . Louis was "reciprocal" in his concern for privacy. . . . Open to all, deadlines would kill him. . . . No waster of time, but it was never evident that he was in any rush. . . . If the conversation ever dwindled down to common talk, he would cut it off fast and definitively. . . . His spirituality wasn't porcelain perfection . . . he rarely used the word "perfection" in his later years. . . . His spirituality was a deep realization of God's mercy. . . . He spoke like a truck driver, his language was always concrete and direct. . . . Mercy was a life-theme for Louis. . . . He had a Gallic sensibility, he could be very earthy, no Anglo-Saxon Puritan. . . . He had a tremendous sense of humor, that is what saved him at Gethsemani. . . . He was really interested in only one topic, "Man's search for God." . . . His message was presented in such a way that he wasn't in the foreground. . . . He had an innate modesty, always reluctant to talk about himself. . . . There were no "Merton followers" in the Community, nor did he encourage it in the least. . . . He was reluctant to talk about prayer because it would reveal too much about him-

self . . . a great sense of privacy in his talks to
the Community. . . . He respected persons and
their freedom and didn't dig.

Many of his "spiritual books" and vocation pamphlets
hold out the ideal to which he was trying to guide his
charges. A deepening and refining of that ideal is evident from a chronological reading of his many writings
on spiritual direction.

A very personal eulogy was preached by Abbot Flavian
Burns at Gethsemani on December 11, 1968, the day
after news arrived of Merton's death at Bangkok. He
said, in part:

> His life was far from silent . . . since he was an
> artful minister of the Word. The world knew
> him from his books, we knew him from his
> spoken word. Few, if any, knew him in his secret
> prayer. . . . He was a skillful reader of the
> secret of the souls that sought his help. . . . We
> respected him as the spiritual father of our souls.
> . . . Those of us who had the privilege and the
> pleasure to deal with Father Louis on intimate
> terms, and submit our inner lives to his direction,
> knew that in him we had the best of spiritual
> fathers.[76]

One may legitimately ask, "Why was Louis never
elected abbot?" The answer is simple. He did not want
the position, he had made a vow never to accept an
election, and he had actively campaigned against the
idea. Abbot James Fox had announced his intention of
resigning, so that he too could become a hermit. In
December 1967, just prior to the abbatial election, Louis

posted on the bulletin board at Gethsemani a letter to the community which caused consternation and confusion. In "My Campaign Platform for non-Abbot and permanent keeper of the present doghouse" he listed five reasons why he should not be elected abbot, stated with deep humility that was disguised under a surface of flippant humor. The first reason given: "More than ten years ago I made a private vow never to accept an Abbatial election. This vow was approved by Dom James and the Abbot General, Dom Gabriel Sortais, both of whom accepted it with evident relief as a sign of the Lord's mercy and of his continued determination to protect the Order from disaster. I consider myself permanently bound by this vow and believe that under no circumstances should I consent to a dispensation. . . . My vow and my solitary life are the divine will for me." Quotations from this "Campaign Platform" were published in the *Unicorn Journal,* a copy having been sent by Merton to the editor.[77] So he did not make any particular effort to keep knowledge of his vow an in-house affair.

*   *   *

Merton's "search for God" had led him to Gethsemani. When he died at Bangkok, he was, of course, still searching. During his years at Gethsemani his search gradually developed, despite long and often deeply frustrating opposition, into a new form of modern Trappist monasticism, that of "a hermit's existence." Through his own historical research and writings, first tested out on his own community in conferences, later published in articles and books, he was able to show that the hermit idea had traditional roots in monasticism, particularly in the Cistercian discipline, and that it could be adapted to the needs of modern contemplatives. During his last three years at Gethsemani (August 1965 to September 1968) he was finally allowed to live in his own hermitage regularly and became the first Trappist "hermit" in modern times. As he said in a letter to a friend, "This week [August 20, 1965] I officially began the hermit life. . . . It is quite a step, and something that has not been done thus officially in the Order since the Lord knows when, way back in the Middle Ages."[78]

When he left for the Orient, his former abbot was himself a hermit, the newly elected abbot had already been a hermit for close to one and a half years before his election and a modern trend had been established in the Trappist tradition. Gethsemani now has several hermits living in solitude on the monastic property. Others who feel the need for more solitude are allowed to live as hermits for a time, on a trial basis. A small "communal hermitage" for five monks from the Trappist community has been established on a trial basis at Oxford, North Carolina.

In his early days as a professed monk, Merton's "temptation" was to seek transfer to a "more contemplative discipline" such as he imagined the Carthusians or the Camaldolese to be. In 1953 he took active steps to effect a transfer. He petitioned to be transfered to the Carthusians, and was refused by Roman authorities in the Congregation of Religious. Again, in 1960, a similar petition to be allowed to transfer to the Camaldolese was refused. He had written to the cardinal prefect of the Congregation of Religious asking to transfer to the Camaldolese Order of hermit-monks. He received an eight-page letter in reply, quoting canonical and legalistic reasons why the permission was to be refused. He was both amused and disappointed that one of the supposedly "telling arguments" for the refusal was a quotation from one of his own books in praise of Trappist life. He had also written to the archbishop of Milan, Cardinal Montini (later Pope Paul VI), asking his intervention to expedite the transfer. Cardinal Montini wrote a long, handwritten letter in reply, while on retreat near the ruins of an ancient Camaldolese monastery. The implication of Cardinal Montini's warm, personal reply by his reference to the "ruins" was: "Don't go on beating a dead horse."[79] When Roman permission was refused, Merton then set out to change the Trappist system from within, to allow more true solitude for mature monks who needed it. The theme of greater contemplative solitude was the warp of the fabric of much of his writings on the history of monasticism and on monastic renewal.

Merton wrote about thirteen articles on the history of eremitism in the Church. In 1955 he wrote a Preface to a book in French by Dom Jean Leclercq, O.S.B., on the life of a medieval hermit, later published in English, *Alone With God*, with Merton's Preface in 1961, a book which helped popularize the idea of hermits in the modern Church. Without a doubt, this guide to the hermit way of life and its function in the life of the Church had a great influence on Merton's ideas about the eremitic life.

The purpose of his researches into eremitism was to show that there has been a constant tradition in Western monasticism, and even within the Cistercian Order, which has not only recognized the rights of the solitary vocation in theory, but has even permitted certain simple, concrete solutions within the juridical and institutional framework of the monastic state. It has never been unusual, it has never been an aberration, for monks to seek and find solitude in the shadow of their monastery, without having recourse to indults, and without giving up their monastic vows.

Merton's researches finally convinced his own abbot of the legitimacy of the hermit life for a Trappist, so the abbot defended the motion eloquently in a general chapter of the Trappists in 1965. In *The Man in the Sycamore Tree,* Edward Rice gives a rather slanted view of Merton's long struggle to become a hermit, and the opposition from his abbot. The site for his hermitage was cleared by the novices in 1960, but, contrary to Rice's statement that the novices built the cement-block structure, it was "an outside contract job" according to one of the monks. That could hardly have been arranged, even by Merton, without the abbot's knowledge, since the abbot controlled the finances of the monastery absolutely. Details of the gradual improvement of the hermitage are given in John Howard Griffin's book *A Hidden Wholeness.* Prior to the construction of the hermitage in the woods in the late 1950s, Merton occasionally used an old tool shed five minutes walk from the monastic enclosure for solitude. He referred to it as "St. Anne's Hermitage." Permission to use the already prepared hermitage on a regular basis was soon granted to Merton, and he was released from his monastic administrative offices. He gave a particularly personal conference to the community on August 20, 1965, and retired to a "marginal existence" at his hermitage on the property at Gethsemani, there at last to attempt to find consistent solitude, which he felt he needed for deeper contemplation.

One of his essays reveals much of what he expected from the hermit life, and what he actually attained. He remained in obedience to the abbot, retained his status in the community, lived according to a daily schedule roughly like that of the monks in the community. He was not bound to choral recitation of the office, nor by assignments within the community, so that he had more leisure for contemplation. His life was not one of complete isolation. Rather, he kept up a limited correspondence (it was at this time that he started the custom of regularly mimeographed letters to all correspondents, which he regretted having to do), had a few visitors and limited contact with externs. A partial statement of his life as a hermit included this information: "I am to a great extent living on the margin of life at Gethsemani and concentrating on my own personal task, my own personal development, and my contacts with persons in my field, such as, first, poets and other writers and artists, and second, Buddhists, Hindus, Sufis, people interested in the mystical dimension of religion, whether Christian or others."[80] His own "personal task" and "personal development" surely implied a deepening of his own contemplative prayer.

As a hermit, he had new freedom for literary activity, including continued social commentaries, as the number of articles published during this period attests. But his real purpose was interior development. First of all, a full recovery of man's human and natural measure. He was trying to extricate himself from the myths and fixations which a highly artificial society, even a monastic society, imposed on him. He tried to realize and experience in himself the ordinary values of a life lived with a minimum of artificiality. His hermitage experiment at Gethsemani was only partially successful, however, and Merton sought an even more perfect solitude. One of the secondary reasons for the trip to the Orient was to find a better place for solitude, both for himself and others, for example in New Mexico, along the California coast, or in

Alaska. He sought a greater attentiveness to the Spirit, so that nothing could distract him from the sense of union with "the Christ who dwells in silence." He made it clear that he did not come there into the silences and solitudes of the woods to seek Christ, but rather, he believed, that was where Christ wanted to find him. He was seeking a certain critical distance and perspective by which he could weigh his own life before God in contemplation. It was his contemplative approach to life that gave Merton a unique quality as a social commentator.

* * *

Merton wrote much about contemplation, he wrote practically nothing about his own contemplation. The present consideration of the contemplative aspect of Merton's life will concentrate on the writings of Merton, his attempts to describe and explain the quality of life he sought, for himself and others, admittedly limited about the "inner reality" of the life he experienced.

The contemplative life is first of all life, and life implies openness, growth and development. Merton grew in his concepts of what true contemplation really is. The growth of his ideas can be judged from a textual comparison of two of his books on this subject, *Seeds of Contemplation* (1949) and the revised version, *New Seeds of Contemplation* (1961). Four new chapters were added in the revision, notably, "What Is Contemplation?" and "What Contemplation Is Not." The twenty-eight original chapters were clarified, refined and rearranged, but very little of the original was actually deleted. He explained his hesitation to use the very word "contemplation" in 1961, but continued to use it because his main purpose was to clarify certain obscurities and incomplete aspects of the original. *New Seeds of Contemplation* can be taken as an intermediate stage in the development of his ideas, in which very little evidence of his deep interest in Zen and other oriental ideas was as yet apparent. His active interest in oriental ideas dated from about 1958, and was more apparent in his writings in the 1960s. This growth implies a deeper religious experience, then reflective thought about this experience; finally this experience is woven into the texture of the life of the contemplative. Wisdom gained in contemplation enables the contemplative to realize a whole new dimension of existence, and changes his attitude toward the ordinary life he lives. He comes to appreciate his life more, in and for its very ordinariness.

Merton insisted that contemplation is basically ordinary, and in some degree open to all who are willing to submit themselves to the necessary self-discipline required so that one is free to be open to the mysterious action of God's loving grace. The process begins by learning to accept human values that people usually fear, from which they try to escape, values usually inaccessible to persons living a confused and surface existence. Some of these simple values are solitude, both physical and mental, inner silence, reflective communion with natural realities, simple and genuine affection for other people, admission of one's need of these things, as well as of one's need for contemplation. A little experience in contemplation leads one to realize that the ordinary actions of his everyday life are invested, by their very nature, with deep spiritual meaning. In this sense, prayerful contemplation is in itself ordinary.

In the early stages of the contemplative life one has to simply train himself, aided by God's grace, to a simple awareness, to an ability to see, to feel, to hear, to taste, to enjoy, to realize the love that is behind the reality of

God's loving concern. This prayerful attitude toward ordinary life leads to quiet and detached intuitions about everyday reality, to a simple peace, interior silence and detachment from material things as objects to be possessed or manipulated for selfish exploitation. There should be little or no preoccupation with oneself, and if the contemplative finds himself reflecting too much on himself, such reflection should be cut off abruptly. Simple contemplation involves no tensions, since the contemplative is enabled to let go of himself and everything else, knowing that everything that really matters is in the hands of a loving and merciful God. Such contemplation is not to be exaggerated, distorted or made to seem great in itself. It is essentially simple and humble, and one can enter into it only by a path of obscurity and self-forgetfulness.

One does not reach the summit of a life of personal and spiritual freedom to love without a most active and continual effort to effect a break with all that controls the senses, the emotions and the will on a strictly temporal and material level. Aided by God's grace, the contemplative reaches a certain passivity only after a tremendous struggle with his appetites. He is enabled to be open to love and to be peaceful, because the summit he has reached is lucid, spiritual and full of liberty. The true contemplative realizes in the depths of his being that he is no saint, but rather a sinner in need of God's mercy. Since he gradually frees himself from subjection to appearances and the opinions of others regarding himself, he is in no way anxious to appear extraordinary in the eyes of others. He is seeking to guide himself by the wisdom of God, not because it is contrary to the wisdom of men, but because it entirely transcends it. The more the contemplative considers prayerfully the presence of God in all things and events in his life, the more his life becomes centered on the one thing necessary, the realization of the presence and the infinite reality of the loving and merciful God.

The contemplative finds as he progresses that he becomes first and foremost a lover and his life is deeply imbued with love: love of God, of his fellowmen and the material things that were created in love. That is why contemplation is basically experience in love, mere theory is not sufficient. How can a lover describe or explain his experience in love? The attempt to do so necessarily distorts and limits the reality. Just as true love is attained by self-forgetfulness, so contemplation requires both a basic forgetfulness of self and leads to self-forgetfulness.

The struggle to cut through the falsity and delusion within oneself through the loving self-discipline required for contemplation will enable the contemplative to cut through the deceptive veil of selfish rationalizations by which the "world" adorns and conceals its empty wisdom.

The contemplative life requires a very practical and prolonged struggle against the adversary that is lodged in the exterior self. God's loving grace is necessary to sustain the struggle against the practical evil within oneself. This struggle is also sustained, not by a desire to get something for oneself, but by the desire to be open to love, so that one can give oneself in love. True contemplation is an austere and exacting vocation, yet it leads eventually to a spiritual orientation on which everything else, order, peace, happiness and sanity, must depend.

Contemplation leads not only to a deepening experience of love, but to a radical change in one's way of being and living, and the essence of that change is precisely a liberation from dependence on external means to external ends, to a complete liberation from all dependence on anything but freedom and divine grace. Real contemplation does not blind one to the world and make him unconcerned about his fellowmen in selfish withdrawal, but rather it helps transform one's vision of the world, enabling him to see all men, and the history of mankind, past and present, in the light of God. Contemplative prayer enables one to realize, in an obscure fashion, the infinite love of God which is at work behind the complexities and intricacies of human existence.

The contemplative life is lived in the depths of the subject's own spiritual being and adds a new dimension to his subjective existence, leading to a new kind of self-discovery, the realization of a new self-identity that is found only in the loss of the exterior self. The contemplative experience originates from the totally new kind of awareness of the fact that man is most truly himself when he loses himself. Man becomes himself when he finds himself in Christ. This paradoxical experience also leads to an experience of the transcendent, personal presence of God. The important thing in contemplation is not gratification and rest, but awareness, life, creativity and freedom. In fact, contemplation is man's highest and most essential spiritual activity, his most creative and dynamic affirmation of his divine sonship, the awakening of Christ within him. The contemplative experience is a personal charism which keeps man in touch with that which is most basic in human existence.

Contemplation has nothing to do with ecstatic visions or high states of spiritual enthusiasm. It is really simple openness to God at every moment, and deep peace, a realization in the very depths of one's being that God has chosen him and loved him from all eternity, that he really is His child and that he really is loved by Him, that there really is a personal bond and that He is really present.

The new quality of life, then, which contemplation gives, is an almost constant awareness of one's direct dependence on God so that he can receive from Him directly everything that comes to him, as pure gift, the delicate and personal attention of God to him in His merciful love, as a living and experienced reality. This quality of life is the result of a search for God, not in the abstract exclusion of all outside reality, not in a barren, negative closing of the senses to the world, but in an openness of love. God calls man in the depths of his own heart to an intimate union of His own Spirit and man's innermost self. This union is beyond words and beyond explanation because it is too close to be explained.

What does one actually contemplate? The answer could easily be stated: "All reality." Far from being absorbed in oneself with narcissistic navel-gazing, the true contemplative expands his horizons to include God, God's world and everything in it, past, present and future, and all men in their interrelationships. Nothing is excluded in a prayerful drive for unity, unity in love, knowledge and understanding. It is all part of an intuitive vision, "to see and enjoy God's beauty in creation, and to seek Him in and through that beauty,"[81] no matter how it is expressed, within oneself, within his fellowmen, within the beauty of the creation of a loving and merciful God. This drive for union in contemplation tends to reduce the subject-object relationship between the contemplative and the "object" of his contemplation so that both are drawn into a loving union. The individual temperament and personality development of the contemplative will, in many ways, determine the occasions that will start the prayerful process, whether it be the beauties of nature, an artistic composition (musical, poetic or plastic) or interpersonal relationships, whether human or divine.

It is not to be thought that one who has experienced deep contemplative prayer is always engaged in the depths or heights of contemplation. The "intensity" of contemplation can, of course, vary both in degree and duration, and, just as the experiences of human love are never constantly the same but show a kaleidoscopic variety in all ways, so too contemplative experiences are infinitely variable. An artistic temperament is in itself a good natural endowment for contemplative experience, since the artistic imagination, already well trained, easily leads to a penetration beyond surface phenomena to the inner reality. In order to see rightly, one must recognize the essential interdependence, impermanence and inconsistency of surface phenomena. On the basis of correct perception, one may proceed to a more realistic understanding.

Anything poetic, anything literary, anything creative, is steeped in possibilities of inducing the contemplative process by stimulating the imagination. Imagination has the creative task of making symbols. The imagination is a discovering faculty for seeing new relationships, for probing meanings that are special and even quite new. It enables the contemplative to discover unique present meanings in any given moment of the ordinary day. The imagination does not just create fictions. Very often it is able to discover real meanings, not just delusions. It not only discovers new correspondences and relationships, new symbols and new meanings, but it also creates nuclei around which everything can collect significantly. Without imagination, the contemplative process would be extremely dull and fruitless.

Religious belief colors one's contemplation. A Christian contemplative would see everything from the perspective of his Christian belief. For him it is extremely important that social and political events, even such things as national policy for economic expansion and military defense, be the objects of contemplation and seen in the light of basic religious understanding of total reality. This requires the development of a genuine and deep historical consciousness on the part of the Christian contemplative, since Christ is still revealing Himself in the critical events of our time. Contemplative prayer, informed by a deep sense of contemporary human anguish, will become more real with the growth of genuine compassion. This historical consciousness, seeing events in the light of the *kairos* which Christ has established, will lead to a more maturely human and Christian awareness of the meaning of the events of the contemporary world.

Specifically Christian contemplation is first of all a response to God's manifestation of Himself in His Word. It is at the same time a contemplative understanding of the whole of creation in the light of the Resurrection, the new creation, or the "new aeon." It leads to a spiritual awareness of the mystery of God at work in history, building up the Church as the fullness of Christ. Christian contemplation is thus centered, not on a vague inner appreciation of man's own spiritual essence, but upon the cross of Christ, which gives a deeper understanding of all the kenotic aspects that mature Christian life requires. Just as Christ "emptied Himself," so the Christian contemplative strives to empty himself of self-concern and self-awareness. He tries to get rid of introspection and introversion and go beyond the limits imposed by subjective absorption in his own interiority. All deliberate self-cultivation in contemplation tends to cut one off from the mysterious but indispensable contact with "the way" by which God is guiding him to deeper union with Himself.

A true contemplative is not one who takes himself and his prayer seriously, but one who takes God seriously and tries to see the workings of God in his life. His contemplation is his response to God's mysterious presence and activity within himself. He suddenly realizes that he is confronted with the infinitely rich source of all Being and all Love and responds with an openness and self-forgetfulness that leads to a deeper union in love. This drive for loving union helps the contemplative to penetrate through the reality of his own being, his own life, to enter into contact with the Divine Reality. This loving contact in deep contemplation between the inmost reality of the created person and the infinite reality of God is thought to really occur. The *experience* which accompanies this contact may be a more or less fruitful sign of what has taken place. The symbolic expression of this experience in transcendental, symbolic terms such as Love, Wisdom, Power, Beauty, Light, is something of a problem for the contemplative, if he is interested in trying to express the experience for the benefit of others.

One of the most appealing aspects of Zen is its metaphysical honesty, which seeks a direct, immediate vision of reality in which the subject-object duality is destroyed. The importance of Zen intuition, through its phenomenology and metaphysic of insight and of consciousness, is very great for Western contemplatives. For the Christian, the culmination of contemplation is an experience of the presence of God within oneself which is beyond description. Since the true self, the innermost "I," is the perfect image of God, the "I" awakens to find himself within the presence of Him whose image he is. They are, by grace, as though one single person, neither being seen as object. This is the "quasi-experiential knowledge of God in obscurity" about which the Christian mystics speak, but can never really explain in positive terms. This quasi-experiential grasp of God as present within one's inner self is brought about by a supernatural intensification of faith.

Thus it is that contemplation is the coalescence of life, knowledge, freedom and love into the supremely simple intuition of the unity of all love, freedom, truth and life in their source, which is God. This is the beginning of an awareness of who one truly is before God, an awareness that is necessary if the contemplative is to play his full part in the plan of God.

In the light of his vision into reality which his contemplation gives, the contemplative can look upon all reality as transfigured and elevated. He does not cease to know and experience objects and events exterior to himself, but he ceases to be guided by them. He encounters them in a new way so that they are no longer objects of desire or fear, but rather they are neutral until they are seen in the light of God. So, too, the contemplative does not back away from social reality and evade it. His insight enables him to penetrate through the surface impressions and get to the inner reality behind social contacts and problems. This implies a deepening sense of social responsibility and awareness. The Christian contemplative is not "alone with the Alone," but becomes more consciously aware of his union with all his brothers in Christ. In attempting to draw closer in spirit to the divine source from which flow all the forces that move the world forward, the Christian contemplative seeks to understand the great undertakings of men.

Contemplation helps to attain an experiential awareness of the missions of the Son and of His Spirit, and leads to a more ready reception of the Word who is sent to man as life and as light. This open reception in love of the Gift of God leads the contemplative to co-operate with the Spirit to make all things new, to transform the created and redeemed world, and to re-establish all things in Christ.

The contemplative helps win the earth completely for God by experiencing the life of love and by working together with His power to transform the world. This really deep Christian concept underlies everything that is going on in life, and that is what contemplation is all about. "Not just the realization of an idea, or of something partial, but a realization of the whole thing, that we belong to God and that He has given Himself totally to us. It has all happened, and it is going on now."[82]

The re-establishment of all things in Christ is not brought about by mere passive anticipation of the Parousia but by the action of creative human freedom. The true contemplative, by the fact of his contemplation, is capable of greater interest and greater concern for the social well-being of his fellowmen. His own mission is to be a complete and totally free man, and he has an inner drive to further the wholeness and freedom of others and of all mankind. This he can do, because he can enter more directly into the pure actuality of human life, and his deeper spiritual grasp of what is real and what is actual. It is not that the contemplative has a deeper practical insight into social or political or economic affairs, but rather he has the inestimable gift of appreciating at their real worth values that are permanent and authentically human. One social effect of his contemplation is that he is able to nurture, at least within himself, a sense of personal responsibility before God, and personal independence from collective irresponsibility.

The contemplative can also subject to critical reappraisal the spurious "faith" of everyday life, which is in reality the passive acceptance of conventional wisdom. This false faith is often confused with "religion," with noxious consequences. He is able to examine and reject all prejudices and conventions which make men blind to human injustice. So contemplation is incompatible with complacency and smug acceptance of conventional wisdom or the status quo. Contemplation is no painkiller. It requires an effort to constantly burn to ashes on the altar of truth all worn-out words, clichés, slogans and human rationalizations. Contemplation helps to clear human life of the clutter of idols and graven images of falsehood which separate man from man, and man from the love of God.

Though contemplation could be considered to have both passive and active aspects, some contemplatives are not content with a state of interior recollection. Rather they look upon contemplation as a response to the concrete word of God manifesting His will and His love, not only for the contemplative as an individual, but for the whole family of man. This leads to efforts to share the anguish and hope of a world in crisis, in which millions struggle for the barest essentials of human existence. This sense of human compassion is most necessary for true contemplation. In wrestling with the problems of his age, the contemplative will be looked upon less as a "professional of vision" than as a "professional of crisis and intellectual suffering."[83]

II

THOMAS MERTON
AS SOCIAL CRITIC

Though Merton did not talk or write much about his priesthood or his prayer life and contemplative experience, he did make several references to himself as a social critic. In *Conjectures of a Guilty Bystander*, Merton quoted and discussed a line from Vergil's *Georgics*: "*Felix qui potuit rerum cognoscere causas.*" This urge to "plumb to the root causes" of situations and events in the light of his contemplation was what turned Merton into a social critic. As he said in 1966, "A contemplative will concern himself with the same problems as other people, but he will try to get to the spiritual and metaphysical roots of these problems, not by analysis but by simplicity. This is of course no easy task. . . . I will at least hazard a few conjectures that are subjective, provisional, mere intuitions. They will certainly need to be completed by the thinking of others."[1] A shift of emphasis in his writing and thinking was evident in the late 1950s and early 1960s. Merton became deeply concerned with the trend of international developments. He started writing more and more on social problems and soon found himself recognized as something of a social critic. Many of his early reflections on himself and his limitations in this area were expressed in excerpts from several of his personal letters published in *Seeds of Destruction*, "Letters in a Time of Crisis" (1964).

Merton felt that he could not with good conscience, both as a priest and a writer with a hearing from many people, devote himself exclusively to questions of prayer, devotion and monastic history while Western society was faced with what he considered the most serious crisis in Christian history. He was disturbed that so many more competent writers and theologians were simply ignoring the crisis. He was convinced of the absolute necessity that he take some responsibility for the world's problems and try to do his part. His being a Christian contemplative forced him to take a Christian view of society, at the risk of failing to be a Christian altogether. Since God was working in history, no one could be a true contemplative without a sense of history and of historical responsibility. As a contemplative, he felt the responsibility to reflect on historical events. He admitted his deficiencies as a social critic and realized that he had to be very careful about what he wrote, prudent about his public conjectures with a prudence that does not belong to the mass-mind. He wished he were more "professional" in these areas, in the sense that he felt his lack of sophistication and practical experience prevented him from better serving the cause of truth and peace.

The silence of bishops and theologians in the United States on the real issues of peace and war (and this was in 1961) so distressed him that he felt the need to say as much as he reasonably could from a point of view which was to him just and in accord with the Gospels. His purpose was to stir up more interest and articulate dialogue on the issues of true peace. He had no illusions that he could put forward views that would influence authorities. All he wanted to do was to try to help establish the truth in all simplicity. He feared that, if more competent theologians did not write on the issue, people like himself would ruin the game for the Christian viewpoint. He was aware of the dangers of rashness, short views, taking his zeal too seriously and being carried away on the winds of his own rhetoric. His contribution to the peace dialogue was to help get the very dialogue started. He considered it his part to continue thinking and asking questions, with the hope that asking the right questions would lead to some achievement. As a result of criticism about some of his early published articles on peace and the Bomb, Merton realized the need to be as free as possible from all prejudgments so that he could better contribute to the immense pioneer job of thinking that was required. He realized that his contribution had to be less hortatory and better informed if he were to help bring out the more subtle aspects of the question and establish the basic moral principle with which no one could seriously disagree, and then prepare the ground to work from there. The fact that he wrote from the isolation of his monastery, where he suffered from a certain lack of perspective and was out of contact with current opinions and even events themselves, was admittedly a serious handicap. Since he tended to express his opinion with vehemence on occasion, he sometimes antagonized certain types of persons, who reacted explosively, thus generating controversy, not thoughtful dialogue. Merton realized that this was due largely to deficiencies in his mode of presenting his ideas. He conceded that his outlook was not purely American since he had been born in France and had his early education in France and England before coming to the United States.

This gave him a certain detachment from the American scene. Despite its technical strength, he saw the United States to be spiritually superficial and weak with a great potential for evil in its sense of mass irresponsibility shielded behind a veil of altruism. Because of his early rootlessness, he felt he had no proper place in the world, that his vocation was essentially that of a pilgrim and an exile, a vocation which made him more easily a brother to people everywhere in the world, especially those who were exiles and pilgrims like himself. Added to that was the fact that he could not get along with formalists, since he was alien to them and they to him.

These early reflections on himself, as social critic, made in 1961–62 to a vast variety of friends to whom he wrote on the peace-war issue, were substantiated and reiterated in his later years. His attitude toward himself and his purpose in his social criticism remained basically the same.

He tried to avoid writing simply as a propagandist for any particular cause or for a limited program. He was in no way a spokesman for any contemplative or monastic movement, nor did he look upon himself as purely and simply a "spiritual writer." He spoke only in his own name, and was in no way putting forth official Catholic teaching, which gave him great independence of action. He looked upon some of his early political and social commentaries as "personal manifestoes" or "tracts," as he humorously referred to them in some "anti-letters" to Robert Lax in 1963. He also considered his book *Faith and Violence* (1968) as a "tract for the times." "It will make a lot of people very mad. I don't claim to have final answers to contemporary problems, just opinions which are subject to modification. And maybe by the time the book is out I will have changed many of them myself."[2]

Merton did not look upon himself as a petulant social critic who was angry at the world after the model of St. Jerome, but rather as a self-questioning human person who, like all his brothers, struggled to cope with a turbulent and confused existence which is so subject to built-in change that almost nothing is predictable, in which almost everything public is patently phony despite a wealth of personal authenticity that is all around man. "I am, in short, a man of the modern world. In fact, *I am the world* just as you are. Where am I going to look for the world first of all if not in myself?"[3]

His most unpopular opinions were those against the Bomb, the Vietnam War and, in fact, the whole United States social system. People supposed him, as a monk, to be "anti-modern" and "opposed to technology" because he disagreed with the myth that technology, all by itself, was really solving the world's problems. He was surely not a member of the "Catholic Establishment" because he did not follow any current fashions of thought, and was a nonconformist with a few tastes and ideas of his own. He was such a nonconformist that he deliberately avoided reading Harvey Cox's very popular book *The Secular City* and could not foresee reading it for at least ten years, after it had long since faded from popularity. As Merton said:

> My own peculiar task in my Church has been that of a solitary explorer, who, instead of jumping on all the latest bandwagons at once, is bound to search the existential depths of faith in its silence, its ambiguities, and in those certainties which lie deeper than the bottom of anxiety. In these depths there are no easy answers, no pat solutions to anything. It is a kind

of submarine life in which faith sometimes mysteriously takes on the aspect of doubt.[4]

As a monk-writer, he felt that he was real insofar as he managed to achieve a contemporary worldliness, a perspective that was proper to the times, because he was both in his time and *of it,* yet uniquely unworldly because he was in the world but *not* of it. He made no effort to disguise that he spoke from a Christian point of view, but in an "unofficial" way, so that he was at liberty to disagree and even "scandalize" on occasion more traditional Christian types. When asked why Merton took some of the positions he did, one of the monks at Gethsemani answered very simply, "He felt it was the Christian thing to say. He was not undertaking any great campaign or crusade. His viewpoint was simply Christian!"

Merton admitted that even though his political views were limited and without authority, since he had no official position, he did have an obligation to give nonconformist criticism in a spirit of independence. His point of view in political and social questions was that of a nondogmatic, existentialist Christian, in a completely nonconformist evangelical sense. He felt closer to a humanist like Albert Camus, with certain religious reservations, than to rigidly doctrinaire Christians whose Christianity is chiefly a celebration of bourgeois "Christian" culture and the status quo.

Merton's later hermit existence had an unforeseen effect on him. As he said in the spring of 1967, "I am still leading a marginal life in solitude which I enjoy very much, and one of the effects of this is that I find I have less and less to say. When you are alone you take stock of things and see them in an entirely different perspective."[5] But even though he had "less to say," he found it difficult to keep entirely quiet. As he admitted:

> It will not be easy for me to shut up. I am writing less, but still writing. No doubt the writing will tend to get further out and less popular. I still recognize an obligation to take up a position on this or that moral issue of general urgency, not because I claim to have the answer, but because one has to take a responsible stand. Stupidity and evasion are no excuse for complicity in what goes on in the world of today.[6]

That Merton looked upon himself as an intellectual has been established. He surely was not the type of Continental or American intellectual whom Jean-François Revel flays so openly and devastatingly in his *Without Marx or Jesus: The New American Revolution Has Begun,* men who self-servingly detach themselves from mass culture without any real concern for genuine social change. His intellectualist position gave him the freedom to move about independently in the world of ideas. His ideas were his own. He could be original, creative, iconoclastic and independent. Not being caught in an avaricious system, he could be more aware of its inner contradictions and injustices and insoluble problems, and could articulate his awareness without fear of the disapproval which must follow. An intellectual is a man of world perspectives, not confined to narrow, parochial, limited or distorted perspectives like the "average people" who accept uncritically the whole package of ideas, or pseudo-ideas, put out by the Establishment, political or ecclesiastical. The intellectual's awareness makes him more open to dialogue with the underclass, and more able to help it in some measure. Yet as an intellectual, Merton did not look upon himself as a prophet or revolutionary activist. He never claimed that his perspective as a monk-intellectual was the only true one or that he had better answers than anyone else. He did not think that he had implicitly judged others or asserted that he, as a monk, knew more than they. "I feel myself involved in the same problems, and I need to work out the problems of the world with other men because they are also my problems."[7]

One of his last statements about himself as a social critic was written shortly before he left for the Orient. "It seems to me that I have already expressed too many opinions about everything and I wish I could really be silent on controversial issues. Yet I doubt if I can honestly refrain from giving some reaction when I am asked."[8] He continued in the letter to explain why he turned down many requests to comment on the recent assassination of Senator Robert Kennedy. In another letter he said, "I am committed to a life of solitude and meditation. I am less and less inclined to try to sell anybody a line, even in writing."[9]

As Jean Leclercq said in his Introduction to Merton's *Contemplation in a World of Action*, "At the heart of everything he said was his vocation, his monastic experience. He saw everything through a monk's eyes. This was both his limitation and his strength: a limitation, because, after all, monastic life is not the totality of the Church or of society; a strength, because he was a man of single purpose, a lone warrior. It was always the monk in Merton that had the last word."[10]

As a social critic, Merton necessarily fulfilled something of a prophetic function in the Church of his time. In a real sense as a Christian he did help the world judge itself by measuring it against the standard of love. His prophetic function was mainly that of a concerned individual who "spoke out" and called attention to a religious dimension within situations and events that was already there. Merton had a real insight into contemporary times in the sense that he spoke about man's deepest troubles, troubles that were deep within man himself.

Merton was convinced that anyone called to a life of special holiness and dedication had a solemn obligation to understand the true nature of man's place before God in an anguished world and to speak out about it. "The priest, the religious, the lay leader must, whether he likes it or not, fulfill in the world the role of prophet. If he does not face the anguish of being a true prophet, he must enjoy the carrion comfort of acceptance in a society of the deluded by becoming a false prophet and participating in their delusions."[11] Part of the role of the prophet, like that of the poet or the artist, is to be aware of immature and inadequate expressions of ideas that are given currency and refuse to be dominated by them. Poets, artists and prophets have greater freedom and should use it for deeper insights and expressions of the reality of man's human condition. "Unfortunately," he complained in 1966, "the confusion of our world has made the message of our poets obscure and our prophets seem to be altogether silent."[12]

A Christian view of the world not only illuminates the most typical and most urgent problems of the modern world, but indeed this view provides a unique light. This light, which does not shine out all by itself, is not always clearly apparent to the world in the official statements and declarations of the Church. This light must be made evident by the creative activity of Christians themselves as they participate in the solutions of contemporary problems on which the very future of man depends. To these problems, basically ethical as well as economic and political in nature, Christians must contribute something of their own unique insights into the value of man, in his inalienable dignity as a free person. The source of these insights is, of course, the Christian concept of redemptive love.

This notion of redemptive love of the world implies an acceptance of the world as it is, in its confusion and imperfection, with a realistic love and awareness that it is the only world there is, the scene of man's redemption and of his creative response to God's love. The Christian's duty is to help Christianize this world, not with lamentations and prophecies of doom that are often merely unrealistic manifestations of compulsive perfectionism, but with realistic and practical love for his fellowmen.

Merton realized the dangers inherent in fulfilling a prophetic role in the Church today. The role has a deep spiritual base and cannot be undertaken lightly. The prophetic function of a monk depends entirely on his being a man of God who has surrendered himself to the action of the Holy Spirit, the builder of the eschatological kingdom of God. His efficacy as a prophet will depend on his real detachment, his real freedom, his real capacity for independent and outspoken criticism vis-à-vis the injustices, lies and self-contradictions of the world.

The prophet's role was one that did not rest lightly on Merton, as it does not on any true prophet. After almost three years in the hermitage, as he found he had "less and less to say," he made this statement: "I certainly do not think I have a 'task' of social commentator, or preacher, or pseudo-prophet or what you will. My task is only to be what I am, a man seeking God in silence and solitude, with deep respect for the demands and realities of his vocation, and fully aware that others too are seeking the truth in their way."[13]

Merton was a social critic, not only in the books and articles which he published, not only in the prophetic role which, despite his disclaimers, he continued to fulfill, but also in the very life which he led. That his life as a monk was in itself a form of social protest was a theme which can be detected in several of his later writings. He agreed in principle with Father Evdokimov's opinion that a monk should by his unworldliness be not only a nonconformist but provocatively so, since the monk is in revolt against the false claims of the world. His "Signed Confession of Crimes Against the State," a seven-page manifesto against modern totalitarian tendencies, was written in a satiric-ironic style, proclaiming his independence as a monk from conformist pressures.

> My very existence is an admission of guilt. . . .
> All I have to do is think, and immediately I become guilty. . . . Everything that is written is
> a potential confession of crime. . . . The worst
> traitor is the one who simply takes no interest.
> . . . That's me. Here I sit in the grass. I watch
> the clouds go by, and I like it.[14]

He insisted that one of the reasons for the monk's existence is to resist the routines to which everyone else has to conform. He is obliged by his vocation to have at least his own mind, if not to speak out. The monk has to be a free man, a witness to man's freedom as a son of God and to the essential difference between that freedom and the spirit of the world.

That a monk adopts a life which is essentially non-assertive, nonviolent, a life of humility and peace, is in itself a statement of his position. By the personal modality of his decision, such a person gives his whole life a special orientation, to make his entire life a rejection of, a protest against, all political and social injustice. Merton made his monastic silence a protest, and when he spoke it was to deny that his faith and his Church could ever seriously be aligned with the forces of injustice and destruction. "It is true, nevertheless, that the faith in which I believe is also invoked by many who believe in war, in social injustice, in self-righteous and lying forms of tyranny. My life, then, must be a protest against these also, and perhaps against these most of all."[15]

It is evident then that Merton looked upon the life of a monk as a calculated form of relevant challenge to the world to reassess its basic value system. He was not, in his social commentaries, offering blueprints for specific solutions to specific problems. His life and his social writings were designed to highlight the problems and to formulate questions, to bring them out into the open and to stimulate dialogue, with a contemporary awareness of basic humanistic and Christian realities. His social concern was impelled by a deep desire to bring the Christian vision of life to bear on the problematic of our modern age.

What sources of information did Merton have, especially for his social commentaries? The quality and inherent value of his commentaries can in part be judged from the quality of the source materials from which he formed his own opinions. While his ideas on religion and religious experience and contemplation resulted from a combination of both the literary sources he mastered and the lived experience of his own religious life, it is obvious that most of his ideas on social questions, economics, politics and oriental religions came from his own reading.

Though he lived five years of his adult life in New York City and for two years plus two previous summers in Olean, New York, the seven adult years "in the world" before entrance into the monastery were for the most part sheltered in academia. As a youth he had traveled in Europe with his father and grandparents, had toured the Continent during a summer by himself at the age of eighteen and had seen a little of pre-World War II France, Italy, England and Cuba. His mature years were spent in the northeastern United States with relatively little travel except to two monasteries for retreats. He had some limited experience for a brief span as a "social worker" in Harlem. He was never gainfully employed, except as a teacher at Columbia and St. Bonaventure universities, never fully employed in an office or in a factory. His experience of the "rat race" of modern technological man was limited indeed. His "soft job" as guide and interpreter on the observation roof of the RCA Building at Rockefeller Center in the summer of 1936, as well as limited experience as a part-time employee in an advertising office that same summer, does not disallow this statement. Though he was addicted to the cinema as a youngster, as an adult he rarely attended motion pictures, and after he entered Gethsemani, only once. Before his Asian trip Merton saw the Peter Sellers romp, *The Pink Panther*, a satirical farce about a French detective, hardly a source of vital sociological information. Radio and television were just not existent in the Gethsemani of Merton's time. Once he watched a television program in the home of a friend, just prior to his Asian trip. It was a football game. Rather than being concerned about the violence of the sport, Merton saw it through the eyes of an artist, remarking with delight about the "choreography" of the team formations in action.

His travels as a monk were severely restricted. Other than trips to Louisville for United States citizenship in 1951, and for medical treatment several times, he rarely left the monastery. Prior to 1968, he had only two trips: to St. John's, Collegeville, Minnesota, in company with his abbot and Father John Eudes Bamberger in 1956, and a short trip to New York City to interview the Zen scholar Dr. D. T. Suzuki in 1964. In the spring of 1968, the new abbot allowed him to visit briefly monastic foundations in New Mexico and California. His Asian trip, with stops in New Mexico, California, Vancouver and Alaska on the way to India, was, therefore, his only extended travel as a monk. Some visitors who went to Gethsemani to speak with him (more, paradoxically, during his hermit years) were able to help form his ideas in dialogue, but by far the sources of his information were literary.

Merton was an omnivorous reader and read with close attention a large number of books at a very rapid rate, because his time for reading was so limited. An extensive study could be made of the literary sources he used, as well as of the major literary influences on him for the development of his ideas. His "heavy reading," such as his investigations in *Migne* on the Latin and Greek Fathers, was done in the early morning hours; lighter reading was done during one hour later in the day. He would normally skim a book quickly, but many of the books in the library at Gethsemani, which he had for his use, show extensive underscoring. He ranged freely through that well-catalogued modern library of approximately 22,500 holdings.

A brief cross-section sample of his reading will suffice here. Among the English-language books in his possession at Gethsemani, which were very extensively underscored throughout, were: Paul Tillich, *Dynamics of Faith*, 1957; Bernd. Naumann, *Auschwitz*, 1966; Erich Fromm, *Man for Himself*, 1947, *The Sane Society*, 1955, *Marx's Concept of Man*, 1961, *Beyond the Chains of Illusion*, 1962; Gregory Zilboorg, *Mind, Medicine and Man*, 1943; Karl Jaspers, *Man in the Modern Age*, 1951; Mircea Eliade, *Images and Symbols*, 1952; Jean-Paul Sartre, *Literature and Existentialism*, 1962; Frantz Fanon, *Black Skin and White Masks*, 1967; Johan Huizinga, *Homo Ludens: A Study of the Play Element in Culture*, 1950; Gabriel Vahanian, *Wait Without Idols*, 1964; J. Robert Oppenheimer, *The Open Mind*, 1946. Among the foreign-language books extensively underscored throughout were: Sergei N. Bulgakov, *Du Verbe Incarné*, 1943; Jean-Paul Sartre, *L'être et le néant*, 1948; Karl Barth, *La Preuve de L'Existence de Dieu*, 1958; Paul Evdokimov, *La Femme et Le Salut du Monde*, 1958; Simone Weil, *Écrits Historiques et Politiques*, 1960.

A random sample of his notebooks at Gethsemani of extensive excerpts from authors, which he typed himself for future use, contains passages from: Martin Buber, Ernst Cassirer, Eric Gill, Lewis Mumford, Daisetz Teitaro Suzuki, Marco Pallis, Mahatma Gandhi, Shmnel Yosef Agnan. Another notebook devoted to Greek and Russian Orthodox theologians has extensive passages from: Nikolai Berdyaev, five books; Sergei Bulgakov, four; George Florovsky, one; Paul Evdokimov, one. Of Nikolai Berdyaev's books, the excerpts number: *Destiny of Man*, fifty-seven typed pages of notes; *The End of Our Time*, twenty-three pages; *The Origin of Russian Communism*, twenty pages; *The Realm of the Spirit and the Realm of*

Caesar, twenty-nine pages; *Slavery and Freedom*, thirty pages.

A sample of the wide range of books Merton read and condensed can be seen from his *Conjectures of a Guilty Bystander*. He made reference to and discussed passages from at least thirty-four books in this 350-page journal of opinion composed between 1956–65, from St. Anselm to Evdokimov, from Erasmus to Ellul, from Hilary of Arles to Heidegger, from John of the Cross to Heisenberg. His range was cosmopolitan; his selections were invariably weighty and serious.

Besides English, he read widely in Latin and Greek, French, Spanish and Portuguese. A steel cabinet at Gethsemani still has uncatalogued over four hundred books in French, Spanish and Portuguese, mostly on poetry and literary topics, which were in his possession, having been sent to him from admirers and friends over the years, books from which he made his rather extensive translations of French, Portuguese, Spanish and Latin American poetry. He could read German and Italian adequately; he once read a book in Flemish as a challenge. He also tried his luck at learning Chinese in the early 1960s, but had to abandon it for lack of time. Among his effects at Gethsemani is a list of the books on oriental religions that were at the hermitage when he left for the Orient. There were 173 books on this subject, mostly on Zen, Sufism, Yoga and general topics. At least forty-one of them had extensive underscorings; twenty-nine also had personal greetings from the author.

Merton was of the opinion that radio, television and daily papers would only be a source of grave confusion to the contemplative monk who was trying to keep a legitimate contact with the problems of the world. Being cut off from the mass media was a blessing rather than a hindrance. The true answer for Merton was in selected sources of books and quality journals and periodicals. For instance, the Center for the Study of Democratic Institutions at Santa Barbara, California, was the source of highly selected reading materials for him, and a friend there kept him well supplied over the years. Other friends in the literary world, publishers, editors, critics and commentators, knowing his isolated situation, continually sent in books and quality articles for his study and comment. He reciprocated and sent out advanced mimeographed copies of his articles for comment and correction before publication, precisely because he was aware of the disadvantages he suffered in his isolation. For current news he read selectively from *The New York Review of Books*, the New York *Times* "Review of the Week," *The Christian Science Monitor*, *I. F. Stone's Weekly*, *Le Monde* in French and on occasion the Manchester *Guardian* and other selected publications. He avoided the more popular news magazines as a quick way to narcosis.

He felt that, realistically, it would be folly for him to try to write on immediately current topics because of his lack of information, his relatively limited sources and the perennial delays of the then strictly enforced monastic censorship. The prior censorship of his books was mitigated by 1968. *Faith and Violence* and *Zen and the Birds of Appetite* both appeared in 1968 without an imprimatur. His normal procedure would be to wait for several months so that a topic of interest could crystallize before he commented on it from his longer range, contemplative point of view.

As would be expected from one with his range of artistic talent, Merton used a broad variety of literary genre for his social commentaries. His views on topics were expressed in essays, book reviews, art criticism, historical

studies, poetry and anti-poetry, parables, myths and satires, manifestoes, personal letters, peace songs and even
in his calligraphies. His approach was personal, con-
versational, tentative, presenting his own version of the
world in such a way that an implicit dialogue was initi-
ated with interested persons to clarify questions, not to
propose dogmatic solutions. He considered his singular,
existential, often poetic approach to topics the only one
proper for one in his isolation.

The actual mode of composition he used was described
by one of his fellow monks who had been assigned to help
him as a typist for several years. "Louis thought on paper.
He wrote as he talked, the same living style both in conversation and in writing. He would type in the evening
at a furious rate, two fingers, pick and peck. Revision
would be done in the morning, which usually meant in-
serting additional thoughts on a subject. Rarely did he
make corrections for style or additional clarity. He had
no time for such revisions, since writing was only a small
part of his life. But two expert final typists could not keep
up with him. We were always behind."[16]

When one of the monks observed to him that his literary style needed much improvement, tightening it up
to remove the "Spanish moss," Merton replied without
hesitation, "The people who read my stuff aren't styl-
ists!"[17] Yet to another monk who would on occasion
bring up a topic of common literary interest, Merton
stated that the audience for whom he wrote his social
commentaries was "the concerned intellectual, the fel-
lows from around my time at Columbia; I write to their
level."[18] This monk observed that "Father Louis looked
upon his life as a constant dialogue with God, and therefore subject to constant change, so that he was continually being called to something new. His life was not a set

of routine activities which, once learned, became automatic and led to 'perfection.' His life was one of 'total flow.' He did not receive his ideas, his talents, inspirations, graces for himself. What came to him had to go."[19]

The scope and versatility of his social commentaries, fragmentary and tentative as they were, may well disguise the basic unity of his concept of what man before God should be. In fact, everything he wrote expressed his consistent concern to uncover and illuminate the life possibilities for all men under God. Merton's concern for "religious man" is the main object of investigation in this book.

III

RELIGIOUS MAN
IN THE WRITINGS OF
THOMAS MERTON

Merton spoke of God in a standard, biblical way, according to traditional doctrine, fully aware that it is impossible to comprehend the Divinity completely, or to express anything about the Divinity adequately in positive terms. He knew full well also that mythical and poetic statements about God, as well as philosophical concepts, are not in the least adequate representations of God. The Bible records events by which an ultimate freedom, which is at once the ground and the source of man's being, the center of his history and the guide of his destinies, broke through into man's private and complex world. The mysterious word for that freedom is a nonword, and the sacred Tetragrammaton, YHWH, is simply a substitute for the real name that was unspoken and all-holy. The word "God" is then in reality a nonword, but behind it is a presence, a freedom, a love which the Bible never clearly explains.

God is not simply the final explanation of things that man does not know about the world, nor is He merely the source of ultimate answers to personal and human problems. God is not simply the one whom man meets when he is extended to his own limits, rather God is the ground and center of man's existence, since he starts from Him and remains in Him as the very ground of his existence and his reality. God is not merely "out there" in a vague beyond, He is the very ground of what man knows, and human knowledge itself is His manifestation. Reality itself is His epiphany. The Bible is a "worldly" book in this sense, that it sees God at the very center of man's life. God is never shown in the Bible merely as a supplement of man's power and intelligence, but as its very ground and reality.

Merton rarely used philosophical terminology in speaking of God, but preferred to emphasize the very personal aspects of the basic relationship of love between God and man. Just as infinite sharing of love is the law of God's inner life, so He has made the sharing of oneself in love the law of man's being. God in His loving mercy has called man to a union of love; it is only through love that man can come to God.

The theme of love is woven through all of Merton's writings about God. The Christian idea of love is contained in three words of the Apostle John: "God is love [*ho theos agapē estin*]" (I John 4:18). This revelation of transcendent mystery is couched in human terms because it is addressed to men, but it is a mystery that human concepts can never limit or contain. John's use of the word *agapē* rather than *eros* is intended to show that God's love overflows and gives of its fullness. The love which *He is* is the infinite giving of Himself. But human love can never be pure *agapē*. So it is that for *agapē* to enter into the life of man, God must reveal and give His own love, His own life, to man. The *agapē* of the Christian is, therefore, something essentially different from and more pure than the highest of natural, disinterested love. It is something altogether new, a manifestation of God living in mankind and revealing His own nature by the love with which He has decreed to unite men to Himself and to each other, thus incorporating them into His mystery. Man can enter into the mystery of the Trinity, not by thought and imagination, but only by love.

In an article written in the last year of his life, after much experience in contemplation, Merton attempted to speak of the reality of God in more contemporary terms. He was well aware that the conceptual knowledge of God is inevitably associated with a certain cultural matrix, so he tried to approach the mystery of God's love in a way that was highly concrete and existential. Merton expressed himself in the following manner.

Since God in His intimate essence is beyond all human concepts, the revelation of God as Father, Son and Spirit is in fact a revelation that is totally unique. Nowhere in the sources of revelation is any definition of God to be found. He simply reveals that *He is* (Exodus 3:14). Or rather, He reveals that He is who He is, a presence, an active, living and personal identity. This identity, this "who," is at once Father, Logos and pneuma, living personal presence as utterance of Himself, as communication of Himself, as love, as mercy, as gift, as life. The self-revelation of the Father through the Son in the Spirit discloses an infinite giving and dynamic personal communication. When St. John said "God is love," one can recognize that the God who is love is known to no one except to him who loves. God is Father who gives Himself in love as Son; He is Son who gives Himself as love in Spirit; He is Spirit who communicates to man the immense love which man believes to be Father and Son, so that men themselves, in the Spirit, become sons and give themselves in love to the Father. This is the self-manifestation of God as the infinite personal ground of all love and all being, of God as loving creator of all things, not only infinitely transcendent but also present within the metaphysical depths and goodness of being itself. God thus reveals Himself as the act and the living presence of love from whom all beings receive the loving and gratuitous gift to be real. The divine persons are not numerically three, but they are the inner communication and dynamism of love in which God is present to Himself in being, vision and love, or perhaps one might say in reality, in realization and in ecstatic delight. Just as God is loving, so too He is merciful in an infinite variety of ways. His mercy is shown in His "inconsistency," in His unexpected gifts of love.

Commenting on the statement of St. Irenaeus—"*Gloria Dei est vivens homo* [Man alive is the glory of God]" —Merton was of the opinion that today it is important to get away from the *idea* of God, the *attributes* of God, merely as objects which man contemplates, then praises. The glory of God is within man, not as a spectacle to be contemplated but as a reality to be lived. Even though man may see nothing of God, still his life may be filled with God. Merton observed, "To say that we will know this in another world is all right, as long as we remember that we do not know precisely what we are talking about."[1]

One's concept of God colors his entire spiritual attitude. If a person is able to believe in love that God is his loving father, that He has an infinite and compassionate concern for man, then a person can love with confidence. If, however, God is seen to be a stern, cold lawgiver, a ruler, a lord, a judge and not a father, the Christian life would be very difficult. The beginning of Christian life is living the belief that God is one's father.

Man's knowledge of God is a tenuous thing and subject to constant change and deepening through experience. In a personal letter to a friend in 1961, Merton reflected on some instances of heroic love for fellowmen shown in the concentration camps of World War II. His opinion was that Christians have taken Christianity for granted for hundreds of years and now some of them are beginning to wake up to the fact that they have almost forgotten what it means, and that their ideas of God and His ways are far from corresponding to the actuality. Merton's studies in the Prophets brought this truth home forcefully.

The reality of God's presence *to* man and *in* man is perceived by theological faith and hope, not by intuition. Man's awareness of God is not an awareness of nature, but of a personal relationship. As a relationship of love, God's presence to man is personal, existential and free. Once God's presence and existence is in some remote way "experienced," the human response to His being should be a resounding, lifelong "yes" of love.

Man's loving belief in God enables him to attain to God, invisibly present as the ground of his being, to a certain degree, but God remains hidden from the investigating mind that seeks to capture Him and secure possession of Him in order to have power over God. It is absurd to try to grasp God as an object which can be seized and comprehended by the human mind. The best the human mind can do is express knowledge about God in analogies which themselves must be transcended. But the person must transcend himself, as well as the analogies about God, so that the familiar subject-object relationship which characterizes ordinary acts of human knowing can be overcome. One comes to "know God" insofar as he becomes aware of himself as "known through and through by God." God is "possessed" in proportion as a person realizes himself to be possessed by God in the inmost depths of his being. Since man's being is penetrated through and through by God's knowledge and love, his knowledge of God is, paradoxically, a knowledge, not of God as object, but of himself as utterly dependent on God's saving and merciful knowledge and love.

Merton was well aware of the great dangers of facile and thoughtless verbalizations about spiritual reality. All true spiritual disciplines recognize the peril of idolatry in the irresponsible fabrications of pseudo-spiritual concepts which serve only to delude and subject man to deep inner captivity. Traditional theology itself has always recognized the insufficiency of propositions *about* God and *about* redemption which tend to objectify God and set Him apart so that He can be used and manipulated. Such a god is truly only an idol and never really existed anyway. Believers sometimes deal with a god who is made up of words, feelings, reassuring slogans, less the God of faith than the product of religious and social routine. "Such a god can come to substitute for the truth of the invisible God of faith, and though this comforting image may seem real to us, he is really an idol, whose chief function is to protect us against a deep encounter between our own true inner self and the true God."[2]

One's world view has very much influence on one's

concept of God. If the transcendence of God is emphasized because of a particular image of the universe, a cause and effect mechanism puts God "outside" and "above" the universe, acting as absolute first cause, supreme prime mover, uncaused cause. Man's problem is then to enter into communication with the Transcendent by "faith" and "prayer" so that he can share God's plans, participate in His causation and have delegated to himself a secret and limited share of God's activity insofar as he is united to God. God's control and man's obedience tend to be emphasized in this view: love is a subsidiary aspect of the basic relationship.

An image of the universe that is more in line with post-Newtonian physics would tend to emphasize the immanence of God, God's presence to man in a dymanic way, perfecting an ongoing creation, including man, *in* and *through* man's loving co-operation with God. Teilhard de Chardin is a modern witness, among others, of this immanentist understanding of God, which is more in keeping with the Christian contemplative tradition. The real point of contemplation in the Christian life has been a deepening of faith and the personal dimensions of liberty and apprehension to the point where God is appreciated as directly and personally present in man's own being, so that his direct union with God is realized and to some degree "experienced."

For Merton, God was not a "problem" and one could not know God as long as one seeks to solve "the problem of God." God seeks Himself in man. Indeed, man exists solely for this, to be the place God has chosen for His presence, His manifestation in the world, His epiphany. If man once begins to recognize the real value of his own self, he will see that this value is the sign of God in his being, the signature of God upon his being. The love of one's fellowmen is given him as the way of realizing this.

* * *

What was Merton's concept of man? Man has an innate thrust toward the Transcendent, and is brought into the intimate relationship of love by the call of God.

> The Christian concept of man, a concept which is held in common by all religions which can be called "Higher" or "Mystical," is one which sees man as a spiritual or self-transcending being. . . . Man, unlike other animals, does not find his fulfillment or self-realization merely on the level of his own nature.[3]

Merton's concept of man followed traditional Catholic teaching, considering man as a creature of God, endowed with intelligence and free will, created for an eternal union with God in love. Man as a sinner is in need of God's loving mercy which is always lovingly given. By co-operating with God's assistance and by self-discipline in love, man can develop his potential for good, and resist his innately selfish potential for evil.

Though in his earlier works Merton used the traditional body-soul dichotomy consistently, in his later years his developing personalism was more evident. The personal dimensions of man were given more stress, and he ceased to speak of man's "spiritual" aspects. Man's search for true self-understanding, for his true identity before God, was a constant theme with Merton. This search culminates in the union of love, in which man is finally able to know himself in his true identity as personally loved by God, and to know and love God as the source of that identity.

Man's life as an individual person and as a member of a perplexed and struggling race provokes him with the evidence that life must have a meaning. His purpose in life is to discover that meaning and live according to it. The process of living, of growing to maturity and becoming a person is precisely the gradual increasing awareness of what that meaning is. In the last analysis, the individual person is responsible for living his own life and for "finding himself." This self-discovery comes only from within, but it is not achieved by oneself. The full discovery of who one really is is accomplished by his God-given powers in the love of others and of God, so that it can be said that one finds himself only in and through other persons. This discovery of oneself in God, and of God in oneself, by a love which also finds all other men in God with oneself, is not so much a discovery of oneself as of Christ. This self-discovery also implies tolerant self-acceptance, acceptance of oneself with all one's personal limitations, and acceptance of others before God with all their limitations.

Man's vocation is but to co-operate with God in the creation of his own life, his own identity, his own destiny. It requires active participation in God's creative freedom, by choosing the truth and creating the truth of one's own identity. To work out one's identity in God requires close attention to the reality of every moment as God reveals Himself in the mystery of each new situation. Unless a person desires this self-identity and strives to find it with Him and in Him, he will never fully mature. "The seeds that are planted in my liberty at every moment, by God's will, are the seeds of my own identity, my own reality, my own sanctity."[4]

As Merton wrote to a friend:

> This emphasis on man's freedom before God is most important, since man is a being whose reality cannot be left to forces outside himself, to nature, society or events. We become real in proportion as we accept the real possibilities that are presented to us, and *choose them freely and realistically for ourselves.* This act of choice implies some kind of personal philosophy and a personal faith.[5]

So it was that Merton endorsed completely the existentialist insight of traditional monastic theology which stresses man's freedom, since in his basic structure man is *capax Dei.* Man is an openness that is fulfilled only in unconditional consent to an unconditioned love. This openness which is at the very core of man's being, and which demands that he transcend his being, is what the monastic theologians call the "image of God in man." The capacity for freedom and love is the image of God because God Himself is pure freedom and pure love. The image in man seeks to attain a perfect likeness to its original by loving as it is loved. Man cannot, of course, attain this by himself. "But God has given us His own Son that we may be sons in Him. The coming of the Word to take our freedom to Himself turns the 'image' into 'likeness.' When the Word loves the Father in us, then our freedom is transfigured in and by His Spirit, and our love becomes identical with His love."[6]

In a letter to another friend, Merton pointed out that the notion of man has been radically modified by the incarnation, so that man in Christ is more than ever a recipient of divine mercy as a spouse of God and in some mysterious way the very epiphany of divine mercy. Merton would probably agree with a recent theological formulation: "Christ was most completely man by surrendering himself most completely to God. Man understands himself best when he grasps himself as the possible self-expression of God which has become actual in the man Jesus."[7]

Merton's studies in the Fathers of the Church led to the development of his notion of the human person and to the emphasis he put on the human person. This personalist philosophy was in the background of most of his social commentaries of the 1960s. His philosophy of the person was rooted in his notion of man's spirituality. His terminology and philosophical distinctions were borrowed from Gabriel Marcel and Jacques Maritain. He was indebted to Marcel for his existentialist outlook on religious faith. Maritain's notions of the individual, the common good and the person in man were taken over by Merton, but he developed them in a more spiritual direction. His ideas of the individual as equated with the empirical ego and expressed in radical individualism, as well as his notion of mass-man as expressed in radical totalitarianism, were constant themes. Both of these modern philosophies tend to suppress what is most thoroughly human in man, his freedom of initiative, his creativity and his personal responsibility. Merton worked hard to expose the errors and inadmissible consequences of these philosophies in the contemporary world, as well as their spiritual counterparts in religion. He offered a constructive alternative to both idealistic and materialistic philosophies in his own realist spirituality. He was attempting to change man's consciousness, his consciousness of himself and of his own true identity, by emphasizing the dynamism of life itself.

Merton's own brand of personalism was not content with man's drive for mature manhood alone, but went beyond to emphasize the transcendent thrust to achieve the sonship of God to which he is called, the vocation to be like God since he is the image and likeness of God, manifesting the divinity of God through his union with the divinity of the Son in the Spirit. This Christian perfection of the human person is God's greatest gift to man. Thus it can be said that man has a twofold end: to know himself in his true identity, and to know and love God as the ground of that identity.

*   *   *

What did Merton mean by the word "religion"? The interrelationship between God and man in love is commonly called "religion." For Merton, this bond of union between the God who calls man in love and the man who responds in a lifelong "yes" of love was a living, existential reality, not a set of abstract principles and dogmas. Merton was not interested in establishing any theoretical, universal definition of "religion" since he was aware of the difficulties of such an attempt. Because of the various cultural aspects which enter into the notion of religion, basically a Western concept, the word is not universally applicable. Just as the living notion of religion cannot be defined but only described, so too the notion of "religious man" can only be described. Merton did not use the term "religious man" specifically in his writings, but he spoke of the reality of religious man all through his writings in the sense intended here, that is, man before God, living out existentially the relationship of love with God. The social, "horizontal" dimensions of man's life which are consequent upon this bond of love are also of concern in this study. It is obvious that this term "religious man" is not intended here to mean "canonical religious" or people living under vows in a specific mode of "religious life." It is intended to apply to all men before God, living in a way which, with a variety of degrees of consciousness, expresses their innate thrust to the Transcendent.

Though much of his writing on religion (and religiosity) had specific reference to persons attempting to live a fully conscious life of prayer, many of his statements about religion had a universally Christian application to all men before God. In none of his books or articles did Merton attempt any extended discussion of the theoretical or abstract notions of religion, but the living, existential realization of this bond of love with God, expressed by one's whole life, as well as by more formal modes of prayer and liturgy, could well be considered the substance of most of his writing. The closest Merton came to a book-length treatment of any of the theoretical aspects of religion was in *The New Man* (1961), but even there the treatment was very practical, the main theme being "self-realization in God." All of Merton's theology was pre-eminently practical.

Of course, Merton's whole viewpoint on religion and religious man was that of a practicing Christian, for whom union with God through Christ in the Spirit was the exclusive mode of attaining, whether consciously or not, the union with God in love which religious man desires. Because of his practical approach to religious man's quest for God, Merton used the words "religion" and "spiritual life," "union with God in love" and "the life of prayer" as interchangeable terms. Many of his writings on prayer contained his deepest notions of the reality of religion.

His writings showed the qualities he spoke of in reference to the monastic theologies of the Benedictine and Cistercian writers of the eleventh and twelfth centuries, that is, they were not speculative, but based on the deeply lived experience of the mysteries of faith. Merton's writings were concrete, existential, intuitive and deeply rooted in the everyday life of modern times. He was not concerned with abstract ideas about God, but with the living relationship of man with God in Christ, and this meant a concern for the love of man for man, that love by which one is known as Christ's disciple. Without this love for his fellowmen, there is, for the Christian, no "life in Christ" and therefore no true union with God, no true religion, only a religious ideology.

The remarkable thing about this union with God in love is that holy things come to seem natural to the soul, because God creates in man a spontaneity in which God's life becomes perfectly man's, and man's own life God's, so that to act as His children seems to be inborn in man. The spiritual life is the life of man's real self, orienting man toward God, integrating him into the real order established by God, and putting him in the fullest contact with reality. This spiritual life gives one the ability to respond to reality, to see the value and beauty in ordinary things, to come alive to the splendor that is all around him in the creatures of God. Because his life is radically centered on God, a religious man can become in a way indifferent to all that is not of God, finding in God the goodness and the reality of all things. The importance of prayer is that man presents himself as he is before God as He is. This sincerity in prayer helps establish a contact with the God of all truth. This contact will lead man to the truth about himself.

Religion does not simply supply answers to questions

about God and human life, or provide internal, self-satisfied security before God, in the sense that a religious man is pleased with himself, and therefore God must be pleased with him also. Religion brings not peace and palliatives, but interior conflict, enabling man to overcome the spiritual inertia which the appeals of a secular society and a superficial world impose. Religion enables man to live in the presence of the mystery of God, so that he is content to live as God's child and God's friend. As Merton stated, "This friendship is Sonship and is Spirit. You have called me to be repeatedly born in the Spirit of your Son, repeatedly born in light, in knowledge, in unknowing, in presence and in praise."[8]

Speaking in a more broadly ecumenical and not specifically Christian context, Merton brought out the sapiential aspects of religion. In an article about William Faulkner's work and its "religious" implications, Merton stressed that the term "religious" is ambiguous and suggested an alternative term. The idea of religion today is mixed up with confessionalism, with belonging to this or that religious institution, with making and advertising a particular kind of religious commitment, with a special kind of devotion or piety, or even a certain exclusiveness in the quest for an experience which has to be sacred and not secular, as though one's whole experience of life had to be dominated from without by a system of acquired beliefs and attitudes. Merton suggested that, instead of speaking of the "religious" impact of Faulkner, the word "sapiential" be used in reference to an experience of basic and universal values on a level which words can point to but cannot fully attain, since the word "religious" no longer conveys the idea of an imaginative awareness of basic meanings. *Sapientia* is the Latin word for wisdom, which is the highest form of cognition. Wisdom seeks the ultimate causes, not simply the efficient causes which make things happen, but the ultimate reason why they happen and the ultimate values which their happening reveals to man. Wisdom is not only speculative, it is also practical, that is, it is "lived" and unless one "lives" it, one cannot "have" it. Wisdom is also creative, expressing itself in living signs and symbols. It proceeds not merely from knowledge about ultimate values, but from the actual possession and awareness of these values as incorporated in one's own existence. One of the aspects of practical wisdom is that it leads to an awareness of man's life as a task to be undertaken at great risk, in which tragic failure and creative transcendence are both possible. It provides a peculiar understanding of conflict, of the drama of human existence, and especially of the typical causes and signs of moral disaster.

Sapiential thinking has the capacity to bridge the cognitive gap between man's mind and the realm of the transcendent and the unknown, so that without "understanding" what lies beyond the limit of human vision, man nevertheless enters into an intuitive affinity with it, or seems to experience some such affinity. Religious wisdoms often claim not only to teach truths that are beyond rational knowledge but also to initiate a person into higher states of awareness. Such forms of wisdom are called mystical. Certain types of wisdom do in fact lay claim to an awareness that goes beyond the aesthetic, moral and liturgical levels and penetrate so far as to give the initiate a direct, though perhaps incommunicable, intuition of the ultimate values of life, of the absolute ground of life, or even of the invisible godhead. Christian wisdom is essentially theological, Christological and mystical. It implies a deepening of Christian faith to the point where faith becomes an experiential awareness of the realities and values of man's life in Christ and "in the Spirit" when he has been raised to divine sonship.

It was the sapiential aspects of various non-Christian "higher religions" which led Merton to study them. Genuine ecumenism requires the communication and sharing, not only of information about doctrines which are totally and irrevocably divergent, but also of religious intuitions and truths which may have something in common beneath surface differences. Ecumenism seeks the inner and ultimate spiritual "ground" which underlies all articulated differences. Religious traditions have always claimed to bear witness to higher and more personal knowledge of God than that which is contained simply in exterior worship and formulated doctrine.

In all religions one encounters not only the claim to (divine) revelation in some form or other, but also the record of special experiences in which the absolute and final validity of that revelation is in some way attested. Furthermore, in all religions it is more or less generally recognized that this profound "sapiential" experience, call it gnosis, contemplation, mysticism or prophecy, represents the deepest and most authentic fruit of the religion itself. All religions, then, seek a "summit" of holiness, of experience, of inner transformation to which their believers, or an elite of believers, aspire because they hope to incarnate in their lives the highest values in which they believe. To put it in grossly oversimplified language, all religions aspire to a "union with God." This union is described in terms which have very definite analogies with the contemplative and mystical experiences in the Christian, and particularly the Catholic, tradition.

In a similar vein, Merton said that the greatest religions are all, in fact, very simple. They all retain very essential differences, no doubt, but in their inner reality Christianity, Buddhism, Islam and Judaism are extremely simple (though capable of baffling luxuriance) and they all end up with the simplest and most baffling thing of all: direct confrontation with absolute being, absolute love, absolute mercy, or absolute void, by an immediate and fully awakened engagement in the living of everyday life.

True religion, then, is the deep and existential awareness of the bond of love between God and man and the consequent social expression of that love for all one's fellowmen. But there are dangers for religious man in various modern-day expressions of religion, dangers which arise from the ambiguities adherent to the term in the minds of modern man. One of these hidden dangers is "religiosity," or the false and excessive emphasis on externals in the practice of religion. Merton frequently spoke of religiosity in a passing manner throughout many of his works. One of the disquieting features he saw in much modern religion was its tendency to dilute deep faith and substitute for it a "togetherness," a passive conformity with a group as if the "obedience of faith" of which St. Paul spoke were nothing more than a refusal to think for oneself and the renunciation of all loyalty to one's innermost spiritual aspirations.

Pious gestures are not enough to make a person religious. This merely "symbolic" attempt at the love of God and man is insufficient. The mere fact that men are frightened and insecure, that they grasp at optimistic slogans and seek interior peace in cheerful and humanitarian maxims, is no indication that society is becoming religious. Superficial religiosity, without deep roots and without fruitful reference to the needs of men and of society, may well lead to an evasion of imperative religious obligations. Mere external respectability without deeper and more positive moral values brings discredit on the Christian faith.

Any religion that emanates from man and vaguely tends toward God does not really change man or save him. Rather, it brings him into a false relationship with God, since a religion which starts in man is nothing but man's wish for himself. Man wishes himself, magically, to become godly, holy, gentle, pure. His wishes terminate not in God but in himself. Such religion is not saved by good intentions, and in the end it becomes a caricature. What is needed, according to Merton, is the religion which "is born in us from God—which perhaps should not be called religion at all—born in us from the devastation of our own trivial 'self' and all our plans for 'our self.'"[9]

Popular religion has to a great extent betrayed man's inner spirit. The clichés of popular religion have in many cases become hollow. The sin of religiosity is that it has turned God, peace, happiness, salvation and all that man desires into products to be marketed. The common combination of organized jollity, moral legalism and nuclear crusading will not pass muster as serious religion. It certainly has nothing to do with "spiritual life."

The danger of mere exteriority in religion is that one can subscribe in all sincerity to correct dogmatic formulas without the intimate spiritual ground of one's existence being called into question. Formal acceptance of dogmas can often be a substitute in practice for any kind of intimate and personal surrender to God. Religion thus becomes a matter of formalities and gestures. If in practice the function of organized religion is nothing more than to justify and to canonize the routines of mass society, if organized religion abdicates its mission to disturb man in the depths of his conscience, and seeks instead simply to "make converts" who will smilingly adjust to the status quo, then organized religion deserves the most serious and uncompromising criticism. Such criticism is not a disloyalty. On the contrary, fidelity to truth and to God demands it.

The possibility of political exploitation of religion is real. It is true that religion on a superficial level, religion that is untrue to itself and to God, easily serves as an "opium of the people." Whenever religion and prayer invoke the name of God for reasons and needs which have nothing to do with Him, when they become a mere façade to justify a social and economic system, when religion hands over its rites and language completely to the political propagandist and prayer becomes the vehicle for a purely secular ideological program, then religion does tend to become an opiate. It deadens the spirit enough to permit the substitution of fiction and mythology for the basic truth of life. It alienates the believer, so that his religious zeal becomes political fanaticism. His faith in God, while preserving the traditional formulas, becomes in fact faith in his own nation, class or race. His ethic ceases to be the law of God and of love. The "God" which such false religion invokes becomes a mere figment of the imagination. Such insincere religion is a front for greed, injustice, sensuality, selfishness and violence. The obvious cure for such falsity is to restore the purity of faith and the genuineness of Christian love.

The Bible is extremely severe in regard to any kind of "religion" that, on the pretext of mediating between God and man, in effect sets itself up as a substitute for God and as a barrier between man and man. Such a religion is gradually revealed in the Bible to be under judgment. Here, of course, religious worship is not condemned and rejected as such, but only insofar as it is an external formality. The Christian who has "died in Christ" is liberated from merely human religious obligations, ritual customs, taboos and prohibitions based on adherence to a special group.

* * *

Through the course of his life, religious man should have a great variety of religious experiences. In the actual living of his life of love for God and his fellowmen a believer develops a more or less acute awareness of and response to the manifestations of the divine in his life, usually in terms of discerning the divine presence in some fashion, or of a deeper realization of his total dependence on the Divinity. These experiences are transient, varying in intensity and duration and subtle in their temporary or permanent effects on him. These religious experiences can occur on a great variety of occasions: in some human crisis when religious man becomes more acutely aware of his human limitations or his need of divine mercy; when the religious man receives some charismatic grace which allows him to perceive the manifest purpose of God in human events; in the faith encounters of prayer, liturgical worship or sacramental life when he has a deeper realization of interpersonal relationships and exchange with God in love.

The content of these experiences also varies. Religious man has a deeper sense of the presence of God, of his own sense of sinfulness, of sonship of God, of the victory of Christ, of fellowship in Christ, of freedom from existential fear and uncertainty, of entering into a new relationship to the Father in the Spirit through the Son. One result of his religious experiences is that the religious man grows in the practical wisdom needed to lead an ever-deepening life of love for God and his fellowmen, so that his conversion to God is made more progressively complete. The purpose of Christian morality and asceticism is to enable the faithful Christian to grow in his existential communion with God, communion which brings a heightened awareness of participation in religious reality, in the mystery of being, of divine and human love, of redemptive mystery.

Just as an act of love is a mystery which can only be experienced and not explained, and cannot be defined in analytic, abstract or strictly rational terms, so too the personal and quasi-intuitive awareness of the action of the ineffable God in one's life can only at best be communicated in poetical, symbolic and metaphorical language. Whenever Merton spoke or wrote about prayer, contemplation and mysticism he was, of course, referring to religious experience. Though Merton acknowledged the difficulties of writing about religious experiences, he did attempt a few descriptions of his own religious experiences in his early writings such as an experience he had at Mass in Cuba or in the chapel at Gethsemani when he was a novice of only three weeks, the experience of Old Testament type of praise of God in choir or the mind-expanding experience in Louisville in which he realized more profoundly the implications of his love for all men. After these early attempts at description of religious experiences, Merton rarely talked about his own experiences. His own religious experiences would have to be inferred from his many writings on prayer and canonical religious life.

In the discourse to the Apostles at the Last Supper, Christ held out the possibility of Christian religious experience of God: ". . . the Spirit of truth, whom the world cannot receive, because it neither sees nor knows him; *you know him,* for he dwells in you, and will be in you" (John 14:17). This knowledge of God, this indwelling of God, by virtue of the presence of the Spirit within the Christian, implies that deep religious experience is open to all Christians. A person first has this experience as a living reality, then he reflects on its value and meaning. It is in the third step of the process, the attempted communication of that religious experience to others that the problem of the external expression of that experience arises. Yet the experienced reality is there. As Merton said:

> The real mystery of Christian *agapē* [charity] is this power that the Person of the Word, in coming to us, has given to us. The power of a direct and simple contact with Him, not as with an object only, a thing to be seen or imagined, but in the transsubjective union of love which does not unite an object with a subject but two subjects in one affective union. Hence, in love we can, so to speak, experience in our own hearts the intimate personal secret of the Beloved.[10]

The heart of Christianity is a living experience of unity in Christ which transcends all conceptual formulations. Christianity is the taste and experience of eternal life. "We announce to you the eternal life which was in the Father and has appeared to us. What we have seen and have heard we announce to you, in order that you also may have fellowship with us and that our fellowship may be with the Father and with His Son Jesus Christ" (1 John 1:2–3).

One of the results of religious experience is a manifestation of that union that is already in existence between religious man and God, but is not fully realized. In the words of Merton, "We do not see God in contemplation —we know Him by love: for He is pure Love and when we taste the experience of loving God for His own sake alone, we know by experience Who and what He is."[11] In another place he states, "We may truly apprehend something about God's love when we know Him as the source of our being. But we learn, and learn by experience that God is love when we find that we ourselves have become identified with the Son whom the Father has sent, and that the Father sends the Son from within ourselves. . . ."[12]

In the process of his Christian life, a Christian should gradually acquire a new consciousness which is the basis of religious experience. The individual self must cease to assert itself as the center of consciousness. God Himself, the personal God, is the deepest center of consciousness. To fully realize this by the active and creative awareness of love is man's highest good. This awareness of love in the heart of religious man will naturally lead to a more active, practical love for other people and an active concern for their social welfare, so that "the love of my human heart can become God's love for God and man."[13]

It is obvious all through the Scriptures, and in the New Testament especially, that a truly religious man will experience social concern for his fellowmen. For whatever is demanded by truth, by justice, by mercy or by love must surely be taken as willed by God. To obey Him is to respond to His will expressed in the need of another person, or at least to respect the rights of others. For the right of another man is one expression of God's love and

God's will. God is not merely asking man to conform to some abstract, arbitrary law: He is enabling man to share, as His son, in His own care for his brother. Religious man must certainly be detached, but he can never allow himself to become insensible to human values, whether in society, in other men or in himself.

Just as a religious man responds to God's call by surrendering himself in love, so he responds to God by faith, by commitment of himself in fidelity to the God who has spoken His Word. His response of faith is another mode of expressing his love. In his early writings Merton emphasized the intellectual aspect of faith as an assent to the revelation of truth about God, in keeping with the type of theology which he had been taught. But in his later years the emphasis shifted, as it did in Catholic theology in general, to an understanding of faith as a personal commitment to the person of God revealing Himself in love. However, even in his first theological book, Merton realized that the passage from a philosophical understanding of God to faith (as an intellectual assent) is marked by the gift of oneself to God. And the transition from faith to that deeper spiritual understanding which comes from contemplation is the direct consequence of a more complete and radical gift of oneself to God.

Reflecting on the element of intellectual assent to doctrine in the act of faith, Merton stated that if faith were merely an intellectual assent and nothing more, if it were only the "argument of what does not appear," it would not be complete. It is also a grasp, a contact, a communion of wills, "the substance of things hoped for" (Hebrews 11:1). By faith, one not only assents to propositions revealed by God, one not only attains to truth in a way that intelligence and reason alone cannot do, but one assents to God Himself. One receives God. One says "yes" not merely to a statement about God, but to the invisible, infinite God Himself. Too often man's notion of faith is falsified by his emphasis on the statements about God which faith believes, and by his forgetfulness of the fact that faith is a communion with God in light and truth. Faith terminates not in a statement, not in a formula of words, but in God.

Still relatively early in his career, Merton spoke of the interrelation of faith and love when he said that "living faith" is a faith that obscurely responds to the reality of God by the movement of love. It only establishes a living contact between the soul and God insofar as it is vitalized by charity. The more intense the love that moves a person to seek God beneath the analogical formulas of revealed truth, the more vital will be the grasp of his faith upon the hidden reality of God. This connection of faith and love, in the context of the attitudes of faith, openness, attention, reverence, expectation, supplication, trust and joy which prayer gives man, was brought out in one of Merton's last formal works on prayer. "Our living faith tells us that we are in the presence of God, that we live in Christ, that in the Spirit of God we 'see' God our Father without 'seeing,' we know Him in 'unknowing.' Faith is the bond that unites us to Him in the Spirit who gives us light and love."[14]

A deepening of Merton's understanding of faith and its social implications was evident by 1960. In the context of apprehending Christ in our fellowmen he said:

> The transcendent work of Christian love is also
> at every moment a work of faith. Not only faith
> in dogmas proposed to our obedient minds by
> holy Church, not only faith in abstract proposi-

tions, but faith in the present reality of Christ. The phrase, "seeing Christ in my brother," is often subject to a sadly superficial interpretation. By a mental sleight of hand we often do away with our neighbor in all his concreteness, his individuality, his personality with its gifts and limitations and replace him with a vague and abstract presence of Christ. This is a pitiful subterfuge by which we end up trying to love, not Christ in our brother, but Christ instead of our brother. Our faith is given us not to see whether or not our neighbor is Christ, but to recognize Christ in him and help our love make both him and ourselves more fully Christ.[15]

However, formulas and creeds have a place in man's religious life. They are not intended to prove anything. They are not the whole of revelation, but time-conditioned human expressions of what has been revealed. They point to a supernatural truth that is invisible and incomprehensible, God Himself. If one remains content with the formulas or the symbols and makes them alone the object of one's "faith," then he does not really "believe" in the full sense of the word. The purpose of creeds is to define clearly what are the reliable terms in which the revelation of the invisible can be expressed. These formulas and symbols do tell us the truth about God, and they really enable us to enter into contact with Him in the act of faith.

By faith, religious man finds his own true being in God. It is evident that faith is not just one moment in the spiritual life, but it requires that acceptance of God which is the very climate of all spiritual living. In faith religious man has the beginning of communion which gives a dimension of simplicity and depth to his apprehensions and all his experiences, by incorporating the unknown and the unconscious into his daily life in a living, dynamic manner. The function of faith is not to reduce mystery to rational clarity, but to integrate the unknown and the known together into a living whole in which one is more and more able to transcend the limitations of his external self. Man's commitment to God in faith reveals the unknown in his own self insofar as his unknown and undiscovered self actually lives in God, moving and acting only under the direct light of His merciful grace. Faith is not just conformity, it is life. It embraces all the realms of life, and is the only way of opening up the true depths of reality, even man's own inner reality. Until a man yields himself to God in the consent that is faith, he must inevitably remain a stranger to himself, because he is excluded from the most meaningful depths of his own being. He believes in God, not so much because he wants to know, but because he wants to be.

Specifically Christian faith is not just the acceptance of truths about Christ, nor acquiescence in the story of Christ with its moral and spiritual implications, nor merely the decision to put into practice the teachings of Christ. The real meaning of Christian faith is the rejection of all that is not Christ in order that all life may be sought and found "in Christ." Such faith is a dynamic and supernatural power in man's life, a "new creation" revolutionizing man's spiritual and bodily life in its inmost depths. It is the total, unswerving source of salvific power and of new life.

Religious faith alone can open the inner ground of man's being and preserve him from the surrender of his integrity to a totalitarian type of life. The reason for this is that no matter what a man thinks, his thought is based on a fundamental belief. If his belief is in slogans and doctrines which are foisted on him by a political or economic ideology, he will surrender his inmost truth to exterior compulsion. If his belief is a suspension of belief, and an acceptance of physical stimulation for its own sake, he still continues to "believe" in the possibility of some rational happiness. Man must believe in something, and that in which he believes becomes his god. To serve some material or human entity as one's god is to be a slave to that which perishes, and this is to be a slave to death, sorrow, falsehood and misery.

Christianity is a religion of the Word. The one Word which God speaks is Himself. Speaking, He manifests Himself as infinite love. That one Word is heard only in the silence and solitude of the selfless, undivided heart, the heart that is at peace, detached, free, without care. Faith is misunderstood if it is considered to be a means of information alone. Christian doctrine cannot be grasped adequately without being centered on love since the object of faith is one, God, love. The various doctrines must converge upon love as the spokes of a wheel converge on the hub.

The Bible does not present faith in terms of dogmatic propositions about God. Biblical faith is presented in terms of personal event and encounter which revolutionize one's entire sense of being and of identity. In Merton's teaching, the question of identity is not raised merely in psychological and ethical terms, but as self-commitment, that is, as a faith that becomes a personal encounter with the unknown for whom there is the nonword "God" and also the more concrete, humanly biased name "Father." But somehow Christ immediately cancels the word "Father" with the word "Son," for the two are identical and later theology understands the immense importance of that identity.

Is biblical faith possible for modern man? It is no doubt quite true that modern man cannot easily grasp the symbols and images, still less the abstract concepts in which the Church spoke of God in the past. But it is not true that modern man is incapable of faith. Faith is not dependent on this or that psychology, culture or set of symbols. Faith is a divine gift which can break in upon the mind of any man at any time and in any culture, in any language. Of course, if it is to be a fully and articulately Christian faith, it must be a response to Christian preaching of the gospel message. And here indeed man needs a contemporary language. There is no doubt whatever that the conventional and well-worn images in which his relations with God and with Christ are expressed are sometimes irrelevant to the modern world. But yet, where does the trouble really lie? In the "myths" of the Bible? Or rather in the tired, jejune experience of Christian truth? If modern man really entered into these truths, really lived them in his "contemporary" life, they would transmute themselves naturally into terms which would reach his contemporary fellowmen. Much of modern atheism is due to the lamentable example of pseudo-Christianity in which Christians, in the words of Vatican Council II, "must be said to conceal rather than reveal the authentic face of God and of religion."[16]

What is required of Christians is that they develop a completely modern and contemporary consciousness in which their experience as men of the century is integrated with their experience as children of God redeemed by Christ. The weakness of the Christian language lies not so much in the theology and formulated belief as in the split which has hitherto separated man's Christian faith from the rest of his life. In order to prevent this split in one's life between belief and action, continual Christian experience, deepened by prayer, is necessary. Speaking in the context of the modern feeling of the "absence of God" and the apparent inability to believe, Merton reminded religious man that this may well be a sign of authentic Christian growth and a point of decisive development in faith. The way to cope with it is not to regress to an earlier and less mature stage of belief, to stubbornly reaffirm and reinforce feelings, aspirations and images that were appropriate to one's childhood. One must, on a new level of prayer, live through this crisis of belief and grow to a more complete personal and Christian integration by experience. This experience of struggle, of self-emptying, of letting go and of subsequent recovery on a new level is one of the ways in which the cross and resurrection of Christ take hold of a person's life and transform it. Merton was not speaking of "mystical experience" or anything new and strange, but simply of the fullness of personal awareness that comes with a total self-renunciation, followed by self-commitment on the highest level, beyond mere intellectual consent and external obedience. Real Christian living is stunted and frustrated if it remains content with the bare essentials of worship, fulfilling one's external duties and merely being respectable. The real purpose of prayer, in the fully personal sense as well as in the Christian assembly, is the deepening of personal realization in love, and of the awareness of God. This results in the exploration and discovery of new dimensions of freedom, illumination and love, and in the deepening of one's awareness of his life in Christ.

Deep Christian faith helps a religious man to be fully adult and mature, securely assured of his own identity before God. His judgments concerning his personal experiences are based on his own awareness of what takes place within himself. A truly religious man will not allow himself to be treated as an alienated and helpless individual whose inner experience is dictated to him by another and imposed on him from outside. It is the surest sign of immaturity to be imposed on entirely by the ideas and ideals of others and substitute these for one's own true personal experiences and judgments of life. The faith of the Christian is the inner adherence to a truth which is not imposed from outside. Rather it is a free, personal adherence of love "in the Spirit" and it gives power to resist all external compulsions in the realm of thought as well as of life. This truth makes one truly and authentically free.

In one of his Christmas letters to his friends, Merton referred to the social aspects of loving faith in relation to the "problems of life."

> The heart of man can be filled with much pain even when things are exteriorly "all right." It becomes all the more difficult because today we are used to thinking that there are explanations for everything. But there is no explanation of most of what goes on in our own hearts, and we cannot account for it all. No use resorting to the kind of mental tranquilizers that even religious explanations sometimes offer. Faith must be deeper than that, rooted in the unknown and in the abyss of darkness that is the ground of our being. No use teasing the darkness to try to make answers grow out of it. But if we learn to have a deeper inner patience, things solve themselves, or God solves them, if you prefer: but do

not expect to see how. Just learn to wait, and do what you can and help other people. Often in helping someone else we find the best way to bear with our own trouble.[17]

So, Merton did not accept the erroneous, axiomatic viewpoint that a life of faith brings total security and an absolute lack of any questioning or of uncertainty on any point whatsoever. Reflecting on the notion that "love conquers all," Merton brought out the inner connection between faith and love:

> Easter celebrated the victory of love over everything. If we believe it we still understand it, because belief is what opens the door to love. But to believe only in systems and statements and not in people is an evasion, a betrayal of love. When we really believe as Christians, we find ourselves trusting and accepting people as well as dogmas. Woe to us when we are merely orthodox and reject human beings, flesh and blood, the aspirations, joys and needs of men. Yet there is no fruit, either, in merely sentimental gestures of communion that mean little, and seek only to flatter or placate. Love can be tough and uncompromising in its fidelity to its highest principles.[18]

One of the results of the commitment to God in faith and love is the conversion of religious man. Surrender to the person of Christ in faith leads to a conversion of man's whole being, a *metanoia*, an entire change of heart which brings a new relationship to God and the world and the discovery of a new identity, a new experiential awareness in his life of love which embraces all men. This commitment of his whole self and his whole life to the reality of Christ present in the world is effected by the Holy Spirit, the Spirit of love. Christian faith, or more precisely conversion to Christ, also has the social function of radically liberating man from the delusions and obsessions of modern man and his society, of protecting man against the absorption of freedom and intelligence in the crass and thoughtless servitudes of mass society. Conversion involves the actual transformation of religious man so that his attitudes are changed, his modes of thought are continually focused on God, and the quality of his life takes on a new dimension of loving fidelity. The intellectual, moral, religious and Christian commitments of his life are altered and strengthened so that one could say that the continual process of conversion changes the whole world for religious man and his relations to it. His horizons are broadened, his capacity for love is expanded and his social consciousness is made more existentially real.

The liberation from self-concern which the process of conversion involves leads to new levels of spirituality and opens religious man to deeper intimacy with God. In the words of Merton:

> We die on the external level of our being in order to find ourselves more alive and more free on another, more spiritual level. We become aware of ourselves as being quite different from our normal, empirical selves. At the same time we are vividly conscious of the fact that this new mode of being is more truly "normal" than our ordinary existence. It is more natural for us to be out of ourselves and carried freely and entirely toward the Other, toward God in Himself and in

other men, than it is for us to be centered and en-
closed within ourselves. We find ourselves to be
more truly human when we are raised to the level
of the divine. We transcend ourselves, we see
ourselves in a new light, by losing sight of ourselves and no longer seeing ourselves, but God.[19]

The deep interior conflicts which underlie all Christian
conversions require a turning to a freedom based, not on
social approval and relative alienation, but on a deep dependence on God in loving faith. The endless series of
large and small conversions or inner revolutions which
living Christian experience requires leads finally to a total
transformation in Christ. The Christian life is in reality a
perpetual conversion, a turning to God and to the community of men in love.

The best summary statement of Merton's ideas on
what religious conversion involves for religious man was
an extended commentary on the statement of Christ to
Nicodemus, "You must be born from above" (John 3:3).
These words of Christ reveal the inner meaning of Christianity. Spiritual rebirth is the key to the aspirations of
all the "higher religions" which attempt to answer a
deeper need in man to be liberated from mere natural
necessity. There is in man an instinct for newness, for
renewal, for a liberation of creative power. To be "born
from above" is not to become somebody else, but to become himself. The deepest spiritual instinct in man is
this urge of inner truth which demands that he be
faithful to himself, to his deepest and most original
potentialities. Yet, in order to become one's true self, the
false self must die and disappear. The new birth of
which Christ speaks gives definitive meaning to life. It
awakens a deep spiritual consciousness which takes man

beyond the level of egoism into Christ. This rebirth is not a single event but a continuous dynamic of inner renewal, a "passover" in which man is progressively liberated from selfishness and not only grows in love but in some sense "becomes love." The perfection of the new birth is reached when there is only love in the religious man, there is only Christ in him. To allow the love of Christ to shine in him is the maturity of the "new man."

This rebirth of religious man in Christ and in His Spirit leads to a new historical consciousness and has eschatological implications since it is a rebirth into a transformed time, the time of the kingdom, the time of the Spirit, the time of the "new aeon." It means the disintegration of the social and cultural self, the product of merely human history, and the reintegration of the real inner self in Christ.

Prayer is one means of continual conversion in love and to love. Prayer is man's response to God seeking man's love, a response to and discovery of God within himself. As such, it is always clouded in mystery. It is an experience of man's complete dependence on the hidden and mysterious God. In prayer, man can come close to God who seeks to do him good, to give him His mercy, to surround him with His love.

Christian faith, then, is not to be seen as a set of abstract doctrinal propositions, but is rather to be experienced as a unified life in Christ. This unified life can be seen within the framework of the Lord's Prayer, which embraces the whole of Christian life. It covers all man's relationships with God and his fellowmen, and brings him face to face with his most elemental and most profound responsibilities. Prayer, knowledge, worship, intelligence, devotion and purity of life are all brought together by consideration of the prayer given to man by Christ in the Gospel.

Merton continued on this theme of the Lord's Prayer in a conference given at Darjeeling, India, in November 1968. He said:

> Prayer is not so much something we do, but an expression of who we are. Our very being expresses itself with prayer because prayer flows from our relationship to God and other people. A person can *be* a living prayer without ever saying a formal prayer. This whole life of prayer relates us to God within us. Prayer comes from a deep sense of our incompleteness as creatures. We are a living incompleteness. The very nature of our being as creatures implies this sense of a need to be completed by Him from whom we come. To cultivate a life of prayer is to cultivate this sense of our relationship with God, the sense of being totally suspended from the loving grace of God, a realization of God's alliance with us. Prayer leads to a desire that His will be completely fulfilled in us, so that the essence of Christian prayer comes to be, "Thy Will be done—Thy Kingdom come." Our Christian life of prayer is centered toward the fulfillment of God's will, not only my good, but the good of all creatures. That is what God wants and plans, and has promised. So, as we go on in a life of prayer, we progress from a sense of incompleteness and loneliness to a sense of fulfillment and confidence, not based on anything in myself, but Jesus Christ, risen, in whom God's

promises are fulfilled and for whose manifestation we are waiting.[20]

The divine love, which underlies the mystery of creation and redemption, is a free gift of God to men. As
Merton said, "God has willed that men should know
Him, not in esoteric secrets and strange philosophies, but
in the announcement of the Gospel message which is the
message of His love. 'This is my commandment, that you
love one another as I have loved you'" (John 15:12).[21]
The practicality of this commandment of love is brought
out in the New Testament, which shows with the clear-
est evidence that the preaching of Jesus and the teaching
of the Apostles was directed against what has come to be
known as religious alienation. The fact that Jesus worked
miracles on the Sabbath emphasized the priority of
human values over conventional "religious" ones. Jesus
decided for the person, and against the claims of a legal-
ist religion. All through the New Testament is found the
explicit contrast between a merely abstract, mental, institutional religiosity and that love which in uniting man
to his brother of flesh and blood thereby unites him to
the truth in God (for example, James 1:27; John 13:34–35;
1 John 4:7–11).

How does man attain to a real union of love with his
brother? Not merely by abstract agreement about truths
concerning the end of all things and the afterlife, but by
a realistic collaboration in the work of daily living in the
world of hard fact in which men must work in order to
eat, as St. Paul showed in the two Epistles to the Thes-
salonians. Paul protested against a religious alienation
which substitutes a mental life of religious ideas for a
practical Christian life of love in the midst of everyday
realities. The fact that the New Testament provides a

theological basis for the practical life of love among men does nothing to weaken that love and certainly does not make it abstract. The Christian loves because God is love, and because God is manifested in actual love, not in pious ideas and practices. "Religion clean and undefiled before God is this, to visit the fatherless and widows in their tribulation . . ." (James 1:27). This is precisely the "new commandment" which is the heart of the new relationship between man and God, the very essence of the teaching of Christianity. The teaching of the Gospel is that men are no longer servants of God, no longer bound by complex natural observances and obscure legal systems known only by experts. They are sons of God and brothers of one another, united in a community of freedom and love for one another. Ideally, this Christian love embraces all men, and not only fellow Christians.

Speaking of the Bible as one source of the knowledge of the bond of love between God and man, Merton stated that the Bible reveals to man the basic dynamism of human existence under God, a dynamism of awareness and response in which lies "salvation." This dynamism is expressed in literary terms, based on the religious experience of the authors of the books of the Bible, an experience that is in many ways prophetic and mystical and eschatological, yet grounded in history and ordinary life. These experiences are more than aesthetic, are even beyond "religion," beyond the devout and cleansing awe of initiation into ritual and mystery, beyond the healing and transforming sense of moral self-transcendence.

In order to express properly this dynamism of human existence under God in a life of prayer it is necessary for man to cultivate a healthy and realistic view of human life which will help insure a genuine occupation with God that is based on living faith and common sense.

Prayer is in reality a simple yearning for the presence of God, for a personal understanding of His word, for a knowledge of His will and for a capacity to hear and obey Him. It is thus something much more than uttering petitions for good things external to man's own deepest concerns. Man's encounter with God in prayer is a discovery of both his deepest freedom and his own true identity, an encounter in which his freedom emerges in the depths of nothingness and underdevelopment in response to the call of God. Prayer is freedom and affirmation opening out of nothingness into love. It is not only dialogue with God, it is the communion of man's freedom with His ultimate freedom, the elevation of his ultimate freedom into the infinite freedom of the Divine Spirit, and of the Divine Love.

Though Merton was addressing contemplative monks in the following passage about their being living witnesses to the bond of love that exists between God and man, his message has a universal Christian application. To Merton, what is of importance today is not to get modern man to accept religion as a human and a cultural value but to let him see that he is a witness to Christ, of the new creation, of the resurrection, of the living God, and that is something that goes far beyond the cultural phenomenon of religion. The contemplative life will, therefore, need to be understood, not in terms of religious observances which dramatize the more devout attitudes of a bygone society, but in terms of living experience and witness, in terms of complete Christian authenticity, as disciples who have found Him whom the Father has sent into the world and are able to bear witness to His reality by their characters, by their lives and by the transformation of their consciousness.

The man of prayer gives living witness to the bond of love which exists between God and man, and gives a message of hope which aids contemporary man in finding his way through the jungle of language and problems which seem to surround God today. For the man of prayer has in his heart and at the very ground of his being a natural certainty which is coextensive with his very existence, a certainty which says that insofar as he exists he is penetrated through and through with the sense and the reality of God even though he may be utterly unable to believe or express this in philosophical or even religious terms. His very existence is a sign that God loves him and the presence of His love creates and sustains him. Whether he can understand it or not, the man of prayer realizes that God loves him, is present in him, dwells in him, calls him, saves him. A life of authentic prayer can lead one to the intimate union in the depths of his own heart between God's spirit and his own secret, inmost self, so that he and God are in all truth one Spirit.

In a life of prayer, a Christian discovers what he already has. As Merton said, "You start where you are and deepen what you already have, and you realize that you are already there. We already have everything, but we don't know it, and we don't experience it. Everything has been given to us in Christ. All we need is to experience what we already possess."[22]

This experience is not to be restricted to highly trained contemplatives. As Merton said:

> Union with God in love also implies a profound and existential grasp of His presence; indeed it should normally imply some such intuition, however vague this might be. Nor is this intuition, even when supernatural, necessarily "mystical" in the full sense of the word. The experience of living faith, the "sense of the presence of God" which many faithful Christians

enjoy without being mystics is a supernatural intuition of God's loving presence and care, granted with the gift of mature faith.[23]

* * *

Religious man expresses his fidelity to God not only in his private prayer and devotion, but also through a communal aspect of his life, namely the liturgy. His religious commitment to God, as expressed in the many artistic forms of community liturgy, be they poetic, literary or musical, enhances the very quality of his whole life of love.

The liturgy is the Church's great school of prayer. In the liturgy, Christ Himself, by His Holy Spirit, prays and offers sacrifice in His body, the Church. Active participation in the liturgy is a mystical participation in the prayer and sacrifice of Jesus Christ, the new Adam and the high priest of the new creation. Liturgical worship is symbolic, and much more than communication, it is also communion. Worship is symbolic communion in mystery, the mystery of the actual presence of Him who is Being. It is religious man's communal recognition of the fact that "in reality we cannot be without Him, that He dwells in us, and that because He is in us and we in Him, we are one with one another in Him."[24]

Liturgical worship of God is man's way of expressing above all his celebration of having found God in his life. He shares his joy in finding God by celebration with those he loves. The Church, which is a community of lovers, is composed of individual men, but it is also a Mystical Body composed of many who are one in Christ and share in His own divine life.

But this cannot be so unless we who are the Church experience in our lives the mystery of

Christ. That is why the liturgy would have us constantly go back to the beginning and work our way down to what we are through the types and figures which foreshadowed the Whole Christ, the Head and members, the Jesus who died on Calvary and lives in us, who dies in us that others may live in Him. The fruitful use of the liturgy can be summed up in this experience of the mystery of Christ. Liturgical prayer does not attempt to raise us up to something we are not. It reminds us that we have already been to some extent transformed. It assures us that the beginnings of transformation are a pledge and foreshadowing of its completion. The liturgy reminds us not merely of what we ought to be but of the unbelievable truth of what we are. It will tell us over and over again that we are Christ in the world, that He lives in us and that what was said of Him has been and is being fulfilled in us. It is itself a manifestation of His presence and power on earth. The liturgy tells us that God's Kingdom has already come. It is established in the midst of a godless humanity.[25]

The more the individual Christian enters into the spirit of the liturgy, the better he is able to understand the personalism of the Christian faith. The real root of personality is that which is incommunicable, genuinely unique, on the deepest spiritual level. Personalism is the discovery of this deep reality. One is a more truly Christian person when his inmost secret remains a mystery shared by himself and others in a way that is at the same time secret and public. Christian personalism is the sacramental sharing of the inner secret of personality in the mystery of love, the discovery of one's inmost self and the inmost self of one's neighbor in the mystery of Christ. This discovery respects the hiddenness and incommunicability of each one's personal secret while paying tribute to his presence in the common celebration. Thus the Christian finds himself and his brother in the communal celebration of the mystery of Christ. "But what is manifested, proclaimed, celebrated and consummated in the liturgy is not my personality or your personality. It is the personality of Christ the Lord, who, when two or three of us are gathered together in His Name, is present in the midst of us. This presence of Christ in the liturgy leads to our discovery and celebration of our secret and spiritual self."[26] The Christian community both celebrates its identity and develops that identity by constant redefinition in love. It is above all aware of itself as a community when it celebrates the mysteries of unity in Christ's redemptive love.

Thus, in the Christian liturgy, the people of God both celebrate and express their self-awareness as a redeemed people. It is the action of Christian persons in the process of achieving full development. In liturgical expression men affirm their divine sonship and exercise their rights as citizens in an eschatological and redeemed community of those who are one in love, freed from the bonds of sin and death. As Merton said:

> Participation in the liturgy implies that we are friends and collaborators with Christ in His great work of redeeming and sanctifying the entire world. For liturgy is not only a way in which the Christian community becomes aware of its existence and its relationship to God in order to praise Him. It is also a work in which the Church

collaborates with the Divine Redeemer, renewing on her altars the sacred mysteries which are the life and salvation of men, uttering again the life-giving words that are capable of saving and transforming us, blessing again the sick and the possessed, preaching still His Gospel to the poor. In the liturgy we meet the same Christ who went about doing good and who is still present in the midst of us. We meet Him by sharing in His life and His redemption. We meet Christ in order to be Christ, and with Him collaborate in saving the world.[27]

Religious man can also find himself and his right relationship to God and the world of men in his daily work. This self-discovery in his work is aided by his liturgical participation, because there man learns both a theology of life and a theology of work. The liturgy plants seeds of self-understanding and wisdom that will flower in his life's work and center him in his present reality. For only in the present can man come in full contact with the truth willed for him and in him by God. With this deepened self-understanding and better appreciation of what his life's work really is, religious man is better able to collaborate with Christ and his fellowmen in changing the world of men.

Liturgy is, therefore, rooted in life. Sharing in the living and spiritual bread is meaningful and spiritually fruitful in proportion as it maintains its vital connection with the most basic activities of man: work, sharing the fruits of work, communion with one's fellowmen in the responsibilities, trials and joys of common social life. Religious man, by his liturgical participation, experiences a communal responsibility and reciprocity which, after taking a religious form in the sacred cult, afterward incarnates itself in work characterized by a similar responsibility and reciprocity. To be worthy of being offered to God in worship, work must be a valid and responsible contribution to the common good of the society in which man lives. Hence to participate in the liturgy should mean a living testimony of the fact that he is dedicated to peace, to reason, to justice for all, and that he is always ready to obey Christ's command to love one another. In signifying these moral and religious aspects of his social life and work, the liturgy exercises a powerful transforming action upon that life and work.

The social dimension of the liturgy then is more than the power to produce a feeling of solidarity and fellowship with those who participate. It expresses more than the current social needs and aspirations of the Christian group. In the liturgical mystery religious man has a ritual and symbolic expression of the redemptive and life-giving union of Christ with His members in all the aspects of their social existence in the world. The Eucharistic mystery then, expressed in the liturgy, is both an expression and a consecration of religious man's total life.

Indeed, the Eucharistic liturgy has dimensions that are not only social but even cosmic and eschatological. They reach out to the limits of man's actual world. For man is in nature not merely as part of nature. By his spirituality, his intelligence and his capacity for wisdom in the Divine Spirit, man can contain within himself all the truth, the goodness, the light and meaning of the cosmos. Man is in the cosmos as the eye is in the body. He is the "light of the world" not only because he is capable of understanding the world, but because he is able, by the right use of his freedom, to give the whole world its ultimate spiritual and religious significance. For the truly Christian religious man, then, Christianity is more than a moral code, a philosophy, a system of rites. It is a life that is lived and expressed in action. The action in which it is expressed and experienced and lived is called a mystery. This mystery keeps ever present in history the sacrifice which was once consummated by Christ. Christian life is then the life, death and resurrection of Christ going on day after day in the heart of the individual man and in the heart of his society.

In striving for self-understanding and self-realization religious man comes to a deeper awareness that everything in his life is a divine gift: his life, freedom, vocation, his openness to love. He realizes that he is the subject of the divine mercy so that, despite his alienation from his true self and the rest of the family of man, God loves him as he is. As one loved by God, religious man achieves a deeper awareness of the power of love in his own life and realizes that divine and human love are the keys to the understanding of himself before God and his fellowmen. The divine Lover presents religious man with gifts, forgives and reconciles him in mercy, and gives him the very power to respond in love to God and to all men.

These three themes of "gift," "mercy" and "love" are so constantly woven through the texture of all Merton's writings that they truly could be said to constitute his "theology of grace." As in all of his writings, Merton was not speculative in the development of these themes, which constitute the essence of Christian life, rather he was very existential in his approach. Rarely did he develop these themes at any great length, but they were constantly referred to in the whole body of his writings. A cumulative index of Merton's published works would show the following entries recurring most frequently, in descending order: one—God; two—Man; three—Love; four—Mercy; five—Gift. Though he did have some explicit articles on the topics of love and mercy, these by no means encompass all he had to say on these subjects.

The divine gifts and divine mercy go together. As Merton said:

> In religious terms, this is simply a matter of accepting life, and everything in life as a gift, clinging to none of it, as far as you are able. All life tends to grow like this, in mystery inscaped with paradox and contradiction, yet centered, in its very heart, on the divine mercy. Such is my philosophy, and it is more than a philosophy, because it consists not in statements about a truth that cannot be adequately stated, but in grace, mercy, and the realization of the "new life" that is in us who believe by the gift of the Holy Spirit. Without the grace of God there would be no unity, no simplicity in our lives, only contradiction.[28]

The Christian, made aware by his life experiences of the mystery of evil which stands between himself and God, is committed to the belief that love and mercy are the most powerful forces in the world. Indeed, it is the very task of a Christian to be a witness of mercy.

> Above all, we must understand the critical importance of forgiveness as the heart of Christian humanism. Christianity is not merely a religious system which attempts to explain evil. It is a life of dynamic love which forgives evil and, by forgiving it, enables love to transform evil into good.

The dynamic of Christian love is a dynamic of forgiveness and the true secret of Christian humanism is that it has the divine power to transform man in the very ground of his being from a miserable slave and confused being into a son of God. This divine transforming power is forgiveness, Christian mercy. Where this mercy is absent, there can no longer be any claim to an authentic Christianity.[29]

To receive mercy and to give it is to participate in the work of the new creation and of redemption. It is to share in the eschatological fulfillment of the work of Christ and the establishment of the kingdom of God. The reality of God's mercy is around man if he has but the insight to perceive it. Religious man is able to do so.

In introducing a photographic study of his own monastery, Merton made some penetrating remarks that can easily be extrapolated to all human life. Stating that "one lives amid the accumulated memories of past mistakes," Merton went on to describe the dynamism of God's good, green earth: "And when we think that we have won a victory for our own partial conception of newness and of order we find that the honeysuckle has triumphed over the abandoned gate; the ivy is coming in the windows; the hollyhocks are running wild along the clotheslines; the trumpet vines have crawled up to the very foot of St. Joseph; the discarded church bell in the vegetable garden provides a magnificent frame for the distant steeple." Even the weeds (of evil) grow up everywhere "full of tiny flowers." Then one remembers "it is the honeysuckle, the hollyhocks and the rest that are really alive and that they have something very appropriate to say about the mercy of God. For His mercy covers everything and turns mistakes, oversights and forgetfulness into a riot of new creation. Now, for once, the camera has caught sight of all the fugitive and symbolic beauty in the very heart of all that is ordinary."[30]

An interesting insight into Merton's personality and the reason for his stress on divine mercy in his writings was given during an interview with one of his fellow monks who had known Merton extremely well and had worked with him for years. When asked, "What was Merton's self-image? Did he consider himself primarily as a poet, a writer, a theologian?" the monk hesitated for a thoughtful moment and replied simply, "I'm convinced that Louis looked upon himself first of all as a sinner in need of God's mercy."[31]

*　*　*

What is the function of love in Merton's thought? Through the power of love religious man is enabled to understand both himself and the true purpose of life. The key to understanding life and oneself is love. Love is man's whole reason for being and until he loves God, man does not really begin to live. Man fulfills the purpose of his existence when, by conformity to Christ, he realizes his own identity by becoming perfectly free both in love and through love. In loving God, he comes to know himself. Since in reality he loves God by loving other persons, in the mutual exchange of love he comes to know himself as loved by God.

> Love is not a mere emotion or a sentiment, it is a certain way of being alive. Love is a lucid and ardent response to a person, and that response creates an aura in our lives which gives both

meaning to life and self-understanding of our
own personhood. It is a fact of experience that we
do not find meaning within ourselves alone, but
in the response of love for another. A person
transcends himself in the encounter, the response and the communion of love, and this
communion and self-transcendence become the
real purpose of life. We do not become fully
human until we give ourselves to others in love,
which creates in us this very capacity for self-
giving, for sharing, for creativity, for mutual care
and spiritual concern. Love itself becomes our
true destiny, and we find it, not in ourselves, but
in another. The meaning of life is a secret
which has to be revealed to us, and it is revealed
in love by the one we love.[32]

The transcendent spiritual power which love confers is
the root of freedom and creative response to life, bringing with it an appreciation of life as value and as gift.
Love responds to the full richness, the variety, the fecundity of living experience itself. One knows by experience the inner mystery of life. Lovers become different
people, more alive, more understanding, more enduring
and seemingly more endowed with humanity. They are
made into new persons, transformed by the power of
love. This transforming power of love creates a deeper
unity within the persons of the lovers and with the realities of life.

The transforming power of human and divine love enables religious man to collaborate with God in redeem-
ing and transforming the world of men. For love is not
only the source of personal salvation and the key to the
meaning of one's existence, but it is also the key to the

entire creation of God. The reality of love is judged by its power to help man get beyond himself, to renew himself in transcending his present limitations. The function of love is not only to give man loving possession of God in eternity, but also to enable man to collaborate in extending the reign of God on earth. In building up this spiritual kingdom of unity and peace, religious man becomes not an exploiter of creation but truly its spiritual head and king.

The whole problem of the modern world is the lack of love for one another. "The reason why we hate and fear one another is that we secretly or openly hate and fear ourselves. We hate ourselves because the depths of our being are a chaos of frustration and spiritual misery. Lonely and helpless, we cannot be at peace with others because we are not at peace with ourselves, and we cannot be at peace with ourselves because we are not at peace with God."[33]

Christian religious man finds the answer to interior and social turmoil in the gospel message of love and peace: "This is My commandment, that you love one another." The Indian philosopher Mahatma Gandhi could say in truth, "Jesus died in vain if he did not teach us to regulate the whole of life by the eternal law of love."[34] The deepest and most fundamental exigency of the divine law, written in the heart of man, is that he find his own personal and social fulfillment, and the true meaning of life, in loving others.

Not only does the power of love give meaning and purpose to life, it also confers self-understanding. A precondition for the experience of God's love is the human experience of being loved. The realization that one is loved by others leads to the discovery of one's own true self in love. "Since persons are known not by intellect or by principles alone, but only by love, so in the highest expression of my own personality and freedom which love is, I come to know my real self."[35] Religious man discovers himself in others by discovering the sources of freedom and love which God has given him. Just as in loving God he discovers his true self in relation to Him, so in loving others he discovers his true self through them and through their love. In the cumulative experience of love, the lover is able to give himself completely to another because he is his own to give. As a free, loving agent he knows what is his to surrender, and he comes to know who he is in himself, in relation to God and man.

Thus man's attitude toward life is reflected by his attitude toward love. And his conception of himself is profoundly affected by his notion of, and experience in, love.

> For our love, or lack of it, our willingness to risk it or determination to avoid it will in the end be an expression of ourselves, of who we think we are, of what we want to be, of what we think the purpose of life is. Love becomes a self-revelation, to ourselves and others, of our deepest personal meaning, value and identity. This revelation is possible only in love of other persons. I cannot find myself in myself and by myself, but only in the persons I love. My true meaning and worth are shown not in my estimate of myself, but in the eyes of the persons who love me.[36]

A complete theology of love would also consider the all-important ideas of the cross, suffering and resurrection, which bring human love into the context of Christ's love for man, and the redemption and transfiguration of human love in Christ.

Religious man believes in the transforming power of love because he recognizes that his whole being is grounded in love. When man attempts to live by and for himself alone, he becomes a little island of hate, greed, suspicion, fear and desire. Then his whole outlook on life is falsified. But where there is a deep, simple, all-embracing love of man, of the created world of living and inanimate things, there will be respect for life, for freedom, for truth and justice, and there will be true love of God.

Merton's own trust in the revealing, unifying and transforming power of human and divine love remained in him to the end of his life. This was brought out on the closing day of the Spiritual Summit Conference, which he attended in Calcutta, October 22–26, 1968, sponsored by the Temple of Understanding. This is an educational organization, based in Washington, D.C., which initiates dialogue among the philosophers of the major world religions in order to achieve understanding and reconciliation among peoples of all religions, thus fostering brotherhood and peace. In a final assembly at the Botanical Gardens on the banks of the Ganges, Merton was asked to offer a prayer to God on behalf of all present, which included representatives of all major world religious groups. After a few minutes of silent meditation he began:

> Oh God, we are one with You. You have made us one with You. You have taught us that if we are open to one another, You dwell in us. Help us to preserve this openness and to fight for it with all our hearts. Help us to understand that there can

be no understanding where there is mutual rejection. Oh God, in accepting one another whole-heartedly, fully, completely, we accept You, and we thank You, and we adore You, and we love You with our whole being, because our being is Your being, our spirit rooted in Your Spirit. Fill us then with love, and let us be bound together with love as we go our diverse ways united in this one Spirit which makes You present in the world, and which makes You witness to the ultimate reality which is love. Love has overcome. Love is victorious. Amen.[37]

Religious man is basically a lover. But, in a sense, he has to find himself before he can truly give himself in love. Finding his true inner self is a lifetime search and an ever-deepening love is both the process of the search and the result of the search. The expression of his love in his entire spiritual life, and especially in his life of prayer, is the means of discovering his inner self. From this self-discovery comes acceptance of himself as he is before God and acceptance of his fellowmen.

It is in the experience of love, then, that a person comes to know his inner self and attains better self-identity. Religious man's search for his "true self" or "inner self" in love is a leitmotif which is recurrent through much of Merton's writings. He expressed this theme rather crudely in 1941: "The measure of our identity is the amount of our love for God." It is of interest to note that Merton's concept of the inner self developed from a rather static notion to a more dynamic, existential understanding.

Since love is relational, the true self of religious man will be discovered in his relations to nature, to his fellowmen and to God. "There is only one problem on which all my existence, my peace and happiness depend: to discover myself in discovering God. If I find Him, I will find myself, and if I find my true self, I will find Him."[38] The true self that Christian religious man ultimately finds is Christ, living and loving in him. He discovers his real self by living for others in Christ. Merton went on to say:

> But then, our vocation is not simply to be, but to work together with God in the creation of our own life, our own identity, our own destiny. As free beings and sons of God, we should actively participate in His creative freedom in our own lives and in the lives of others, by choosing the truth. We are called to share with God the work of creating our true identity. The secret of my full identity is hidden in Him. The seeds that are planted in my liberty at every moment, by God's will, are the seeds of my own identity, my own reality.[39]

The inner self is not a part of man's being, it is his entire substantial reality, on its highest and most personal and most existential level. This true self, which is the source of man's deepest liberty, is not easy to find. It is hidden in obscurity and "nothingness" at the center where he is in direct dependence on God. The dormant, mysterious and hidden self, which is always effaced by the exterior self, does not seek fulfillment. It is content to be, and in its being, it is fulfilled because its being is rooted in God. The inmost self exists in God, and God dwells in it. Man recognizes his true self, in the divine image, in the process of being known and loved by God.

Merton's best description of the inner self was given in existential terms. In response to the question "Who am I?" he answered:

> I am a word spoken by God. Can God speak a word that does not have any meaning? Yet am I sure that the meaning of my life is the meaning God intends for it? Does God impose a meaning on my life from outside, through event, custom, routine, law, system, impact with others in society? Or am I called to create from within, with Him, with His grace, a meaning which reflects His truth and makes me His "word" spoken freely in my personal situation? My true identity lies hidden in God's call to my freedom and my response to Him. This means I must use my freedom in order to love, with full reciprocity and authenticity, not merely receiving a form imposed on me by external forces, or forming my own life according to an approved social pattern, but by directing my love to the personal reality of my brother, and embracing God's will in its naked, often unpredictable mystery.[40]

The real self is utterly simple, humble, poor and unassuming. It is not to be confused with an ideal self fabricated to measure up to some social pattern or self-image. The real inner self is just simply oneself and nothing more, stripped of all masks and pretensions, as it exists in the eyes of God. For religious man, to discover the true inner self in the love of God and others is to tap the source of his deepest liberty. Just as man has a deep inner self, so he often projects a false, superficial, social self that is really a mask behind which he can hide from himself, from reality, from responsibility and from love. The human problem for religious man is to see himself as he truly is before God, so that he can honestly respond in love. In plumbing to the depths of his personality to get to the core of himself, man is able to attain a basic honesty before God and uncover the root of his liberty for social freedom and responsibility.

Man may be said to create his own identity, in the sense of one's own authentic and personal beliefs and convictions, based on experience of oneself as a person, experience of one's ability to choose and reject even good things which are not relevant to one's life. Identity in this deep sense is something one must create for himself by choices that are significant and that require a courageous commitment in the face of anguish and risk. It means a belief to stand by, certain definite ways of responding to life, of meeting its demands, of loving other people and, in the last analysis, of serving God. In this sense, identity is one's witness to truth in one's life.

*　*　*

Where does the notion of sin come in as an obstacle to finding one's true self-identity? Merton's ideas on original sin were very "traditional" in his early writings. In his later writings, following changes in theological thought, he referred to the "fall" of man and the resultant "brokenness," man's inability to love, in more existential terms. The radical sense of sin besets even religious man who is striving to love God and others. It is not the same as guilt, which is the sense of oppression from outside, an anxiety one feels when he fears he is to be called to account for his misdeeds. The sense of sin is deeper and more existential, an awareness of evil within oneself when he has been deeply and deliberately false to his inmost reality, his likeness to God. Man realizes that he is in some way exiled from himself and from his true self, he is an exile in a world of objects so that his mind is enslaved by concerns which are exterior, transient, illusory and trivial.

The story of the "Fall" tells in mythical language that "original sin" is a basic inauthenticity, a predisposition to bad faith in man's understanding of himself and of the world. It implies a determined willfulness in trying to make things be other than they are in order to make them subserve, at any moment, his individual desire for pleasure or for power. Christianity is a religion for men who are aware that there is a sickness at the very heart of man's being. However, the traditional Christian doctrine about original sin is, if properly understood, optimistic. It does not teach that man is by nature evil, but that evil in him is unnatural, a disorder, a "sin." The great reality is not man's wickedness, but the goodness and mercy of God. The function of Christian love is to destroy the evil which is in man and in his society. The reorientation of all human life in a direction which is not immediately perceptible to the natural intelligence of man is the characteristic work of Christ as the second Adam.

As a result of original sin, man finds himself in a state of separation, separation from his inner self, from his fellowmen and from God. In socio-psychological terms, he is an alienated man. When such a man is reduced to his empirical or his outer self, and confined within its limits, he is excluded from himself, cut off from his own roots, condemned to spiritual death by thirst and starvation in a wilderness of externals. Without true self-identity, the alienated man is in a hell of meaninglessness, of obsession, of complex artifice, of systematic lying, of criminal evasion and neglects, and of self-destructive futilities.

In existential terms, the alienated man is one who, though "adjusted" to society, is estranged from himself. He lives in a world which is cluttered with his possessions, his projects, his exploitations, his machinery, but from which he himself is absent. The precise nature of the society in which he lives promotes this alienation. He is no longer capable of experiencing the truth that he is himself rooted and grounded in God's love. The inner life of such a mass-man, alienated and leveled in the existential sense, is a dull collective routine of popular fantasies maintained in existence by the collective dream that goes on, without interruption, in the mass media. He is, in effect, a human being who is systematically kept, or allows himself to be kept, in a social system in which he exists, not for himself, but purely and simply for somebody else. The alienated man, one who lives superficially, is always outside himself, never "with" himself. The alienated man can conceive of only one way of becoming real, that is, by cutting himself off from other people and building a barrier of contrast and distinction between himself and other men. He does not know that reality is to be sought not in division but in unity. The man who lives in division is not a person, but only an individual.

For religious man, there are many specific obstacles to the freedom of his love, both within himself and in others, as well as within the social structures which support his life. Such evils as excessive individualism, legalism, formalism and fanaticism and the social injustices built into the culture in which he finds himself inhibit his freedom as a son of God, evils which must be confronted and overcome by love. For some religious men there is a very real danger of an externalism which vitiates their love for God. Such religiosity enervates the power of their love to effect any real social change for the betterment of their fellowmen, and rests content in complacent self-satisfaction and passivity. As Merton said:

> This is particularly true of the negative, lachrymose and "resigned" Christianity of those who manage to blend the cult of the *status quo* with a habit of verbalizing on suffering and submission. For such as these, indifference to real evil has become virtue, and preoccupation with petty and imaginary problems of piety substitutes for the creative unrest of the truly spiritual man. A few phrases about the Cross and a few formal practices of piety concord, in such religion, with a profound apathy, a bloodless lassitude, and perhaps an almost total incapacity to love. It is the indifference of a man who, having surrendered his humanity, imagines that he is therefore pleasing to God.[41]

Christian religious man has an obligation to struggle against evil, whether it be moral or physical. The Christian can only resign himself passively to the acceptance of evil when it is clear that he is powerless to do anything about it. Hence it is an utterly false Christianity which preaches the supine acceptance of social injustice.

Where then is the evil to be situated which religious man confronts in his efforts to love his fellowmen in freedom? The roots of evil are first of all within himself and within all mankind. The obstacle is within man himself, that is, in the tenacious need to maintain his separate, external, egotistical will. It is when man refers all things to this outward and false self that he alienates himself from reality and from God. Thus, it can truly be said that "evil is within us all."[42]

In reference to the "dance of death" which is in man's "blood" Merton said:

> This "death dance," this hidden propensity to pestilence, is something more than mere mortality. It is the willful negation of life that is built into life itself; the human instinct to dominate and destroy, to seek one's own happiness by destroying the happiness of others, to build one's security on power, and by extension, to justify evil use of that power in terms of "history," or of "the common good," or of "the revolution," or even of "the justice of God." Man's drive to destroy, to kill, or simply to dominate and to oppress comes from the metaphysical void he experiences when he finds himself a stranger in his own universe.[43]

But some of the evil to be confronted and overcome by love is also built into the social structures of our time, structures which perpetuate injustice flowing from the evil will and accumulated inheritance of past mistakes and past sins. There is an objectively evil force, objective in the sense that it transcends individually personal ill will, almost a demonic force, which is rooted in negation and injustice, which sustains itself on the vast cruelty of an alienated and alienating social system.

It is, then, the evil within himself and his fellowmen, as well as within the structures and institutions of society, that religious man must confront in his social life and overcome by love if he is to co-operate in his freedom in creating a better world for himself and for all mankind.

Man before God finds himself in a specific mode of existence. His existence as a son of God is primary to him, all other modes of existence being made subordinate. This primary mode of existence determines his life-style and behavior and leads to a definite integration of his personality. An integrated personality is one that is authentic, that is, in harmony with one's life situation. An unauthentic personality results from a mode of existence that is in disharmony with the realities of daily life. An integrated person steadily grows in his own uniqueness before God and men within his own life situation, accepting his personal life with all its possible and actual modes of being a person. The primary motivation in his life is love and the exercise of his freedom as a son of God. All other motivations in life are deliberately rejected. Religious man, as a lover, integrates his personality by his life of love. As his personality develops under the primary motivation of love, the quality of his life and his behavior become more unified and simple. His value system, and the very meaning which he gives his life, are integrated by his love for God and his neighbor.

To give himself to God and others in love, religious man must first belong to himself, must first have that degree of self-possession required for the exercise of his freedom without interior turmoil and interference from baser motives. This requires that he be a living unity, an integrated personality. For he is not united to God in love just in his mind and will, but in his whole personality, imagination and senses, heart and spirit. In leading a balanced spiritual life by striving to love God fully, religious man is helped to become one complete man who is in

God. He is one complete man in whom God is all in all, in whom God carries out His will without obstacle.

But religious man must face the existential fact of disunity within himself, and his disunion from God and his neighbors. The achievement of an integrated personality is a lifelong process. It is only in unity with others in love that his own interior unity is naturally and easily established. To be preoccupied with achieving interior unity first and then going on to love others is to follow a logic of disruption which is contrary to life. As Merton said: "To start with one's ego identity, and to try to bring that identity to terms with external reality by thinking, and then to act on reality from our privileged autonomous position, in order to bring it into line with an absolute good we have arrived at by thought, is the way we become irresponsible. This implies no real respect for reality, for other persons, for their needs, and no real respect for ourselves."[44]

The function of prayer in attaining an integration of one's personality is important. As Merton said:

> Prayer gives an existential awareness of our life situation as sons of God, as loved and supported by God, and leads to a wholeness, a completeness, a simplicity in our inner selves and in our lives. Prayer is not something that we do, not just an activity in life, but it becomes something that we are. And in proportion that we become whole, we pray. The root of wholeness before God is, then, the gift of the Spirit. The Spirit is given us, not that we may see Christ, but that we may be Christ. At the same time that we are called to be Christ we are aware of ourselves as sinners before God, and we have to be ourselves and have

to be sinners. The Spirit gives us courage to be at the same time fallible, sinful people and Christ, "sons of the Father in the Spirit." This seems to be a division, but it is here, in fact, that our wholeness is found, and it is here that we become our prayer. Prayer is the constant re-establishment of the unity and wholeness of this "split Christ" which we are. Prayer is constant recourse to the Spirit bringing us to the roots of unity and wholeness which are in ourselves and in God at the same time, a returning to the source of our being which is in us and from which we are, no less, separated. Prayer is this constant healing of the split and wound of our being.[45]

The interior wholeness and integration that flows from man's life of prayer is also called "purity of heart," the unconditional and totally humble surrender to God, a total acceptance of himself and his situation as willed by Him. It implies renunciation of all deluded images of himself, all exaggerated estimates of his own capacities in order to obey God's will as it comes to him in the difficult demands of life in its exacting truth. This acceptance of his own true inner self as he is in his existential situation before God enables religious man to exercise his full freedom as a son of God.

A religious man who has attained some degree of adult maturity and integration as a result of his experience in a life of love is one who is serenely assured of his own identity. His judgments concerning his own experiences are based on his own awareness of what takes place within himself. The truly adult person will not allow himself to be treated as an alienated and helpless individual whose inner experience is dictated to him by another and imposed upon him from the outside. He has reached a state of maturity far beyond mere social adjustment, which always implies partiality and compromise. He is in a certain sense identified with everybody, so that he can become "all things to all men." He is able to experience their joys and sufferings as his own, without, however, being dominated by them. The integrated man reaches a state of insight so that he is no longer limited by the culture in which he has grown up. He accepts not only his own community, his own society, his own friends, his own culture, but all mankind. He does not remain bound to one set of values in such a way that he opposes them aggressively or defensively to others. He is fully "Catholic" in the best sense of the word. The integrated man has a unified vision and experience of the truth shining out in all its various manifestations, some clearer than others, some more definite and more certain than others. He does not set up these partial views in opposition to each other, but unifies them in a dialectic or an insight of complementarity. With this view of life he is able to bring perspective, liberty and spontaneity into the lives of others as a peacemaker and unifier among all men.

* * *

One of the aspects of self-integration for Christian religious man is the realization of a basic fact, that he has been given the internal capability of being transformed in Christ. The degree of this transformation will depend on his awareness and the living response he makes to what the love of God has effected in his life through Jesus Christ in His Spirit. This transformation of his life is not a repudiation of ordinary life, but a definitive recovery in Christ of what true human life should be, depending on an individual's freedom to experience life as it should be experienced. Transformed religious man has the freedom to be more constantly sensitive to areas of experience that his "new life in Christ" opens to him. Transformation does not mean that one is called to be like Christ, rather it means that religious man has the capability to be Christ in his own life and in the lives of others. The ontological basis for this transformation of human life into divine life is given in the incarnation of the Word of God in Jesus Christ. Through the power of the Spirit, Christ lives and acts in Christian religious man in a union brought about by faith and knowledge and especially by love. The Holy Spirit, the gift of God to man, becomes his spiritual and divine self, and by virtue of His presence and inspirations religious man is and acts as another Christ. By and in the Spirit, religious man has a new immanent spiritual principle of life, love and activity which, when activated, transforms religious man into Christ. The man who lives and acts according to the power of Christ dwelling in him acts as another Christ, as a son of God, and thus prolongs in his own life the effects and the miracle of the incarnation. As St. Athanasius said, "God became man in order that man might become God," thus enabling every man to be united to God in the person of Christ, as a true son of God by adoption.

Because of this interior transformation in Christ, the Christian life becomes a continual discovery of Christ in new and unexpected places and in unlikely persons. Religious man is enabled to live in constant confrontation with Christ in himself and in other men and to recognize Christ both within himself and in his brother. Christian life becomes a continuous and progressive conversion and transformation in Christ in which religious man helps, in some measure, to transform others and allows himself to

be transformed by and with others in Christ. This does
not mean that individual personality is suppressed and
that total conformity and uniformity in Christian life results. The union with Christ is personalized so that each
one's transformation in Christ produces a personalized
version of Christ in him. Christ does not live in each person in a uniform way, since He does not call each one to
an identical role in the Mystical Body. But the norm of
the basic transformation in Christ is the intensity of the
love one has for his brother.

Religious man's transformation in Christ results in a
new life "in Christ." In making man his friend, Christ
dwells in him, uniting man intimately to himself. This
"new man" that is brought into existence by transformation in Christ is spiritually and mystically one identity,
at once Christ and the individual person. The union of the
two natures in the one person of the Word, in Christ, is
ontologically perfect and indestructible. The union of religious man with God in Christ does not have this ontological and inseparable character. It is an accidental union, yet it is more than just a moral union or an agreement
of hearts and wills. It is a mystical union in which Christ
Himself becomes the principle and source of divine life
in man. Christ himself "breathes" in man divinely by giving man His Spirit. The ever-renewed mission of the
Spirit to the person who is in the grace of Christ is to be
understood by the analogy of the natural breath that
keeps renewing, from moment to moment, man's bodily
life. Since the mystery of the Spirit is the mystery of selfless love, religious man receives Him in the "inspiration"
of secret love and gives Him to others in the outgoing of
his own charity. Religious man's life in Christ is then a
life of both receiving and giving. He receives from God,
in the Spirit, and in the same Spirit he gives his love to

God through his brothers. One of the functions of prayer for religious man is to make this transformation in Christ more constantly conscious and all-pervasive in his life.

Among the social effects of religious man's personal transformation in Christ is not only a deepening and broadening of his capacity to love but also a widening of his vision, so that he can see the needs of his brother in Christ and respond to them with greater personal responsibility. He is enabled to see Christ in others and respond to their needs in loving concern and mercy. His transformation makes him no longer an isolated person, rather, becoming one with Christ, he is also one with all men. A new dimension comes into his Christian life so that, instead of living for himself, he lives for Christ in others. His personal transformation leads him to co-operate with Christ, acting in himself and in other men, in the basic Christian project of restoring all things, in Christ, to the Father.

* * *

The broadened vision which religious man attains in his interior transformation enables him to be more consciously aware of the fact of human solidarity. Though all men have a common origin in love and a common destiny, their basic humanity is the most fundamental bond of union. The transformed Christian can appreciate other aspects of human solidarity beyond that basic bond of union, but all other forms of social communion are really consequent upon the fundamental fact of man's common humanity. Man's most fundamental obligation is to be what he is, a human being. All other social commitments are of value insofar as they enable humans to be first of all human. Any form of perfectionism that tries to take mankind beyond his human reality cheats man of his humanity.

An individualism which leads one to think of himself as a completely self-sufficient unit and to assert this imaginary "unity" against all others is a fallacy. This is an affirmation of oneself as simply "not the other." One who seeks to affirm his unity by denying that he has anything to do with anyone else, by negating everyone else in the universe until he comes down to himself, has very little left to affirm. The true way of self-affirmation is just the opposite. As Merton said: "The more I am able to affirm others, to say 'Yes' to them in myself, by discovering them in myself and myself in them, the more real I am. I am fully real if my own heart says 'Yes' to *everyone*."[46]

The thrust to love and to be merciful to all mankind is basic for religious man.

> The climate of mercy which is the climate of the
> new creation depends on the realization that all
> men are acceptable before God. All that is re-
> quired for man to be acceptable before God and
> a recipient of His mercy is for him to be a man
> and a sinner. We ourselves are not entitled to be
> more demanding than God. Whoever is accept-
> able to Him is, therefore, acceptable to us.
> This is the test of our faith and our obedience
> to Him.[47]

Christian religious man often sees the basic reality of human solidarity in the context of the doctrine of the Mystical Body of Christ. All men are members of a race which is intended to be one organism and "one body," so:

> Every other man is a piece of myself, for I am a
> part and a member of mankind. Every Christian

is part of my own body, because we are members of Christ. What I do is also done for them and with them and by them. What they do is done in me and by me and for me. But each one of us remains responsible for his own share in the life of the whole body. Charity cannot be what it is supposed to be as long as I do not see that my life represents my own allotment in the life of the whole supernatural organism to which I belong. Only when this truth is absolutely central do other doctrines fit into their proper context. . . . Nothing at all makes sense, unless we admit with John Donne that, "No man is an island, entire to itself; every man is a piece of the continent, a part of the main."[48]

Merton became more existentially aware of the fact of basic human solidarity on his Asian trip. He ended his extemporaneous talk at the Spiritual Summit Conference at Calcutta, October 22–26, 1968, with these words: "Not that we discover a new unity [by communication and communion], we discover an older unity. My dear brothers, we are already one, but we imagine that we are not. And what we have to recover is our original unity. What we have to be is what we are."[49]

There is another bond, mystical in its nature, but still no less real, founded on the fact of the incarnation of the Word of God in Jesus Christ. All men are either actually or potentially united to each other as members of the one Christ, the whole Christ, in a union of the Mystical Body of Christ, head and members. As Christ died and rose for the sanctification of all men in a union of love, so Christian religious man strives to build up the one body of Christ by loving union in Christ with all men. The primary aspect of Christ's risen life is His life in the souls of His elect. He is now not only the natural Christ, but the mystical Christ, uniting in Himself all who believe in Him. Mystically and spiritually Christ lives in man from the moment that he is united to Christ in His death and resurrection, by the sacrament of baptism, and all the moments and incidents of the Christian life. This union is not merely a moral union, nor an agreement of wills, nor merely a psychological union. Christ mystically identifies His members with Himself by giving them His Holy Spirit. In this context, Merton quoted Father Prat: "The natural Christ reconciles us to His Father, the mystical Christ unifies us in Him."[50]

The Mystical Body of Christ is the body of those who are united with one another and with the Father and the Son by a union of charity so close that it is analogous to the circumincession in which the Father dwells in the Son and the Son in the Father. Indeed, religious man's status as a son of God depends on the fact that his unity with Christ makes the Father dwell in him as He dwells in the Son, while religious man dwells in the Father as does the Son. The man, therefore, who enlightened by the Spirit of God, discovers in himself this union with the Father in the Son and with all men in Christ, is at the same time unified in the highest possible degree within himself and perfectly united with all men who are one in Christ. The force that holds this unity together is charity. Christ's union with the Father depends on the love of the Father for Him.

> Our union with Christ depends on His love for us, which is simply an extension of the Father's love through Him to ourselves. The charity of Christ goes on through us to those who have not yet known Him, and unites them, through Christ

in us, to the Father. By our Christian love for other men, we enable them to discover Christ in themselves and pass through Christ to the Source, the Beginning of all life, the Father, present and hidden in the depths of their own being.[51]

The essential task of Christianity is to spread this union of love in Christ's Mystical Body. For Christianity is not merely a doctrine or a system of beliefs, it is Christ living in men and uniting men to one another in His own life and unity. In becoming man, God not only became Jesus Christ, but also potentially every man and woman that ever existed. In Jesus Christ, God became not only "this" man, but also in a broader sense, yet no less truly, "every man."

In a rare reference to himself, Merton summarized his writings thus:

Whatever I have written . . . can be reduced to one root truth, that God calls human persons to union with Himself and with one another in Christ, in the Church which is His Mystical Body. . . . If I have written about interracial justice or nuclear weapons, it is because these issues are terribly relevant to one great truth: that man is called to live as a son of God. Man must respond to this call to live in peace with all his brothers in the One Christ.[52]

What then is the function of the Church in achieving this union of all men in Christ? Christian religious man, called to unity with God and his fellowmen in the Mystical Body of Christ, finds himself in a community of lovers known as the Church. God reveals Himself to the world not only in one's own heart but also through this community of love. The Church's main concern is this revelation of God's saving love for man. This saving love is visible to the world in proportion as Christians seek peace and unity with one another and with all men.

The Church has a dynamic transforming power to bring about the total renewal and regeneration of human society on a divinely revealed and eschatological pattern. This task of renewal is part of the undivided and indivisible whole, the life of Christ, the life of the Holy Spirit, in the whole Church and in each Christian. Man's social role consists in being not only a good citizen but also in being "another Christ." The Church, or *ecclesia*, is built up of those people who have been "called together" and have gathered in one community to hear the word of God, to praise Him and to offer the sacrifice of their worship and mutual love. All Christians have responded to the same mysterious action of love brought about by the Holy Spirit. No one Christian has to realize in himself all the truths and all the mysteries of the Christian faith. All are members of one another, and what one cannot do, another does for him. The real Church is the union of hearts in love, sacrifice and self-transcendence. The strength of this depends on the extent to which the Holy Spirit gains possession of each person's heart in freedom.

So it is man's freedom, therefore, that is the instrument of divine redemption and reconciliation. This work of reconciliation requires the formation of a living body of men who are united by the Spirit of God. The Church is made up of men who recognize themselves to be sinners in need of reconciliation and pardon. All men are involved in each other's lives, not by choice but by necessity, and everybody is affected by the evil that is in the heart of one. The

Church, as a community of pardon, is not so much a body of men who never offend, but who frequently err and offend, and have received from God the power to forgive one another in His name. The Church, which Christ has "purchased with His blood" (Acts 2:29), is called to keep alive on earth this irreplaceable climate of mercy in which the creative and life-giving joy of reconciliation in Christ remains not only possible but is a continuous and ever-renewed actuality. The power of mercy is the power that makes men one in Christ, destroying and healing all divisions, in bodies, spirits, society and history. It is the only force that can truly heal and save.

The communal aspect of reconciliation is very clear in the Bible. The Bible acknowledges no permanent chasm between men and God, and does not seek to bridge the gulf by mere religious acts. On the contrary, the reconciliation of man with God is seen in more deeply mysterious and existential terms as a spiritual identification in pardon, worship, grace, freedom, love and community. To say that the Bible goes beyond religion is to say that it preaches *kenosis,* or the self-emptying of God and His identification of Himself with man as person and as community in Christ. The word of God is able to prove itself by its transforming power, which brings love, unity, peace, understanding and freedom where before there was prejudice, conflict, hatred, division and greed. The message of the Bible is, then, that into the confusion of man's world with its divisions and hatreds has come a message of transforming power and those who believe in it will experience in themselves the love that produces reconciliation and peace on earth. Religious man receives reconciliation with God in and through his brother.

The union of Christians is a union of friendship and mercy, a bearing of one another's burdens in the sharing of divine forgiveness. Christian forgiveness is not confined merely to those who are members of the Church. To be a Christian, one must love all men. Christians themselves must bring love, mercy and justice into the lives of their neighbors, in order to reveal to them the presence of Christ in His Church. This is only possible if Christians love and serve all men.

Christ will teach men to understand, not only His love for them, but His love for their neighbor. In Merton's words:

> He will teach us to see into the depths of our brother's heart, by humility and self-effacing compassion. He will teach us that it is not enough to bear with the frailties and the sins of others, we must love them even unto the death of the Cross. As Christ came to die for us when we were all His enemies, we no longer have any excuse for willfully hating any man. As Christ came to overcome evil with good, so we too must learn that the charity of Christ is strong enough to reach out and embrace even our enemies and His, strong enough to turn them from enemies into friends.[53]

The whole question of social life for the Christian religious man then is the reconciliation of all men with one another in Christ, because ultimately, in the Christian view, all other men are Christ.

* * *

How does Merton understand the biblical concept that man is created in the image of God? The basic image of

God in man is his existential freedom to love and to be loved. The image is clouded in man by his selfishness, separation and sin. Religious man recovers his image of God, his freedom to love in the actual process of opening himself to love, by his striving for self-integration and self-realization as one transformed in Christ, as a member of the Mystical Body of Christ, living in a community of love and reconciliation. The actualization of the image of God within him enables religious man to exercise his power to love God and his fellowmen in total human freedom. The life of religious man can be seen as a process of growth in love, of transformation in Christ and supernatural self-realization in the Mystical Body of Christ so that he can fully express himself as the God-like image which he is.

Man is in his basic structure *capax Dei*. He is an openness, a capacity, a possibility, a freedom, whose fulfillment is not in this or that isolated object, this or that circumscribed activity, but in a fullness beyond all objects in the totality of consent and self-giving which is love. Man is an openness that is fulfilled only in unconditional consent to an unconditioned love. This openness, this freedom, which is at the very core of man's being, and which imperiously demands that he transcend his being, is what the monastic theologians call "the image of God in Man." The capacity for freedom and love is the image of God because God Himself is pure freedom and pure love. The image in man urges him to attain a perfect likeness to its original by loving as he is loved. He cannot attain this by his own nature, but God has given His Son so that man may be a son in Him. The coming of the Word to take man's freedom to Himself turns the "image" into "likeness." When the Word loves the Father in man, then man's freedom is transfigured in and by His Spirit, and man's love becomes identical with Christ's love.

It is necessary for religious man to overcome his own sensual, selfish and exterior self to be really capable of true love. But when he does this he discovers his own interior, simple, inner self, his God-like self, the image of God, "Christ in him," and he becomes capable of loving God in freedom, returning to Him in all simplicity the gift of love which He asks.

The image of God in man is, then, man's interior potential for freedom in love. The likeness of God is the actualization of this capacity for love. The likeness of God is fully restored in man when man's freedom is perfectly united with the divine freedom, so that man acts in all things as God acts, or rather when God and man act purely and simply as one. To attain this pure and disinterested love, man must continually rid himself of the self-concern which makes him aware of himself as a separate, insecure subject of subordinate needs. The perfection of disinterested love is possible, of course, only in the ultimate union with God in glory.

This recovery of the image of God in the individual Christian religious man also has a community aspect, since man does not love God in isolation, but in and through other men. The full sense of the Christian person is found in this recovery of his likeness to God in Christ by His Spirit. This in turn is attained only in the relationship of personal love that is established in the Church, with all those who have heard the same message and have responded to it in the one Spirit. The Church can be considered as the "one man" in whom the "new Adam" has restored the image of God, extending this recovery of freedom objectively and potentially to all mankind.

The capacity for freedom in love and merciful understanding that makes religious man the living image of

God is the key to his divine sonship and to his own interior perfection.

> If we are to be perfect as Christ is perfect, we must strive to be as perfectly human as He is, in order that He may unite us in love with His divine being and share with us His Sonship of the Father. Hence, sanctity is not a matter of being less human, but more human. This implies a greater capacity for concern, for suffering, for understanding, for sympathy, and also for humor, for joy, for appreciation of the good and beautiful things of life. To be perfect, then, is not so much a matter of seeking God with ardor and generosity as of being found, loved and possessed by God in such a way that His action in us makes us completely generous and helps us to transcend our limitations and react against our own weakness.[54]

Man, created in the image of God, has a basic freedom, a capacity and openness to love. Religious man, because of his fundamental relationship to God and his fellowmen in love, develops his capacity to love and, in the process of loving, develops his own existential freedom. Love is perfect in proportion to its freedom. His loving relationship to God which helps man find his own inner self and integrates his human personality in conformity to Christ also liberates man from his false self so that he is free, as a self-possessed and responsible person, to give himself more completely in love to God and his fellowmen and to exercise his freedom as a son of God. Religious man frees himself from himself so that he is more truly free for love.

> We are created for freedom, for the options and self-dedications implied by the highest kind of love. We discover and develop our freedom precisely by making those decisions which take us out of ourselves to meet others as they really are. . . . The Spirit of God, penetrating and enlightening our own spirit from within ourselves, teaches us the ways of freedom by which alone we enter into vital spiritual contact with those around us. In this contact we become aware of our own autonomy, our own identity. We find out who we really are. And having made the discovery we are ready for the love and service of others.[55]

God is the source and guarantee of man's freedom, not a force standing over him to limit his freedom. Man's encounter with God leads to the discovery of his own deepest, spiritual freedom. Without encountering God, man's freedom never develops fully. The personal encounter with God in response to His word is the drawing forth and calling out of man's deepest freedom and helps establish man's true identity as a lover. This means that religion, on its deepest level, is a liberating principle. Love of God leads to a freedom from any control that is not in some way immanent and personal, that is not associated with the power of love, that is in any way less than man or exterior to him. One who loves God can experience a freedom which makes him no longer fully and completely subject to the forces of nature, to his own bodily and emotional needs, or to the merely external and human dictates of society.

The world of men is therefore more real in proportion

as the people in it are able to be more fully and more humanly alive by their being better able to make a lucid and conscious use of their freedom. Basically, this freedom is expressed in the capacity to choose their own lives and to find themselves on the deepest possible level. A superficial freedom to wander aimlessly here and there, to taste this or that, to make a choice of distractions is simply a sham. They may claim to have a freedom of choice when they have in reality evaded the basic task of discovering who it is that chooses. They are not really free because they have been unwilling to face the risk of self-discovery.

The law of life can be summed up in the axiom "Be what you are." As son and image of God, man must have no higher or more urgent obligation than to resemble Him in the purity, the universality and the perfection of his freedom in divine love. Man, then, can be said to be fully alive only when he becomes conscious of the real meaning of his existence, when he experiences something of the intelligence, spirituality and freedom that are actualized within him. It is only a religious man who becomes conscious of the reality and inviolability of his own freedom and is made more aware of his capacity to consecrate that freedom entirely to the purpose for which it was given him, that is, to live a life which transcends his individual needs and subsists outside the individual self in the absolute, in Christ and in God. The true meaning of his life is revealed in his freedom in love, a freedom transcending the self and subsisting in "the other" by love.

The doctrine of pure liberty is at the very heart of the New Testament. It is in Christ and His Spirit, and in the Church living by His Spirit, that true freedom is found. One of the chief functions of the Church is the preservation of man's spiritual liberty. Not only does true freedom under God open religious man to the possibilities of responsible love, it also liberates him from himself, from excessive self-awareness and self-concern, as well as from the chains of sin and separation, and even from the tyranny of time.

IV

THE SOCIAL DIMENSION OF RELIGIOUS MAN

In Merton's thought, what is the relationship between religious man and the world in which he lives? He does not live and develop to maturity by himself but in society. As a mature person, he takes a personal interest in other persons and in their welfare. As a lover, religious man is open, open to other persons, open to change, to development and to growth, both personal and societal. The society in which he lives may well be limited to a particular time and place and to a particular cultural milieu. But his horizon of concern goes beyond his own social limitations and embraces the welfare and growth of all mankind in freedom and love, especially in this age of global communications, global politics and global conflicts. However, as a religious man, his viewpoint remains basically religious, considering himself and his immediate fellowmen in their relation to God and to all mankind in a historical and eschatological framework. For religious man realizes that his own ultimate personal fulfillment is intimately connected with the growth, development and fulfillment of all his fellowmen in freedom and in love.

The question of the relationship of the person to the social organization in which he lives is one of the most important problems of modern times. Every ethical problem of modern times can be traced back to this root question. The problem is met everywhere, but since men are tending more and more to be "organization men" (in the West) or "new mass-men" (in the East) modern man is becoming so conditioned that he fails to recognize his own personal relationship to his immediate society as a personal problem. Modern man has moved very close to losing his personality and freedom in a general wave of conformism and passivity.

It is important to distinguish between an individual and a person. An individual can be considered to be an isolated human unit functioning for himself and by himself. The person can never be properly understood outside the framework of social relationships and obligations, for the person does not exist merely to fight for survival or to function efficiently or to overcome others in competition for the world's goods. The person finds his reason for existing in the realm of truth, justice and liberty. For a person to be fully alive, he must direct his actions by free decisions made in the light of his own thinking. These decisions promote his intellectual, moral and spiritual growth. Not only do they make him more aware of his capacities for knowledge and free action, they also expand and extend his powers to love others and dedicate himself to their good, for it is in this that he finds his fulfillment. He fulfills himself not by closing himself within the narrow confines of his own individual interests and those of his family, but by his openness to other men, to the civil society in which he lives and to the society of nations in which he is called to collaborate with others in building a world of security and peace and freedom. In his openness, understanding, empathy and commitment, religious man becomes in a sense "every man."

The Christian religious man, in his loving concern for others, faces the complicated problems of modern society with a deepened sense of personal responsibility since he is aware that God works in history and reveals Himself and His will in history. He is bound to search history, that is, the intelligible actions of men, for some indication of their inner significance and relevance to his own commitment as a Christian. He is forced to take a Christian view of society and accept some responsibility for the workings of society at the risk of failing to be a Christian altogether.

The work of collaborating with others to establish the reign of God in the hearts of men is not the work of individuals or of mass-men, but of persons who have reached not only natural maturity but their full stature as free Christians. The spiritual and eschatological character of the kingdom of God cannot be made a pretext for ignoring the temporal happiness and welfare of all men in this present life and in contemporary society.

The Christian, as one who is on a pilgrimage "out of this world to the Father," should have a different viewpoint and horizon in reference to social problems. He should have an expanded horizon of concern for anything that touches the well-being and development of men, because his true viewpoint is that of the eschatological kingdom of God. His collaboration in establishing the reign of God in the hearts of men calls for special understanding and compassion for all his fellowmen in this age of alienation. It is not that the Christian religious man has a complete set of solutions to the world's problems worked out in advance, but his feeling of solidarity with all mankind opens him to communication, dialogue, mutual understanding and trust which will help shed light on those problems.

Religious man, as a collaborator with God working in history, is called to help build a better world here and now by his free co-operation with his fellowmen in love. All men need food, shelter, protection, comradeship and work. Man's personal and family happiness depend in large measure on his ability to provide a normal and reasonable standard of living for himself and his family, to take part in the political, artistic and intellectual life of his world, and also on his freedom to love and serve God in the service of others. God reigns in the hearts of men through love, but where freedom, justice, education and a decent standard of living are not to be had in modern society, love rarely flourishes. The religious man, then, should collaborate with other men in building a world of justice, decent living, honest labor, equitable distribution of goods, peace and truth, so that the love of others and of God may flourish and man may be delivered from servitude.

Christian social action conceives man's work itself as a spiritual reality which has a very definite religious dimension. As Merton said:

> Christian social action is first of all action which discovers religion in politics, religion in work, religion in social programs for better wages, etc., not at all to "win the worker for Christ" but because God became man, because every man is potentially Christ, because Christ is our brother, and because we have no right to let our brother live in want, or in degradation or in any form of squalor whether physical or spiritual. In a word,

if we really understood the meaning of Christianity in social life, we would see it as part of the redemptive work of Christ, liberating man from misery, squalor, subhuman living conditions, economic or political slavery, ignorance and alienation.[1]

Such social action implies three great emphases: first, emphasis on the human as distinct from the merely collective or technological, and affirmation of man as opposed to production processes, a liberation of man from tyranny in any form; second, emphasis on the personal, and personal values, which are essentially spiritual and incommunicable, and which promote respect for man's right to be himself, to think for himself, his right to freedom, friendship, creativity and love; third, emphasis on a sapiential viewpoint that enables man to see life in its wholeness, with stability and purpose. This view is rooted in the patterns of the cosmos itself, and makes it possible for man to live according to the light of wisdom immanent in the processes of nature, as opposed to the uprooted condition of technological man whose life is geared to production, the consumption of goods and the exploitation of natural and human resources.

A socially concerned religious man will weigh social ideas and programs in the light of the word of God to identify and reject any program which compromises the standards of justice and mercy demanded by the Gospel. His norm of acceptance or rejection of any program will be the measure of authentic respect and love it manifests for the human person.

Man can be said to live in a variety of "worlds," physical, social, economic, political, intellectual. All these worlds affect him in a variety of ways, and man can by

his freedom, his knowledge and his love affect the worlds
in which he lives. Many factors in his worlds are beyond
his control and to that degree he is determined. But other
elements in his life are the result of free choice. Depending on his uses of his freedom, man can to some degree
inrcease or decrease good or evil in his own life and in
the lives of others. The challenge for religious man is to so
activate his powers of love that he can by his free choices
multiply the good and minimize the evil in his various
worlds. It is this project of creative free choices in love
that determines the quality of his personal and social life,
his own happiness and the happiness of others. Religious
man should freely embrace his various worlds and attempt to renew them with the power of his love.

The social world of religious man with which this study
is primarily concerned is not the physical globe covered
with a great variety of people. It is the complex of responsibilities and options composed of the loves, the hates,
the fears, the joys, the hopes, the greed, the cruelty, the
kindness, the faith, the trust, the suspicion of all men.
The world is beset with problems inasmuch as everybody
in the world is a problem to himself. The world is a problem insofar as all human beings add up to a big collective
question, because the world is full of problematic and self-
doubting freedoms. What religious man can do when
faced with these "problems of the world" depends very
much on his ability to love.

A deepened understanding of the social implications of
the incarnation leads the Christian religious man to realize that he cannot be a stranger to the real world of men.
If he were, he would really be estranged from Christ
and from the people of God. The unworldliness to which
he is called by the Gospel requires separation from the
whole realm of selfishness and inhumanity. It certainly

does not refer to the world of everyday reality, of common duty, the world in which men are called to work out their destiny as sons of God. True love for the world means love for the common lot and the task of man, and above all, is love for man himself, and therein love for Christ. True Christian unworldliness is not a rejection of man or of God's creation, rather it is a firm and ardent faith which is strong enough to find Christ in man and in man's world. Such a faith can see a hidden meaning and a divine message in the needs and struggles of the men of today. It can see Christ suffering in the people who starve, who seek their just rights, their freedom, their chance to develop and build themselves a new civilization. This awareness of Christ in the world today is the basic intuition upon which the work of renewal must be built. To be a stranger to the needs of one's fellowmen and to the hopes and perils of this moment of history is to be a stranger to Christ Himself.

The task for the Christian is to seek and find Christ in the modern world of men as it is, not as it might be. The fact that the world is other than it might be does not alter the truth that Christ is present in it, and that His plan has been neither frustrated nor changed. Certainly it is not Christian to reject the world which is the cosmos created by God, and is destined to be transformed with man in the new eschatological creation. So, too, the world was given by God not to ideally perfect men, but to human beings as they are, with strengths and weaknesses, powers to love and powers to hate. The Christian task is to find meaning, order, truth and love in this world of men. Man's freedom and creativity must be worked out in the human and personal encounter with other men, often with the stranger seen as one's other self, as another Christ.

One of the essential tasks facing religious man in the modern world is reorganizing his world view in such a way that his ideas of God, man and the world are no longer dominated by a static model of a sacred and hierarchical cosmos in which everything is decided beforehand and in which the only choice is to accept gladly what is imposed as part of an immobile and established social structure. In "turning to the world" modern man is admitting that his world view can become a matter of choice, a decision about the attitude he will take in determining the mode and extent of his participation in the living, ongoing events of his own personal world. To choose the world is to accept a task and a vocation in the world, in history and in time. To choose the world is to elect to do the work one is capable of doing, in collaboration with one's brothers, to make the world better, more free, more just, more livable. It has become obvious that the automatic "rejection of the world" and "contempt for the world" are in fact not a choice but the evasion of a choice.

In collaborating with his brothers to transform the world, religious man will often be opposed by many people who constitute a power structure which resists the transformation of the world and who wish to maintain a status quo in which their power is rooted. In his confrontations and dialogues with those who oppose and resist change and transformation in the world, religious man will be forcefully reminded that he has to live and work in this present, imperfect world, that it is here God has placed him, and here that he has a task to accomplish. If he rejects and disparages this world as it is and seeks some "ideal world," he will not be doing the task God asks of him. Religious man must also stand back from the power constellations of the world which demand his absolute submission and servitude. This refusal to submit and this declaration of independence from power structures will bring to the forefront of his conscience painful and complex ethical decisions which are far from easy to make because of the many ambiguities of life in the modern world. But when Christian religious man comes to recognize the world as already redeemed by Christ and enters into a personal relationship with all other persons in his own world, seeing them as loved and sought by Christ, he realizes that he has a spiritual power to help free the men of his world from the tyranny of their own selfishness. There is no simple ethical answer to the problems arising from this attitude of acceptance and dialogue with his fellowmen. The Christian religious man does not learn a new set of unworldly laws which put him in opposition to the ways of those who believe differently from him, but by the cross and the love of Christ, and the indwelling Spirit of freedom he learns to live in the world as Christ did, in perfect liberty and with unlimited compassion and service.

What is the personal world in which religious man lives and works? Obviously the physical world is limited for each person to the human and subhuman environment in which he finds himself and in which he is called to establish certain definite relationships. The dimensions of this physical world can be narrow or broad depending on his personal circumstances, his freedom for movement and travel, his opportunities and his personal inclinations to meet and communicate with a wide variety of his fellow human beings. But it is the intentional world of religious man that is of concern here. Depending on his mental horizons and the development of his viewpoints, a person can live in a very narrow world or have a truly global viewpoint and truly world-wide horizons of concern. The world in which a religious man lives and works will depend on his own intellectual, moral and religious development. A religious man who is consistently conscious of the basic affinity between the human world in all its dimensions and God as loving creator and father maintains a basic religious viewpoint in his life, and can expand his mental horizons to include concern for all mankind within his intellectual grasp. The personal world of religious man can thus be described as that totality of relationships on the intellectual, moral and religious level with which the subject is consistently concerned.

Christian religious man has a capacity for still further development through his transformation in faith into the life of the Spirit by his union with the whole Christ in the Mystical Body. The degree to which Christian religious man is open to the power of love and growth in the Spirit either narrows or expands the horizons of his personal Christian world. Continual growth in love and the expansion of his Christian horizon is, of course, desired until he is able to consciously embrace all mankind in his loving concern for their human well-being. Christian love demands a specifically Christian response to human problems on a world-wide scale and leads the Christian to select, to choose and to decide for that which promotes true human welfare in the world, and also to reject and oppose that which is detrimental to human development. The Christian, aware of his human and mystical solidarity with all men through Christ, either potentially or actually, can develop his compassionate concern so that he can identify himself more with the human problems of all mankind.

Thus it is that religious man can truly say "I am the world, just as you are. Where am I going to look for the world first of all if not in myself?"[2] The Christian's attitude toward the world of men should not be that it is a hostile force bearing down on him from outside, from which he is totally alienated, but rather that the real world is in him, with him and for him. In the deepest ground of his being, religious man remains in contact with the whole of creation of which he is only a small physical part. Through his senses and his mind, through his loves, his needs and his desires, he is implicated without possibility of evasion in this world of matter and of men. Religious man is not only affected and changed by the physical and human world but by his life and his love he can himself change and affect the world of men, and give to his human relationships a deeper human meaning and significance.

The world as pure object is something that does not exist. It is not a reality outside of man for which he exists. It is not a firm and absolute objective structure that has to be accepted on its own inexorable terms. The world has in fact no terms of its own. It dictates no terms to men. Man and his world interpenetrate. The whole human reality which of course transcends man, individually and collectively, nevertheless interpenetrates the world of nature and the world of history. But this reality, though "external" and "objective," is not something entirely independent of the individual human person which dominates him from without through the medium of fixed laws. It is an extension and a projection of man himself, and if he attends to it with respect, while attending also to his own freedom and his own integrity, he can learn to obey its ways and co-ordinate his life with its mysterious movements. The way for religious man to find the real world is not merely to measure and observe what is outside of himself but to discover his own inner ground. For that is where the world is, in his deepest self. This ground, this "world" where he is mysteriously present at once to himself and to the freedoms of all other men, is a living, self-creating mystery of which he himself is a part. Of course, personal memories, personal experiences and personal culture must be considered in establishing a set of meanings and values which help constitute a personal world view.

In developing his own personal world view, religious man comes to a deeper tolerance and understanding of his fellowmen through his identification with them in their problems. He is better able to accept them as persons to be embraced in love even though he may not accept their own particular world view. The fact that their world view may be limited to material and temporal concerns does not mean that he denounces or denigrates them personally, rather that he has liberated himself from their delusions, from their relatively vain concerns so that he can devote himself more completely to the quest for meaning in life through love and union with his fellowmen in peace. By his personal love and understanding, religious man can be in the world of his time as a sign of hope for the most authentic human values to which his time aspires.

The Christian religious man, with his world view that includes an eschatological dimension, holds out to mankind a Christ-like hope of still deeper meaning in human life. For Christ is not merely the risen Christ dwelling with the Father. He is above all the Mystical Christ, living and working in mankind. The Christian's vocation is therefore no evasion from the physical world. He is to be in the world, but not merely of the physical world, by being Christ himself in the world, and collaborating with his fellowmen in bringing the whole of creation to the Father in Christ. His communion with Christ is not merely Eucharistic in a limited, personal sense, but broadly Eucharistic in that his everyday life is meant to prolong his personal participation in the Eucharist by a renewed and intensified communion with Christ in His creation. This prolonged communion with Christ is primarily a matter of work. The Christian is called to help renew all things in Christ, not only in his private and liturgical prayer, but above all in his Christian work in the world of men, thus helping transform and consecrate the world of men in the divinizing power of the Spirit of Christ.

The work of Christ is not to save men from the physical or the economic world of men but to liberate men from the sinful use of created things and from the great complex of illusions and obsessions which organize human activity in the service of power, egoism and inhumanity. To assume that all human and temporal existence, all work, all social life, all sexual and procreative love, all technology, all forms of human knowledge, are by their very nature damnable and "worldly" is unchristian since it removes all these necessary aspects of human life from the power and influence of Christ working in the world of men today. An added dimension of wisdom is necessary for a world view which includes all human traditions, not only the Christian and Western view, but also oriental cultures.

Just as his love of God and his fellowmen helps religious man to achieve true self-integration, so too a proper understanding of his true relationship to the world enables religious man to have an integrated world view as a guide for his life and activity. Unfortunately, the older, established religious world view tended to induce a false, static dualism in life, emphasizing a separation between God and man, heaven and earth, the sacred and the secular, the supernatural and the natural, grace and na-

ture, the "spiritual" as opposed to the "merely human."
Modern religious man needs a view of reality which over-
comes these false dichotomies and unifies his life of love
and service into one integrated whole. A world view
which maintains a stereotyped dualism of God, the supernatural and the sacred in opposition to the world, the
natural and the secular no longer seems valid today.

Modern man needs a whole and integral experience
of himself and his life on all levels, bodily as well as
imaginative, emotional, intellectual, spiritual. There is no
place in modern life for the cultivation of one part of
human consciousness, one aspect of human experience,
at the expense of others, even on the pretext that what is
cultivated is sacred and all the rest profane. The old
dichotomy divided man's life between two worlds,

> one visible, comprehensible, the other invisible
> and incomprehensible, one familiar, the other
> frightening and strange, one where you could be
> yourself, and another where you must strive to
> be unnaturally "good," one which you instinctly
> took to be real, but which you must repudiate
> for the other which is truly real. This divisive
> and destructive pattern of life and thought is not
> the Bible message at all. The message of the
> Bible is precisely one of unity and reconciliation,
> an all-embracing and positive revelation from
> which nothing real is excluded, and in which all
> receives its full due and ultimate meaning.[3]

Any attempted cleavage between the "inner life" and
the rest of man's existence may be nothing but an attempt to evade reality altogether. Under the pretext that
what is "within" is in fact real, spiritual, supernatural,

one cultivates neglect and contempt for the "external" as worldly, sensual, material and opposed to grace. Instead of accepting reality as it is, such a man tends to reject reality in order to explore some perfect realm of abstract ideas which in fact have no reality at all. A false supernaturalism which imagines that the "supernatural" is a type of Platonic realm totally apart from and opposed to the concrete world of nature offers no support for a genuine Christian life.

It is in the quest for meaning in life that religious man uses the concept of the sacred. The "sacred" and the "secular" are intentional categories imposed on reality in an attempt to make life more meaningful. Religious man strives to attain an integrated world view in which all aspects of reality are given due consideration. For him, God is real, both as transcendent and as immanent in the world. The world is real, and religious man living in the world has a living, dynamic relationship to God that is vitally real to him, not just a matter for intellectual speculation. A religious man's attitude toward life includes both the sacred and the secular within his grasp of meaning, aware that in the mystery of life the mercy of God has transformed his apparent nothingness into reality, and that in his own darkness God's light has hidden itself. Ordinary life with its work, its insecurity, its inevitable sacrifices is for the Christian just as much of the sacred realm as anything else, because ordinary life has been consecrated to God by the incarnation, death and resurrection of Jesus Christ.

Only one person is properly sacred, God Himself. Human persons, human actions and material things participate in the sacred only in the secondary sense that they are in some way referred to God. A world view could be considered sacred when it gives proper consideration to both the transcendence and the immanence of God. God is transcendent in that He is separate and distinct from His creation and is not to be identified with it. God is immanent in that He is somehow within His creation through the power of His Spirit. A world view that considers only the material, temporal aspects of the physical and the human world without reference in any way to God as transcendent and immanent could be said to be a purely secular world view. However, a distorted world view that so emphasizes the transcendence of God that it divides the "sacred" from the "secular," the "spiritual" from the "material," tends to discount the immanence of God and reduces the realm of God in His creation to the realm of pure spirituality and cult, a kind of mystic enclave in an otherwise doomed and irredeemable creation. An attitude of mind which separates "spirituality" and "sacredness" from ordinary human life and reduces God's domain to one area of life, that of official "religion," is in large measure to blame for the continued secularization of Christianity and by that fact sets up the world as a secular realm in its own right, independent of God.

A reaction against the overemphasis on the transcendence of God and the exaggerated separation of the sacred and the secular occurred during the 1960s in the theological movements variously described as "radical theology," "death of God theology" or the movement for a "religionless Christianity." Merton wrote extensively about these topics, often with sympathetic understanding of the aims of the movements, even though he did not approve of the logical results which would follow from them. The denial of the divine transcendence, and overemphasis on divine immanence in a very nebulous form was the basis of these movements.

The stereotype of world rejection is now being replaced in some Christian quarters by a collection of equally empty stereotypes of world affirmation. Modern men may affirm the world and its secular values, but the complexity of events responds too often with a cold negation of their hopes. A Christianity which acts as if the hopes of men are really to be fulfilled within this world alone has forgotten the true meaning of the incarnation and the cross. The answer to the question of meaning in life is present in the world, but it is God in the world, not the world of men by itself.

* * *

How did Merton look upon social change? Modern man is living in a rapidly changing world. His physical world is changing due to technological innovation. With the emergence of new philosophies of social organization and development, and the consequent altering of sociological structures, his social world is changing. Many of the aspects of organized religion are also changing, with new emphasis on the communal dimension of religious practice and observance and new awareness of social responsibility. The emergence of new means of mass communication facilitates the spreading of new ideas and new attitudes toward life, and opens up new frontiers of educational and cultural development. All of these types of change can work for the promotion or restriction of true human development, depending on the persons who control and direct the change.

Religious man, in his concern for the social and religious development of mankind, should want to help direct and control the forces of change in the modern world, to enhance and promote true human freedom and develop man's capacity for love. He will accomplish this primarily through his own work, through his social involvement and through his communication and dialogue with his fellowmen. By their work and their love Christians can eliminate the prejudice in the minds of some that Christian moral and spiritual perspectives diminish and frustrate man's true development as man, and that Christianity confines man within the limitations of a narrow set of myths which forbid him to make a creative adjustment to the reality around him. Through his commitment to social change the Christian can show the falsity of the notion that Christians are doomed to obscurantism, retrogression and a flight from human reality. By the very nature of his Christian commitment the Christian is bound to make full use of his natural talents to help create a better world for himself and his fellowmen. Especially since Vatican Council II, Christians are confronted not so much with new tasks in the world but with old tasks seen in a new and more cogent light and in a truly new perspective.

The mystery of Christ is at work in secular events in contemporary history. It is not Christian to despair of the present, putting off all hope to the future. There is also an essential Christian hope which belongs in the present, and it is based on the nearness of the hidden God and of His Spirit in the present. The world of the present has to be accepted as the place where God's love is at work. The Holy Spirit speaks in many ways in the modern world, one of those ways being precisely through the poverty, the limitations and the need for assistance of one's fellowmen. The Church has insisted in recent years that Christians must have a deep understanding of the Christian implications of current problems, whether social, interracial, international, economic or cultural. These problems must not be seen as peripheral, rather Christians must recognize that the Holy Spirit is speaking today in the midst of the world and in the agony of men. Failure to hear Him and failure to react as a Christian in attempting to change the world for the better would be unchristian.

The gospel message which the Christian is called upon to witness by his life is that, if he will, man can respond in perfect freedom to the redemptive love of God for man in Christ, that he can rise above the forces of necessity and evil, and respond to the mysterious action of the Spirit that is transforming the world, even in the midst of violence and confusion that seem to proclaim God's absence and His "death." Christian faith helps to free him from the myths, the idolatries and the confusions of the society in which he lives. His Christian freedom, autonomy and independence from the demands of a world full of illusions liberate him from the psychic determinisms and obsessions of a society that is often governed by the love of money and the unjust, arbitrary use of power. The Christian's first mission is to live his freedom and to show those who want to be free where their freedom really lies.

"Christ taught us that the new command of love was the basic law of human perfection and hence of the world's transformation."[4] The Christian religious man experiences his freedom in love not as an isolated individual but in the mainstream, as a member of society, in collaborating with his fellowmen and as a member of the Body of Christ, the Church. In creating their own lives and fashioning their own destinies, Christians are prolonging the creative work of God Himself and helping to transform the world. The eschatological mission of the Church to witness to the truth and love of God in Christ and to build up the reign of God in the hearts of men has not changed. Nor does this mission entitle the Church to a privileged position among the other institutions of human society. The Church's presence in the world corresponds to Christ's way of being present when He was on earth. The Church is not in the world as a body of people who are separated and unconcerned. The duty of the Christian to participate fully and naturally in all that rightfully concerns human society is clearly affirmed in Vatican Council II, which urges Christians to participate actively in all man's strivings to build for himself a better world.

The notion of dialogue so frequently emphasized by Vatican Council II clearly shows that the Church as a body is both willing to participate and willing to learn from the world. The insistence on the rights of men and in particular of the individual conscience, so strikingly affirmed by the council, shows that the Church is willing to enter into a conversation with men in the modern world. The duty of Christians to help promote social change, and to play a more actively prophetic role in promoting the cause of civil rights, human freedom and especially world peace, is emphasized. All members of the Church, according to their diverse offices and vocations, should collaborate with their fellowmen, even those who are hostile to the Church and distrustful of it, in solving the common and urgent problems of the whole human race, especially poverty, war and social injustice. But the Church recognizes that in matters affecting social change and transformation, she must proceed by means of love, insight and persuasion, and by promoting dialogue and mutual understanding.

In attempting to transform his world, religious man is seeking to achieve a world that is more open to love and to the dynamism of life. A religious world view gives a primacy to life and love, and tries to promote those situations and structures which enable life and love to develop. Religious man has to be "open to love" in the sense that he is ready and available in all possible situations to promote human love, especially in situations of human encounter and exchange. Christians must courageously face the fact that collaborating with others to establish the reign of God in the hearts of men in reality comes down to changing man's human condition by helping to build a better world here and now in which human love and brotherhood are prominent. Such love would be a sign of the presence of the Spirit of love, a sign of openness to all others in love.

The emphasis is on present change here and now, not in the distant future. In promoting change in life, one cannot be too preoccupied with what is ending, or too obsessed with what seems to be beginning. In either case one loses touch with the present, and with its obscure but dynamic possibilities. What really matters is readiness to face the risks and the challenges offered by the present moment, and to embrace them with courage, faith and hope. In this event, courage is the authentic form taken by love. Those who seek to build a better world without the Spirit of love are those who, trusting in money, power, technology and organization, deride the spiritual strength of faith and love and fix all their hopes on a huge monolithic society, having a monopoly over all power, all production and even over the minds of its members. To alienate the spirit of man by subjecting him to such indignity is to make injustice and violence inevitable.

One danger to be avoided in attempting to transform the world of men through love is the "return to paradise" syndrome. Promoting the reign of God in the hearts of men does not aim at establishing a primeval paradise where sin and evil do not exist. The type of world which religious man is attempting to establish accounts for human weakness and evil and tries to minimize evil and its effects by promoting mercy and love. Until the definitive Parousia, Christian religious man is prepared to resist and overcome the evil that is within man because of his selfish lack of love.

The type of world which religious man hopes to achieve by the transforming power of love is one which enhances human life and brings out new qualities in life. If the essence of the material world view is that it promotes, in Faulkner's phrase, "the same frantic steeplechase towards nothing," a religious world view puts a meaning and a quality into life that is capable of ever-deepening realization. It promotes a life centered on people, rather than things, and promotes human unity and love instead of fostering selfish competition with one's neighbor over control of material possessions. Religious man should be able to concentrate more on the quality of life and its mystery, and thus escape in some measure from the tyranny of quantity.

Often the effect of life in society is to complicate and confuse man's existence, making him forget who he really is by causing him to be obsessed with what he is not. The religious viewpoint in life helps to correct that tendency by applying wisdom and experience that are not available to those whose viewpoint is strictly secular. The life of religious man takes on a deeper and more enriched quality because he is brought into communion with the mysterious sources of vitality and meaning, of creativity, love and truth, to which he cannot have direct access by means of science and technique. The religious viewpoint also enhances life with the qualities of celebration, festivity and joy.

The religious dimension also affects the decisions which

man makes to enhance the quality of his life. Decisions to promote a better world must be life-affirming and loving. But life-affirming decisions are not likely to emerge from a thought system that is largely programmed by unconscious death drives, destructiveness and greed.

> A few vital imperatives have to be taken into account: to refrain from the wanton taking of life, to avoid selfish greed and the exploitation of others for our own ends, to tell the truth, to respect the personal integrity of others even when they belong to groups that are alien to us. We must face the challenge of the future realizing that we are still problems to ourselves. Where the religious dimension enters in is not just in pious clichés, but in radical self-criticism and openness and a profound ability to trust in an inner dynamism of life itself, a basic creativity, a power of life to win over entropy and death. We have to learn to be wide open to change, and not closed up in tight little systems and cliques, little coteries of gnostic experts.[5]

The actual transformation of social structures to enhance humanity will be effected by religious man in collaboration with other persons who are striving for the same purposes. This active collaboration is in many ways dependent on a person's ability to communicate and to enter into true dialogue with others. Men with religious perspectives must not collaborate only among themselves but also with others who do not share a religious viewpoint and are seeking to attain the same human values in life.

The modern Christian finds himself more and more in

a "diaspora situation" in that he no longer lives in almost exclusive association with persons of similar religious persuasions. In the past, religious organizations were such that members clustered together for mutual support and security against a hostile world of nonbelievers. This tended to induce a ghetto mentality in that social horizons were apt to be limited to one's own religious group. Recent sociological developments, changes within the institutional churches, as well as mass media communication techniques have helped overcome the ghetto mentality to some extent so that the Christian finds himself in more meaningful human contact with the vast number of his fellow human beings who do not share his own religious convictions. Even though he is in such a diaspora situation, the Christian religious man is still called upon to love all men and promote human freedom and justice for all.

Pope John XXIII, through his encyclical *Pacem in Terris,* and through the convocation of Vatican Council II, helped open up the Christian churches to more active collaboration with each other and with nonbelievers in a spirit of mutual openness and trust. This attitude of openness, understanding and sympathy has enabled the Christian to discover unsuspected values in the world of men and makes active collaboration in common human problems possible among groups that were formerly antagonistic.

It is one thing to believe; it is another to collaborate with others in bringing the social implications of Christian belief to bear on the social structures of the contemporary world. What is required of Christians is that they develop a completely modern and contemporary consciousness in which their experience as men of this century is integrated with their experience as children of God redeemed by Christ. The weakness of Christian practice lies not so much in theology and formulated belief as in the split which has hitherto separated Christian faith from the rest of life.

Rational collaboration is manifestly impossible without mutual trust, and this in turn is out of the question where there is no basis for sure and honest communication. Modern man has marvelous means of communication, but often lacks the desire for honest exchange of ideas and attitudes. Failure of communication leads to a cycle of resentment, distrust, disillusionment and ultimate isolation. Love and friendship are the basis of true communication, and are necessary factors for mutual understanding. If communication is to exist at all it must first of all be human, and ultimately loving. It must have resonances that are deeper than formal statements, declarations and manifestoes. It requires a willingness to acknowledge common human solidarity. Partners in communication have to see each other as mutually in need of God's grace and mercy. Often the other person is not listening for words, but for the resonances of love and understanding behind the words. One thing is certain: if one loves his own ideology, his own formulas and his own opinions instead of loving his human brother, he will seek only to glorify his own ideas and institutions and by that fact make real communication impossible.

Where there is openness, humility, love and the willingness to accept the obvious limitations of common humanity, communication, though never absolutely perfect, becomes more possible and may lead to solidarity. The struggle to achieve human solidarity in a world of confusion and conflict may at times appear hopeless. Man is fatally attracted to nihilism and violence. His peace is constantly threatened by his incapacity to recognize his fellowman as his other self and to enter into frank, simple communication with him.

True communication on the deepest level is more than a simple sharing of ideas, of conceptual knowledge or of formulated truth. It can also lead to a communion in authentic experience which goes beyond the level of words. This depends on the real truthfulness of words. Communication becomes possible, and with it community, once it is admitted that words are capable of being true or false and that the decision on how the words are to be used is largely up to the individual person.

What is needed in the world today is not official statements of programs, or reiteration of propaganda slogans or the repetition of familiar generalizations, but a rethinking of the human situation by a common effort to arrive at new aspects of the truth, in other words, dialogue, in an effort to establish community, not only among persons with religious perspectives, but between believers and nonbelievers as well.

Dialogue is a true reciprocity in communication between persons, each fully respecting the other as a person, with mutual protection of the other's liberty, dignity and rights. Such dialogue requires openness and honesty based on the mutual assumption that there is a complete willingness to accept the other as he is. It also presupposes a willingness to be oneself and not pretend to be someone else. In order to accept the other as he is and love him as oneself, it is necessary to begin by accepting oneself as one truly is before God. This openness and acceptance of the other also includes acceptance of his viewpoint as the initial basis of the dialogue. In the event of a dialogue with a person who is initially antagonistic and inimical, the person should still be accepted as an equal and as a brother. If he is accepted as a brother, there is a basis for Christian love.

In the past there has been an exaggerated obsession with the difference between adversaries on the level of theory and ideology. The time has come to take a more humane attitude toward one's adversaries. Religious man should not be afraid of adversaries, but should be willing to enter into genuine dialogue with them, precisely those who in the past were most to be feared and were most liable to condemnation. When adversaries engage in dialogue, the possibility of new attitudes is considered, ideas are clarified, friendships are formed, individuals get to know and understand each other, ways are opened for mutual respect and co-operation in certain areas. It is necessary to communicate in dialogue with others who hold different ideologies when all men are confronting common problems which can only be solved in collaboration. This would extend to all adversaries, even atheistic communists. All members of the Church, according to their diverse offices and vocations, should collaborate with their fellowmen, even those hostile to the Church and distrustful of it, in solving the common and urgent problems of the whole human race. Initial collaboration and co-operation with an adversary in economic, social or cultural matters leads one to realize that his adversary is not totally inhuman, wrong or unreasonable.

The purpose of dialogue is not to convert others to one's religious point of view, but human collaboration. Conversion might well follow from the example of love shown, but this is not the prime purpose. Dialogue is a process of mutual learning and understanding, and one must be willing to truly learn from an adversary. If the adversary is able to expose new facets of the truth, they should be accepted. Religious man can give to his adversaries in dialogue what they most want, love. Not simply good will and piety, but Christian love, shown by a readiness to co-operate in all efforts for the betterment of the world and human order.

Merton made a forceful statement on the problem of the insincerity of some men in dialogue in an article entitled "Apologies to an Unbeliever." He said:

> I think this apology is demanded by the respect I have for my own faith. If I, as a Christian, believe that my first duty is to love and respect my fellowman in his personal frailty and perplexity, in his unique hazard and his need for trust, then I think that the refusal to let him alone, the inability to entrust him to God and to his own conscience, and the insistence on rejecting him as a person until he agrees with me, is simply a sign that my own faith is inadequate. I do not (in such a case) believe in the love of God for man, I simply itch to impose my own ideas on others. Claiming to love truth and my fellowman, I am really only loving my own spiritual security, and using the Gospel as a gimmick for self-justification.[6]

The dread of being open to the ideas of others generally comes from one's hidden insecurity about his own convictions. But mature and objective openmindedness, viewing a problem from a basically different perspective, may lead to a discovery of one's original truth in a new light and with a new appreciation. One's willingness to take an alternative approach to a problem may perhaps relax the obsessive fixation of the adversary on his view, which he believes is the only reasonable possibility and which he is determined to impose on everyone else by coercion. It is the refusal of alternatives, a compulsive state of mind which one might call the "ultimatum complex," that makes wars in order to force the unconditional acceptance of one oversimplified interpretation of reality. The mission of Christian humility in social life is not merely to edify but to keep minds open to many alternatives.

The possibility of meeting his adversary on the ground of dialogue and reason is now recognized as a great opportunity for a religious man to develop an understanding of his contemporaries and, in so doing, to deepen his understanding of himself in relation to Christ, by seeing Him in his adversary, even if he be a godless and material-minded man. The religious man can, by humility and lucidity, awaken in his partner in dialogue a sense of his real identity and restore to him a hope of sanity and peace. As Merton said:

> For one of the basic truths of our time is the mysterious fact that the full spiritual identity, not only of cultures but of individual persons, remains a secret gift that is in the possession of others. We do not find ourselves until, in meeting the other, we receive from him the gift, in part at least, to know ourselves. The religious person must proceed by means of love, insight and persuasion, by dialogue and mutual understanding, to collaborate with others in transforming the world of men.[7]

* * *

In attempting to change the social structures of his world through collaboration, communication and dialogue so that persons can better be themselves and express themselves more freely in loving union with their fellow-men, religious man comes up against vested interests. He is confronted with people in power structures who resist change and wish to maintain the status quo, since change of structures would be detrimental to their position of power. These power structures are evident in various areas of human life, but they particularly affect religious man in politics, economics and in the area of religious organizations, where they block development and maintain established patterns in the interests of those who know best how to profit from the use of power at the expense of everyone else.

Power in itself is morally neutral, and can be used to promote or thwart the development of human freedom and love. It is the abuse of power for ultimately selfish reasons that is confronted by religious man. Abuse of power is a type of force which is destructive of love, which produces division rather than union, alienation rather than personal wholeness. Pope John XXIII in *Pacem in Terris* tirelessly repeated the principle that force is not and cannot be the valid basis for any authority over another person. The proper basis for authority is reason and conscience, guided by the fundamental principle of love. Power can guarantee the interests of some men, but it can never foster the good of man. Power always protects the good of some at the expense of all others. Only love can attain and preserve the good of all. Any claim to build the security of all on force is a manifest imposture.

The scriptural basis for the Christian struggle against the powers of enslavement is to be found in the New Testament, especially the Apocalypse. The modern Christian religious man is concerned with the defense of the dignity and the rights of man against the encroachment

of massive power structures which threaten either to en-
slave or to destroy him. As Merton said, "In a world where
God is indeed 'dead' in the lives of many men, we see that
the void left by His absence is filled with a variety of demons, demons of ruthless exploitation, of genocide, cynical and barbarous travesties of justice, perversions of every human and natural instinct. Truth is subverted to
power, and persons become subservient to things. Heaven
is empty, and earth is delivered up to power without
principles."[8]

In the political sphere, modern religious man has to con-
tend more and more with a tendency to totalitarian power
control, even in countries not under communist domina-
tion. More and more a managerial power elite makes all
the decisions and passes the decrees down to the lowest
strata of society. This totalitarian and absolute concept
of authority based on force implies a completely pessimistic view of man and of the world. It is for one reason or
another implicitly closed to human values, distrustful or
openly contemptuous of reason, fearful of liberty which it
cannot distinguish from license and rebellion. It seeks security in force because it cannot believe that the powers
of nature, if left to grow spontaneously, can develop in a
sane and healthy fashion. Nature must be controlled with
an iron hand because it is evil, or prone to evil. Man is perhaps capable of good behavior, but only if he is forced
into it by implacable authority.

In the past, the Christian attitude toward politics
tended to be abstract, divisive and highly ambiguous.
Political action was by definition secular. Because of
abuses of political power in the past, such a passive attitude toward those in political authority can no longer be
cultivated. Religious man, in concert with like-minded
individuals, can stand up against political power and by

dissent and protest can help bring about political changes. The pre-eminent example of a religious man who in modern times has wrought significant change by challenging the power structure in the name of truth and nonviolence is Mahatma Gandhi. Two other religiously minded men who stood up against the power structure and were martyred for their stand were the Austrian peasant and conscientious objector Franz Jägerstätter and Father Max Josef Metzger. In recent times, perhaps the Berrigan brothers could be taken as examples of religiously minded men who are fighting the power elite in their own way.

At times political power is used to manipulate public events and public information for political reasons. Facts are distorted or suppressed, information is withheld so that well-informed opinions become close to impossible. The individual stands alone and helpless before the power class, deafened by the noise of propaganda that the power elite turns out. Freedom, peace, plenty, joy are all enthusiastically invoked, but prove on closer examination to be their opposite. There is seemingly only one choice, to submit to the decision handed down by an authoritarian power which defines good and evil in political terms. It is, therefore, no longer reasonable or right to leave all decisions to a largely anonymous power elite that is driving all, in their passivity, toward ruin. Religious man has to make himself heard.

Another type of power that is often used to repress human liberty and manipulate human lives for profit is economic power. The concentration of wealth and economic power in the hands of relatively few managerial types who control faceless corporations tends to increase the gap between classes of people and produces as a by-product a class of alienated people, fit subjects for further exploitation. Almost unlimited freedom is allowed to the big corporations, whereas little concern is shown for the human liberty and human development of the people subject to economic power. When the expression "the free world" is used, it implies primarily that business is free. The freedom of the person comes after that, because often the freedom of the person is dependent on money. For many, money and possessions become the sole concern in life, to the neglect of the development of their own human personhood. Their estimate of their true worth is likely to be made in monetary terms.

For many, business can become a substitute for religion. Some large corporations tend to force on persons a new kind of faith, faith in a process and a product that leads to a mystique of things. Belief in the corporation and its product and promotion of the corporation and its product can lead to an idolization of the corporation. Through the product, one communes with the vast forces of life, nature and history that the commercial enterprise symbolizes. The process is climaxed by advertising that treats all products with the reverence and the seriousness due to sacraments. Man's whole life becomes commerce oriented, and material things become his "god."

Economic power has often been used for exploitation of the Third World nations, thus increasing the gap between the vast mass of the world's poor and the absurd affluence of the few more economically fortunate. Gestures at remedying the inequitable distribution of the world's wealth are often a camouflage for further exploitation and support of repressive military regimes which are intent on maintaining the status quo. That continues the economic dominance of the few, and the misery of the masses of mankind.

Another source of opposition which religious man meets in trying to attain full human freedom and integral development in love for himself and others is often the religious power structure built into ecclesial communities. A Church is human in that it is a community composed of men, organized by and for men, structured and ruled by them. The Holy Spirit of love is present within the human beings who compose the community and rule the community in the Spirit of love. He is not to be considered present in the human structures and laws and regulations by which the community fosters its community growth and development in love. The authority which some in the community have to teach, to rule and to sanctify is founded on love and service in the Spirit, not on the human laws and sociological structures which have developed within the ecclesial communities in the course of time. If as the community develops, the primacy of love of persons is forgotten, and priority is given to human structures, to human laws, to human authority and power to rule, the ecclesial community is faced with the need of sociological change and renewal. Religious man should work and collaborate with others in the community to insure and promote that necessary change and renewal within the community of love.

That an ecclesiastical power structure based on secular models exists within some parts of the Christian community is evident. These power structures are remnants of a past era when the temporal involvement of the Church in community organization and rule was much more pervasive. In modern times the Christian community can much more effectively perform its service of love without a political power base. The medieval symbols of a secular power which no longer exists within the Christian community could well be eliminated without any harm to anyone, but with great gain to the credibility of its message of disinterested love and service. The modern sociological organization of the Christian community should be a function of its self-understanding of its role in the world of men today. The Church should be present in the world today in the same way that Christ was present, as one who came to love, to serve, not to rule. The Father's love sent Christ into the world to use His freedom to save men. It is out of love for the Father that Christ chose the way of humiliation and total renunciation of power, in order to save men by love, mercy and self-sacrifice.

In the past, the Christian Church was too often identified with political power structures. This identification with the status quo made it very difficult for leaders of the Christian communities to combat effectively various forms of social injustice in a meaningful way. Too close an identification of political and religious structures in the past gave a religious dimension to merely human structures in the minds of the people, and this sacralization of political structures was maintained by those in political power to their advantage as an aid in preserving their rule. This identification of religious and political structures with the sacred often meant that the structures were preserved as ends in themselves.

The Church's identification with the status quo has muted the liberating force of the gospel message. Often those with power in the Church have been afraid of antagonizing those with political or economic power in a country even though these people were responsible for injustice and even crimes. Institutional complacency, with its established public situation, often led to the submergence of the Christian social conscience in the complex and dubious cares of an existence that was ultimately inauthentic because it was merely sociological rather than Christian. As the world proved itself capable of getting along without reliance on religious power, the Church became in reality less and less demanding in the social sphere. Christianity issued less and less of a challenge to those in power roles. More and more the demands of the Church resolved themselves into demands for formal and exterior gestures of pious allegiance to God and to the authority of the institutional Church. Today, religious man lives in an irreligious world in which the Christian message has been repeated until it has come to seem empty of all intelligible content to those closed to the word of God. In their minds, Christianity is no longer identified with newness and change but only with the static preservation of outworn structures.

In many sociologically advanced countries today, Catholics—the hierarchy, the clergy and the ordinary middle-class Catholic people—accept and identify with the conservative establishment. Their ideology and world view are simply that which they have acquired from the establishment. They uncritically accept the establishment view of things. Many of those who rule the Church are men whose sense of business administration is certain but whose ardor for sociological change is faint. It is not sufficient to issue formal condemnations of social injustice in broad, general terms for world-wide application. What is needed is that the local leadership of the Christian communities produce practical programs to combat social injustices on the local level. As Merton said:

> We are very good at coming out with declarations and resolutions, usually a little late. . . . On the whole the Church is too cautious, too inert, and too slow to have a really creative influence in social affairs. She seldom leads. She usually follows, often with rather pathetic attempts to scramble on to the back of somebody

else's bandwagon. In one word: The Church is involved in the political life of the world but seldom as a creative or constructive force. When a showdown comes she tends to become reactionary because she is too often already committed to the *status quo*. The conclusion seems to be that Christians are sufficiently content with the comfortable compromises of their worldly situation and have no real motive for action that will radically alter that situation, even though there may be definite indications that Christian morality and conscience demand a radical change.[9]

One of the grave problems of religion in the present time is posed by the almost total lack of protest on the part of religious people and clergy in the face of enormous social evils. These people are no longer fully capable of seeing and evaluating certain evils as they truly are, as against God and the Christian ethic of love. Excessive emphasis on the authority of Church leaders to rule has induced a passivity in the Christian layman in the face of grave social evils. In situations where the conscience of the Christian should play a positive and decisive role, he waits to be instructed by Church leaders who often issue statements devoid of practical moral seriousness. This results in an abdication of responsibility and passive submission to an evil that ought to be identified, denounced and resisted. In his general letter to his friends, Septuagesima Sunday, 1967, Merton said:

The present institutional structure of the Church is certainly too antiquated, too baroque, and is often in practice unjust, inhuman, arbitrary and even absurd in its functioning. It sometimes imposes useless and intolerable burdens on the human person and demands outrageous sacrifices, often with no better result than to maintain a rigid system in its rigidity and to keep the same abuses established, one might think, until kingdom come.[10]

During an interview in 1967, Merton was asked about the problem of freedom and authority in the Church itself, "Is it not the problem that too often power is mistaken for authority? Ought not true authority derive from a theology of love rather than a theology of power and legalism?" Merton replied:

There can be no question that the great crisis in the Church today is the crisis of authority brought on by the fact that the Church, as institution and organization, has in practice usurped the place of the Church as a community of persons united in love and in Christ. On the one hand, love is announced and "instilled"; but, on the other, it is equated with obedience and conformity within the framework of an impersonal corporation. This means too often that in practice love is overshadowed by intolerance, suspicion and fear. Authority becomes calculating and anxious, and discredits itself by nervously suppressing an imagined opposition before the opposition really takes shape. In so doing, it creates opposition. The Church is preached as a communion, but is run in fact as a collectivity, and even as a totalitarian collectivity. Hence its proneness to ally itself with dictatorships and to demand that its members obey these dictator-

ships as God Himself. To go to war for them is
to go to war for God. This situation is really
apocalyptic, but few Christians can see it. Wait
a little. It may mean the complete destruction of
the Church as a powerful institution.[11]

The paradox about the Church is that the Christian
community is at the same time traditional and essentially revolutionary. The Christian community is traditional and conservative in that it preserves within itself
the authentic Christian message of God's love for all
mankind. The Christian community is revolutionary in
the sense that it attempts by means of love to change
any social structures which delimit and restrain the human person's freedom in love. So the Christian community should be willing to collaborate in any efforts
to change entrenched social structures in any way which
will promote true human freedom. Christian liberty is not
only concerned with human freedom of choice, but also
involves freedom as responsibility, responsibility for one's
own actions, and also responsibility for others in loving
concern.

The Christian's mission in the world today is not a
mission merely to consolidate his own position and to
establish and protect Christian institutions in a world in
full revolution. It is a mission to witness to the love of
Christ in this changing world, to see Christ in modern
man, so that the Christian recognizes that his duty is
more to his fellowman, whether he be Christian or not,
than to Christian institutional advantage and prestige.
The Christian message of love is a liberation from every
rigid legal and religious system which restricts man's
freedom to love his brother. This is attested with such
categorical force by St. Paul that one ceases to be a

Christian the moment his religion becomes slavery to "the law" rather than a free personal adherence by loving faith to the risen and living Christ present in one's fellowman.

Love is measured by its activity and its transforming power. Christianity teaches man to give himself to his brother and to his world in a service of love in which God will manifest his creative power through men on earth. Man is in the midst of the greatest revolution his world has ever seen. This revolution is not merely political but scientific, technological, economic, demographic, cultural and spiritual. It affects every aspect of human life. This revolution in its broadest aspects is something that cannot be stopped. The great question is whether it can truly be directed to ends that are fully compatible with the authentic dignity and destiny of man. Science alone, politics alone, economics alone, the power of nuclear weapons cannot do this. There must be a full and conscious collaboration of all man's resources of knowledge, technique and power. But the one hope of their successful co-ordination remains the deepest and most unifying insight that has been granted to man: the Christian revelation of the unity of all men in the love of God as his one Son, Jesus Christ.

Now above all is the time to embody Christian truth in action even more than in words. What is needed now is the Christian who manifests the truth of the Gospel in his social life, with or without explanation. The more clearly his life manifests the teachings of Christ, the more salutary it will be. Clear and decisive Christian action explains itself, and teaches in a way that words never can. A Christian should seek to follow Christ perfectly, not only in his own personal life, but also in his political commitments and in all his social responsibilities. At this point,

Christian social action must be decisive, and Christians must speak by their actions. Their social action must conform to their deepest religious principles by putting into practice the teachings of Christ in the social context of the modern world. Christian social action is not so much a question of "doing something" as of "being someone." The Christian religious man must realize that, before he can do anything truly effective to transform the world of men, he must be what he claims to be, a Christian, a person reconciled to God and to all men.

V

SPECIFIC SOCIAL CONCERNS OF RELIGIOUS MAN

Religious man, in collaboration with his like-minded fellowmen, is confronted with problems of social change in specific areas of life. These areas of particular concern are those in which his freedom to love is restricted, namely, the political and the economic, the area of institutionalized religion and certain cultural aspects of life. Guided by his basically religious world view and attitude, religious man can help to emphasize the human dimensions of specific social problems, guarding man's basic freedom to love in peace, which is man's right as a son of God.

Religious man's efforts to bring about social change for the betterment of mankind require not only collaboration, communication and dialogue, but also on occasion more active means such as dissent, protest and active non-violent resistance to social forces which inhibit social change. Religious man, by his very commitment to God and his fellowman in love, should be in constant dissent from policies and practices which promote social injustice and disturb peaceful living, on a local, national or international level. The adversary is not time or history, but the evil will that is in some men and the accumulated inheritance of past untruth and past sin. Responsible persons are morally obliged to dissent from and protest against practices of injustice which are built into the structures of their society.

The challenge for religious man in his public dissent and protest is to maintain clarity, objectivity and openness even in resisting manifest error and injustice. Constructive, consistent and clear dissent is needed to recall people to their senses, to make them think more deeply, to plant in them the seed of social change and to awaken in them a profound desire for truth. Such dissent implies belief in openness of mind and in the possibility of mature exchange of ideas rather than a passive acceptance of an "official viewpoint" that does not concern itself with social justice. The immediate purpose of dissent and protest is to help each other to a new openness, to think and speak and act as brothers and to awaken a new social conscience. It is also to awaken the conscience of any social or political oppressor to the reality of his injustice and to help identify the source of the injustice, both in the social structure and in the injustice and hatred that are rooted in the heart of man himself.

The ultimate purpose of dissent and protest is to speak words of hope, to help keep a human measure in public policies and to help protect the freedom of man for openness and love, which is the image of God in man. The mature religious dissenter is careful to maintain a concern for people rather than ideological conformity. He is not so much interested in accusation and the condemnation of social injustice as he is in breaking a way through to communication and dialogue which will constructively promote social change.

More active forms of protest are on occasion required, above and beyond a habitual attitude of dissent from social policies which promote or sustain social injustice. The important aspect of public protest is not so much the short-range possibility of changing the direction of specific social policies but the longer-range aim of helping everyone gain an entirely new attitude toward social injustice. Every individual religious man has a serious responsibility to protest clearly and forcefully against policies which lead inevitably to social injustice. There should be no abdication of responsibility or passive submission to social evils that ought to be identified, denounced and resisted.

Ambiguity, hesitation and compromise are no longer permissible. What is required is that religiously minded persons speak out with such clarity and force against social injustice that there can never be the slightest doubt in the heart of even the simplest man that a specific injustice has been condemned and the need for social change publicized. Such protests from those who are loyal but who hold unpopular opinions are necessary to correct some social evils. If enlightened and responsible protest is not allowed and encouraged, people will become more and more passive instruments of huge power structures. Without the right to protest actively, man is reduced to despairing trust in political and social "experts" in whom he has no real confidence and he is left in a state of passive helplessness by the consequences of judgments made in high places over which he has no control. However, a religious man should be careful not to let himself be carried away by movements and pressure groups that put more faith in words and tactics than they do in the Spirit of God. A religious man in his dissent and protest should be one who refuses to accept, with passive and unthinking resignation, a diminution of authentic and living possibilities. He should not be resigned to letting his life be mutilated in the name of something else, whether it be business, politics, money, revolution or religion. The religious protestor simply refuses to be alienated.

Nonviolent resistance on the Gandhian model has been effective in the past and could be used effectively in the present to promote social change if the technique is properly understood and consistently applied. The classical Gandhian approach to nonviolent resistance is really an expression of religious humanism which seeks to apply the ideals of traditionally religious civilizations to the resolution of conflicts and the solution of social problems. It claims that, instead of revolutionary violence and the overthrow of established structures by force, a more efficacious method is to appeal to the deepest moral idealism of a civilized tradition to effect reform. In Merton's opinion this appeal to the highest ethical motivations is based on a fundamental respect for social order, even though it singles out a particular unjust law as the source of a particular disorder and as the object of demonstrations of civil disobedience. The classical theory of nonviolent resistance claims to respect the values and structures of civilization even more than does the social establishment which has become involved in the routine of retaining power and making money. Both the strength and the weakness of nonviolent resistance are that it is a religious humanism and a mystique of reform. Such a theory of nonviolent social change is opposed by professional revolutionaries who advocate outright use of force to bring about social change as well as by the entrenched political establishments which call it "anarchy" because it advocates reform and protests against injustices.

The cornerstone of all of Gandhi's life, action and thought was respect for the sacredness of life and the conviction that love and truth are basic to man's being. Gandhi believed that the acceptance or rejection of the basic law of love and truth which has been made known to the world in traditional religions and most clearly by Jesus Christ is the central problem of the modern world. The spirit of love and truth is strong enough to heal every division within mankind. The greatest of man's spiritual needs is to be delivered from the evil and the falsity that are in himself and in his society. On many occasions, social evil and falsity are most effectively overcome by nonviolent resistance. The fabric of society is not finished but is made up of constantly changing relationships. Nonviolence tries to change those relationships that are evil into others that are good, or less bad. The only real liberation is that which liberates both the oppressor and the oppressed at the same time from the same tyrannical automatism of an unjust social system.

Nonviolence belongs to the very nature of modern political life for religious man. It is not possible for a truly religious man to ignore the inherent falsity and inner contradictions of a society that tolerates organized greed and systematic oppression. The first principle for valid political action in such a society is nonco-operation with its disorders, its injustices and more particularly with its deep commitment to untruth. If social change cannot be brought about by other methods of persuasion, nonviolent means of resistance should be used. Devotion to the power of truth (Satyagraha) is meaningless if it is not based on the awareness of the profound inner contradiction of all social structures that are based on force.

Very often objections are raised to nonviolent resistance because it seems to imply a passive acceptance of injury and evil and is therefore a type of co-operation with evil. But there is a difference between nonviolent resistance and nonresistance. The genuine concept of nonviolent resistance implies not only active and effective resistance of evil, but in fact a more effective resistance. The only way to overcome an enemy is to help him to become other than an enemy. The resistance is aimed, not at the evildoer, but at evil at its source. Not only does nonviolent resistance resist evil, but if it is properly practiced it often resists evil more effectively than violence ever could. Ideally, nonviolent resistance is the only really effective way of transforming man and human society in the face of injustice and evil.

Nonviolent resistance is in fact a very practical and pragmatic technique of social change. Its purpose is to restore a different standard of practical judgment in social conflicts. It is a desirable alternative to what is now considered the only realistic possibility, political manipulation backed by force. The advantage of nonviolent resistance is that it presents more humane alternatives for possible political action. The nonviolent resister is persuaded of the superior efficacy of love, openness, peaceful negotiation and, above all, truth. Nonviolent resistance maintains respect for the personal conscience of the oppressor and works for his good also. It is a way of insisting on one's just rights without violating the rights of anybody else. It aims not at the disruption and disintegration of society, but at a more real and living collaboration based on truth and love. Nonviolent resistance is a type of language, a restoration of real communication on a human level. It communicates love, not in word, but in act. Above all, it is meant to convey and defend truth that has been obscured and defiled by political double-talk. Nonviolence is not for power, but for truth.

Religious man's resistance to the forces of social evil and human oppression can in many ways be encouraged by new developments in Christian theology which are bringing out the inherent dynamism of the Christian message for promoting social change. These developments are known variously as Theology of Social Change, Theology of Resistance, Theology of Liberation, Theology of Revolution. All through the Bible the groundwork for a theology of human liberation and resistance can be found. The "people of God" to whom the message of liberty was directed in the Old Testament was in fact a small nation or a minority in exile, called upon to resist the massive power of invaders or oppressors. But they were to do so in a spiritual way, trusting not the alliances with big powers but the hidden, yet firm promises of God. It is precisely in the soil of oppression and in the call for spiritual resistance that God sows the seed of radical biblical humanism. The prophetic vision of a united, peaceful mankind, of justice for the poor and helpless, blazed out in what was essentially a dark and tragic situation.

The essence of the New Testament message is the reconciliation of all mankind to God and to each other in love. But a theology of love and reconciliation cannot afford to be sentimental and opposed to social change. It cannot preach edifying generalities about love while identifying "peace" with established political power and legalized violence against the oppressed. A theology of love cannot be allowed to serve only the interests of the rich and powerful, justifying their wars, their violence and their bombs, while exhorting the poor and the underprivileged to practice patience, meekness and long-suffering and while urging them to solve their problems nonviolently. A theology of resistance must seek to deal realistically with the evil and injustice in the world, not merely to compromise with them. It involves a refusal of evil and at the same time emphasizes reason and humane communication rather than force. Such a theology does, however, in Merton's opinion, admit the legitimate possibility of force in a limit-situation when everything else fails. Merton, at the same time, cautioned against the simplistic interpretation of the notion that "Christianity is a revolutionary force" which results in Christians promoting organized violence.

Christian openness to the world means a willingness to accept the reality of revolutionary change in the modern world. Violent revolutions are in fact taking place, but there are other, nonviolent revolutions in the sense of sudden and dramatic changes in social and cultural patterns which affect religious man and which he should attempt to influence and direct. It is in this sense that religious man can in many ways be a rebel, as distinguished from both the conformist who accepts the conservative establishment and its injustices and the violent revolutionary who in the name of an ideology and an abstract utopian humanism consents to the alienation and destruction of his fellowmen. The revolt of this type of a rebel against the power structures that resist social change is based on love and springs from the warmth and authenticity of human solidarity and compassion. Since it is based on love, such a revolt is defined by risk, limitation, uncertainty and vulnerability. The logic of such a revolt demands dialogue, openness and speech, as opposed to the conspiracy of official silence which, both under totalitarianism and under capitalism, attempts to seal men's lips so that they cannot protest against organized international murder and violence.

The various peace movements that are working to establish international peace and justice for all mankind are of deep concern for religious man. As Pope John XXIII said:

> The great tasks of magnanimous men are: to establish with truth, justice, charity and liberty new methods of relationship in human society and to bring about true peace in the order established by God. It is an imperative of duty; it is a requirement of love.[1]

Ignoring the problem of peace and war could of itself be a political act and could involve religious man in complicity with evil. Religious man co-operates with peace movements both to protect the right of men to live freely as sons of God and to protect mankind against the criminal abuse of the enormous power which military regimes have acquired. Religious man as a peacemaker is not to be considered a doctrinaire pacifist. He does not allow himself to be integrated passively into a war-making society. The hope for peace which is his is rooted in true love for his fellowmen in collaboration with whom he tries to work out alternatives to violence as means to settling national and international problems. Peace cannot be built on exclusivism, absolutism and intolerance, nor on vague liberal slogans and pious programs.

The real source of war is the instinct for violence and for force which has become inveterate in the human race. Just as the roots of evil are in the human heart, so too the roots of peace are within man himself. If religious man is to work for peace, he must first hate the injustice, tyranny and greed which are in himself. He must be willing to sacrifice and to restrain his own instinct for violence and aggression in his relationship with other people. He must first face this responsibility himself. His first task is to understand the psychological forces at work in himself and in his society. Religious man, in collaboration and dialogue with others, should try to obtain information and form his own conscience so that he can effectively contribute his share of intelligent political action which will promote the cause of peace.

It is of vital importance for religious man to develop a forceful and articulate position in favor of peace rather than a permissive and silent attitude toward the possibility of war. In the face of the moral passivity of so many well-intentioned men today, religious man should accept the responsibility for the present and for those present actions and attitudes from which future events will develop. Therefore, as Merton said:

> It is extremely important that we get a grip on ourselves and determine that we will not relinquish either our reason or our humanity, that we will not despair of ourselves or of man, or of our capacity to solve our problems, that we will make use of the faculties and resources we have in abundance, and use them for positive and constructive action. We will resist the fatal inclination to passivity and despair as well as the fatuous temptation to false optimism. In a word, we will behave as men, and, if Christian, then as members of Christ.[2]

Religious man is helping to establish the truth and is acting as a true disciple of Christ when he works for peace, justice and liberty on earth. The actual work to be done requires radical changes in society, not merely superficial adjustments. He should keep himself open to rational perspectives in relation to the problem of world peace, and be willing to re-examine with others certain fundamental assumptions on which political and military policies have been formulated. He will try to help create a general climate of rationality in political life, and preserve a broad, tolerant, watchful and humanistic outlook on the whole of life and on all mankind, precisely in order that rash and absurd assumptions may not have too free a circulation in his society. With his freely questioning mind, religious man, in union with others in peace movements, can bring a note of urgency and protest against national policies which would lead to war.

Religious man has a duty to contribute everything he can to help in this great common work of finding non-military and nonviolent ways of defending human rights, human interests and human ideals. It is a problem of evaluating the critical situation of humanity in its totality, so that the problem of war can be seen in this context, and alternative solutions to national and international problems can be worked out. Fanatical nationalism and racism are the prime causes of the moral blindness which prevents men from seeing each other as brothers. The irrational forces of a nationalism which sets up the state as the final object of man's allegiance were the causes of wars in the past. These forces have to be confronted and overcome by mutual understanding, dialogue and openness on the national level.

Religious man should take the lead in helping to discover in practice the efficacy of nonviolent methods of defense by the transformation of attitudes and methods which now govern political and military action. They should support every kind of action which involves serious dialogue, genuine reciprocity, international understanding and world social justice to remove the causes of war and social unrest. A study and investigation of the positive meaning of nonviolent defense, its efficacy as a defense policy, its clarity in stating the will to resist aggression and its opportunities for heroism and dedication, are vital.

The problem of racial conflict and the repression of minorities presents another challenge to religious man in his struggle to promote greater justice and openness to love for all mankind. Religious man is faced with the problem of promoting social change both in personal attitudes of people and in the structures of society to insure greater social equality for people of all races. The cause of the civil rights movement is basically Christian and could be advanced by nonviolent means if the technique of nonviolent resistance were properly understood and applied. If Christian communities do not co-operate in promoting racial justice, the Christian message will ultimately be meaningless for those who are oppressed by racism. The work of Dr. Martin Luther King has set a pattern of what actually can be accomplished in the struggle to achieve civil rights and liberation from racial oppression for minority groups. In 1968, at the beginning of his trip to Asia, Merton expressed his opinion on the feasibility of nonviolent resistance. He said, "There seems to be a general impression that nonviolence in America has been tried and found wanting. . . . I might as well say bluntly that I do not believe this at all."[3]

The problem of racial conflict and the suppression of minorities is not limited to the United States alone but is widespread throughout the world. This engages the concern of religious man for social justice wherever it is violated and wherever human freedom is denied. The racial problem in the United States is, however, symptomatic of the social sickness which is destroying the humaneness of man's society all over the world.

The basic questions of the race issue are not only political and social, they are moral questions of fundamental social justice. As Merton said:

> Our ways of coping with the racial problem are an essential part of the problem itself. We do not ask relevant questions. We talk as if we were concerned with right and wrong, but this often turns out to be sheer verbalism and rests on no serious moral judgments at all. The basic issue is one of rank, crass, deeply rooted injustice. The only thing that can right the wrong is justice in every sphere, in every level of society, in every branch of social, political, economic and personal life. What matters is that justice be done. It is a matter of righting actual wrongs, paying definite debts, restoring very precise rights that have been ignored or violated.[4]

The problem of racial injustice cannot be solved without a profound change of heart within the individual and the radical restructuring of the social institutions which perpetuate the injustices. The leaders of Christian communities should not be afraid to antagonize rich and powerful groups in society to bring about those needed social changes.

Christianity in the United States is suffering a crisis of identity and authenticity. It is being judged by the ability of Christians themselves to abandon inauthentic, anachronistic social structures and to work for social justice on all levels. The basic challenge for white religious man in the racial question is how to treat Christ in another person when the other person is nonwhite. In Merton's opinion, the Negro has a message for white

America. White America has betrayed Christ by its injustice to races it considered inferior. It has sinned against Christ in its lamentable injustices and cruelties to the Negro and other racial minorities. The time has come to repair this injustice and re-establish the violated moral and social order on a new plane. Merton confessed to having his own identity crisis as a "white man." He once said, "When I read about the race issue I have a tendency to identify with the Negro."[5] In an anti-letter to Robert Lax, October 5, 1963, he said, "I am trying to figure out some way to get nationalized as a Negro, as I am tired of belonging to the humiliating white race."[6] Again on October 17, 1963, "I am going to write to the Government about resigning from the human race, at least from the white part, which is not by all accounts the most human."[7]

The racial problem is fundamentally a problem of persons and personal relationships. Religious man should put emphasis on these personal relationships, supporting those programs and societal structures which liberate the oppressed as persons, making it possible for them to make personal decisions which help build their self-respect, their confidence in themselves and others of their race and confidence in the white man as one who respects their personhood.

* * *

The economic and technological development of the modern world is, of course, of great concern for religious man. Modern technology can do much to make human life better and more free, yet there are many dangers in technological society that man has to guard against, particularly ecological destruction and personal dehumanization.

Was Merton against technology as such? He was often accused by reviewers of being so. He stated quite unequivocally several times that he saw great benefit for mankind in technology if properly used and controlled. What he questioned was the universal myth that technology infallibly makes everything in every way better for everybody, and that technology could, all by itself, solve man's problems. In his opinion, it did not. "What I am against is the complacent and naïve progressivism which pays no attention to anything but the fact that wonderful things can be and are done with machinery and electronics."[8]

Modern man, living in a technological society that is oriented to the production and consumption of goods, often does not show sufficient responsibility and respect for nature, for his natural environment and for the human values of life. Religious man, because of his love for God and his fellowmen, has a respectful attitude toward life and natural processes. Merton once wrote in one of his journals, "If you love God, you will respect His creatures and respect all life because it comes from Him."[9] This attitude of respect for nature and for life developed throughout his entire life and was a constant theme in his writings, particularly in connection with the themes of prayer, solitude and contemplation.

How should religious man experience nature, as something alien and fearsome, to be conquered, subdued and exploited, or as a gift of God, to be understood, contemplated and to be used in proportion to real need? Man's attitude toward nature is simply an extension of his attitude toward himself. As he is free to be at peace with himself and others if he chooses so he is free to determine his attitude toward the natural world in which he lives. Respect for the world of nature and for life itself rests ultimately on a religious sense of being, of gratitude and tolerance, a willingness to let things be themselves. Man should be content to let nature be. Lack of respect for nature leads to a false humanism which ends in violence and destruction.

This attitude of respect for nature carries over into religious man's attitude toward his work. Religious man should be free enough from things to be able to respect them instead of merely exploiting them. He should not only use things, but value their use. With a proper understanding of his work, he should be able to measure and control the effects of his work, not only on the things and persons immediately concerned, but also on others more remote from him. The sense of social responsibility that religious man has toward living and growing things and toward human society in general is most necessary for truly human life. Such an attitude of respect for life and for living things in one's work reflects the creative aspects of God's love.

An attitude of respect for nature and natural processes leads religious man to support programs for conservation on a local and national scale. It also helps religious man to have a kinship with all living things so that he can look at living things not only as good for him but also as good in themselves. Instead of self-righteously assuming that man is absolute lord of all nature and can exterminate other forms of life according to his real or imagined needs, religious man realizes that he is part of nature himself and lives in a balanced ecological system. Without this fundamental respect for nature and for himself as part of nature, man could ultimately destroy himself.

Religious man can develop an ecological conscience which is centered on the awareness of man's true place in nature as a dependent member of the biotic community, an awareness that he is dependent on a balance within nature which he is not free to destroy and that he has obligations to other members of the vital community not to co-operate in its destruction. The affirmation of all life is basic to the ecological conscience, which is, as a consequence, also a peace-loving conscience.

Merton quoted a principle of the ecological conscience as formulated by Aldo Leopold: "A thing is right when it tends to preserve the integrity, stability and beauty of the biotic community. It is wrong when it tends otherwise."[10] He also quoted Dr. Albert Schweitzer: "A man is ethical only when life as such is sacred to him, that of plants and animals, as well as that of his fellowmen."[11] Merton observed, in 1968, "The ecological conscience is not predominant, to put it mildly, in business, in the armed forces, in government, in urban and suburban life, in the academy. It tends to receive some notice from humanistic philosophers, artists, psychoanalysts, poets, conservationists, hippies. I regret to say that it is something about which the Church apparently couldn't care less, at least today."[12]

An ambivalence on the part of some toward nature has come from a misunderstanding of the biblical traditions, a misunderstanding of the implications of some early statements in Genesis, such as "Fill the earth and subdue it, and have dominion over everything that moves" (Genesis 1:28) and "The Lord God took man and put him in a garden of Eden to till and to keep it" (Genesis 2:15). A proper understanding of these texts is that man is to act as God's instrument in cultivating and developing natural creation. But a certain Manichaean hostility toward created nature has come into American culture through the Puritan ethic that had a half-conscious bias against the realm of nature. Puritans hated the wilderness almost as a person, as the extension of the Evil One, an enemy which opposed the spreading of the kingdom of God. The work of combating, reducing, destroying and transforming the wilderness was purely and simply "God's work."

The ideal of human freedom and creativity is in danger of being totally subverted if natural ecological balance is destroyed. Religious man, with his developed ecological conscience, should be aware of the ecological problems which affect technologically advanced countries and should co-operate with programs to eliminate practices which destroy ecological balance. He should support laws designed to prevent technological pollution and damage. The government has the same obligation to protect the land, air, water and natural environment of man against such damage as it has to protect the country against foreign enemies and to protect the individual from criminals. Conversely, every citizen is duty bound to make an effort to understand how technology operates and what its possibilities and limitations are. Religious man should oppose any technological operation based merely on the ethics of expediency and efficiency that does not take into consideration the long-term economic interests of society or even the basic needs of man himself. If technology is not kept subservient to man's real interests, it often degrades man, despoils the world of nature, ravages life and leads to much destruction.

Technology is both a fact of modern life and a necessity for modern life. The problem for religious man is how to maintain that inner peace, personal identity and personal freedom that are necessary to be truly religious in the modern world that is dominated by activism, science, machinery and the drive to acquire power and proficiency. Withdrawal from the world or flight to a rural commune that disavows technology in favor of simple manual work is not the answer for most people. It is most important for religious man to relate the wisdom gained from his religious experience to the technological culture of the present day. He should maintain a critical distance from technology in that he neither one-sidedly accepts or rejects it but makes an effort to study its problems and possibilities and contributes something of his own to a world view that may be highly expert in science but perhaps deficient in wisdom. Certainly the mere rejection of modern technology as an absolute and irremediable evil will not solve any problems. The harm done by technology is attributable more to its excessive and inordinately rapid development than to technology itself. It is possible in the future that there may be a technological society that may be tranquil and equitable for all. Religious man should contribute to that development.

Religious man cannot acquiesce passively in the many dangers and evils attendant on technological development. His openness to the world means a willingness to accept the challenge of the world that is being changed rapidly by technology. It means an acceptance of man's desire to better himself and his world by science, but science that is put at the service of man and not just at the service of power. Religious man should not oppose such change by being attached to outdated forms or to the antiquated or the obsolete merely because such forms are "traditional." The improvement of the quality of his life is one of the challenges facing modern man. Technology can help man to improve his life by providing an abundance of goods and services in a quantitative way, but it provides no guarantee by itself of improving the quality of human life. In fact, unless technological development and operation are controlled by foresight and wisdom, technology can in many ways contribute to de-humanizing life.

The rapidity and sophistication of technological growth mean greater wealth, greater military capacity, a higher standard of living and, above all, the power to exploit and dominate others. Technology is the key to the power struggle. It can also alienate those who depend on it and live by it, deadening their human qualities and their moral perspectives. Gradually everything becomes centered on the most efficient use of machines and techniques of production. The style of man's life, his culture, the tempo and manner of his existence respond more and more to the needs of the technological process itself. It often happens that what is good for the process is bad for man. Thus man comes to serve his machines instead of being served by them. A basic law of the technological process is that once a quicker and more effective mode of production becomes possible it becomes necessary. The danger is that technology becomes an end in itself and arrogates to itself all that is best and most vital in human effort. The more corrupt a social system is, the more it tends to be controlled by technology, since technology assures greater wealth and power to those who serve technology at the expense of authentic human interests and values, including their own human and personal integrity. Religious man must face the question of how to control technology instead of being controlled by it.

In a highly organized technological society, considerations of persons are subordinated to the processes and techniques of production. The person is valued more for the position he occupies, the influence he wields, the money he earns and his general usefulness in getting things done than for himself. His personal identity is dependent on his function, his income, his possessions, not on what he is in himself. If he has nothing, he does not count, and what is done to him or with him ceases to be a matter of ethical concern. The problem for man in the mass society which modern technology produces is to achieve personal authenticity and responsibility. He desperately needs to give a personal meaning to a life which is so easily reduced to an empty routine by the alienating pressures of commercial and technological organization. A way must be found to separate technology from the uncontrolled profit motive and from the manipulations of power politicians. Instead of contributing to the idolatrous cult of technology and power, religious man should co-operate with others in directing and controlling technology to subserve man's real needs from motives of human solidarity and love.

Another area of concern for modern religious man is the spiritual crisis of so many of his contemporaries. Deprived of the traditional patterns of religious belief and practice by the dehumanizing effects of modern technology and urban living, many modern men find themselves devoid of any value system which gives meaning and purpose to their lives. Religious man, by his openness and love, should stand as a witness of hope to his contemporaries in their search for life's meaning.

Religious man is also concerned about the worsening economic situation of so many of the world's poor and the mass migrations of the landless poor into large city slums where they are subjected to economic exploitation. The living conditions in slums and ghettos further increase man's dehumanization and alienation. In spite of technological development, poverty is becoming worse for vast masses of people. The human misery that exists in so many parts of the world is by no means to be attributed to the "will of God" but to the effects of incompetence, injustice and the economic and social confusion of our rapidly developing world.

One of the most pressing social problems for men today is to help solve the problems of human misery in the underdeveloped nations of the world, in Asia, Africa and South America, where the landless peasant is subject to extortion, illiteracy and practical serfdom, a condition that leaves him open to communistic exploitation. Religious man has an obligation to work in collaboration with others to insure the rights of small and emergent nations and of racial minorities to enjoy their full rights as members of the human race. He must show genuine concern for social justice toward people who have been shamelessly exploited and toward the races that have been systematically oppressed. Never before has there been such a distance between the abject misery of the poor, still by far the majority of mankind, and the absurd affluence of the rich. Much of the foreign aid from technologically advanced countries goes into the pockets of corrupt politicians and military dictatorships who maintain the status quo, of which the oppressed condition of the poor is an essential part.

* * *

Religious man is also concerned with preserving and extending a religious attitude toward life and promoting religious freedom for all mankind. His openness to others in love also makes him open to dialogue with those who do not share his own particular religious viewpoint but who do share common human goals with him, namely, to find meaning and purpose in life through religious experience. Just as dialogue with others is necessary to promote mutual peace and understanding and to bring about change in the political and economic spheres, dialogue with others on topics of mutual religious interest is most important to promote peace, mutual understanding and brotherhood in the sensitive area of religion.

The purpose of ecumenical dialogue is not to convert someone to a particular religious point of view but to open oneself to all facets of the truth about man's human condition before God and to deepen one's human understanding through knowledge of the religious experience of others. Interfaith dialogue in a "sapiential" atmosphere helps the individual to enlarge his horizons while giving him a deeper consciousness of his own gifts from God, his own vocation and his own responsibilities.

The "diaspora situation" in which the modern Christian finds himself makes an openness to ecumenical dialogue imperative. Dialogue with members of the Orthodox churches can enrich the Western churches with the contemplative and sapiential traditions which have flourished in those Christian communities. A deeper knowledge of Orthodox theology is also very helpful for members of the Western churches.

A practical way of promoting ecumenical dialogue and understanding between Christian groups is to encourage the exchange of church journals and to publish in the journals of other church groups. Promoting lectures by people of other religious groups is also a practical way of fostering the cause of ecumenical unity.

Dialogue and interfaith co-operation should not be limited to one's fellow Christians. Religious dialogue with Jews is also to be encouraged. Such dialogue can produce, among other benefits, an alleviation of the anti-Semitism which still afflicts some Christians. Religious man could broaden his religious horizon by promoting a serious interest in the various oriental religions and religious philosophies. Dialogue on topics of religious importance is to be encouraged with secular humanists and even with those who are professedly atheists.

Genuine religious dialogue requires communication and sharing not only of information about doctrines which may be divergent but also of religious intuitions and truths which may have something in common beneath surface differences. This dialogue seeks to discover the inner and the ultimate spiritual ground which underlies all articulated differences. Beyond the level of religious beliefs, religious man in dialogue seeks that deeper level which the major religious traditions have always claimed to reach, where they bear witness to a higher and more personal knowledge of God than that which is contained in exterior worship and doctrinal formulations. In all higher religions one encounters not only a claim to revelation in some form but also the record of special experiences in which the absolute and final validity of that revelation is in some way attested. It is generally recognized that this profound "sapiential" experience represents the deepest and most authentic fruit of religion itself. Religious man enters into religious dialogue with others both to understand better the religious experience of others and to gain better self-understanding.

Religious men in dialogue seek to affirm religious truth wherever it is found. Dialogue is not concerned with refutation of error as much as it is in discovering and promoting the truth. This does not imply facile syncretism or indifferentism but it does help avoid the tendency to affirm one's own understanding of truth by denying the truth of others. Anything that prevents efforts at real religious unity and co-operation among religious men, anything which prevents true dialogue with one's brother in Christ, should be eliminated.

Human solidarity and friendship, spontaneity and spiritual liberty are of the greatest importance in ecumenical work, and too much emphasis on organizational questions can inhibit fruitful dialogue. The promotion of ecumenical movements such as Una Sancta is a very important concern of religious man. Dogmatic differences, however serious and important they may be, are not today the main elements which prevent union between some Christian churches, but rather the attitudes on both sides which prevent openness to discovering religious truths wherever they may be. Conformity in religious belief is not the first requisite for persons who are seeking religious truth in dialogue. Sincerity and truthfulness with oneself and others are the things required. Since God made man for the truth, it is necessary for him to be truthful in order to know and recognize the truth. A common desire for truth and enlightenment is what brings religious men together in dialogue.

The Christian churches strive to protect man's highest spiritual, interior and personal freedom. All the other great world religions and religious philosophies aspire to promote the same type of human freedom. This common aspiration brings out the dignity and the grandeur of all religions. Christians should try to understand the other great world religious faiths in their search for the light of truth in all sincerity. They must not reject and despise non-Christian religious traditions as sources of pure error and blind superstition. Rather, Christians should show these great religious traditions the respect implied for them in the Christian Scriptures themselves.

The destiny of the whole human family has been in many ways under the control of the West for about four hundred years. Now the Orient is coming more into its own and aspiring to a more active share in directing the course of civilization and the fortunes of mankind. The majority of the human race lives in the Orient and is still largely untouched by the Christian tradition, which is predominantly Western in its cultural tone. For very practical reasons it behooves Western religious man to investigate the traditional religions and religious philosophies of the Orient. Care must be exercised to avoid facile generalizations and classifications of these ancient Eastern traditions as "religions" in the Western sense. Merton warned that those who are serious about interfaith dialogue with Orientals should avoid any loose and irresponsible syncretism which, on the basis of purely superficial resemblances and without serious study of qualitative differences, proceeds to identify all religions and religious experiences with one another, asserting that they are all equally true and supernatural and differ only in the accidentals of cultural expression. To adopt this view as axiomatic would from the very start guarantee that the interfaith dialogue would end in confusion. Westerners have a tendency to concentrate on doctrine and formulations, on explanations of ideas and philosophical presuppositions which confuse the issues for the Oriental. The common ground for ecumenical dialogue between Westerners and Orientals should be religious experience and an essential dimension is lacking if this religious experience is not taken into account. Fruitful interfaith dialogue requires that one be in touch with human experience itself and resist the tendency to substitute ideas and forms of authentic religious experience.

Any discussion of religious experience with Orientals would of course lead ultimately to the realm of Christian and oriental mysticism. This requires that the approach which the Christian takes toward these oriental religious cultures be personal, singular, existential and humanistic rather than doctrinal. The search for similarities and analogies in the realm of religious experience and technique can lead to a deeper understanding of one's own religious truth in the light of the religious truths of others. As Merton said, "Only Westerners who are still convinced of the importance of Christian mysticism are also aware that much is to be learned from the study of the religious experience and the technique of the Orientals."[13]

Both the Christian and the non-Christian who have deep experience of mystical realities can bear witness to higher religious values and experience in the world of today. They are witnesses to new depths of awareness and meaning in human existence. This dialogue in which the religious experience of both Christian and non-Christian traditions is studied and compared can aid in the general transformation of human consciousness. Both Christianity and the major oriental religious philosophies look primarily to this transformation of man's consciousness, a transformation and a liberation of the truths which are imprisoned in man by ignorance and error. The traditional oriental religious systems have long sought to liberate man from a half-real external existence in order to initiate him into a full and complete reality of an inner peace which is sacred and beyond explanation.

Zen Buddhism, of all the oriental religious philosophies, is the object of considerable interest in the West today, largely because of its paradoxical and highly existential simplicity, which stands as a challenge to the complicated and verbalistic ideologies which have become substitutes for religion, philosophy and spirituality in the Western world. It was Merton's opinion that Zen is at present most fashionable in America among those who are least concerned with moral discipline. Zen has become a symbol of moral revolt. It is true, the Zen man's contempt for conventional and formalistic social custom is a healthy phenomenon, but it is healthy only because it presupposes a spiritual liberty based on freedom from passion, egoism and self-delusion.

Zen is a basic natural attitude of mind, a kind of elemental simplicity and sanity which is not necessarily bound up with any religious creed or metaphysic, but which ought to be found in any spirituality worthy of its name. Dom Aelred Graham said, "Zen is essentially an attitude of directness and simplicity, uncomplicated by self-consciousness."[14] This meeting of Zen and the West has brought out many points in common between Zen and the Christian mystical tradition, but the similarities should not be pushed too far. There is, however, a solid basis for dialogue between the Christian and the Eastern experts on the ways of prayer and contemplation.

One of the purposes of Merton's Asian trip was to meet in dialogue with experts in oriental mysticism, so that "I can bring back to my monastery something of the Asian wisdom with which I am fortunate to be in contact, something that is very hard to put into words."[15] Even though Merton was very interested in oriental religions and in the investigation of their techniques of meditation, there is no doubt that he remained a loyal, committed Christian to the end of his life. On October 27, 1968, six weeks before his death, he gave a conference on prayer to a group of Christian men and women in Calcutta, the entire theme of which was union with Christ, identity with Christ and Christian maturity. All of his concerns in this conference were thoroughly Christian. In his first letter to all his friends from Asia, one month before his death, he said, "I wish you all peace and joy in the Lord and an increase of faith; for in my contacts with these new friends I also feel consolation in my own faith in Christ and His indwelling presence. I hope and I believe He may be present in the hearts of all of us."[16]

* * *

Religious man attempts to promote social change in a variety of cultural ways also. The culture in which he lives may in many respects inhibit his freedom to love his fellowmen in peace, so religious man tries in a socially responsible way to direct cultural change for the better. Those religious men who are intellectuals have a peculiar obligation to direct and control cultural change and to point out by their creative work, sometimes in the form of protest, how the cultural conditions can be changed for the improvement of man's condition. The intellectual has specific opportunities and obligations to help direct social change more than the ordinary citizen. Intellectuals, who are usually in the middle position between those who have more power to promote social change actively and those ordinary citizens who are most affected by social change, should for this reason have a heightened sense of social responsibility. They can ill afford to relinquish their social responsibility and leave the control of social change by default in the hands of those who are more apt either to be self-seeking manipulators or inhumane ideologists.

Intellectuals, who because of their particular abilities are in a unique position to direct and control social change, are liable to be subject to the seductive blandishments of the vested interests within the power structure. They are constantly being offered a privileged position in the societal structures which resist change. An intellectual is asked to surrender his own authenticity, his own freedom of decision. His power of resistance depends on his appreciation of his own gifts and on his desire to use his potential to improve man's condition. He should not be afraid of the independence, the solitude, the risk which his creative work involves. Especially in a technological society the intellectual has a responsibility to keep the liberating and humane aspects of life and the spiritual dimension of man before the public consciousness. The connection between art and culture and the social responsibility of artists were a lifetime interest of Merton, as his many writings on this subject attest.

Primary among the social responsibilities of the intellectual is his responsibility to his own work. If his work is authentic it will speak its own truth, and in so doing it will be in harmony with every other kind of truth—moral, metaphysical and mystical. The intellectual should not allow himself to be used or controlled by society. This requires that he struggle to maintain his artistic freedom to produce works of personal creativity, on their own terms and his, not those of the marketplace or of some political ideology.

Albert Camus was for Merton the prime example of an *artiste engagé* "not in the sense that he put his art at the service of some definite party program, but in the sense that he realized that his art would never be worth much without deep roots in human responsibility. One cannot be an artist if one is not first of all human, and humanity is not authentic without human concern and real involvement in common and critical problems. The lucidity of the artist and the lucidity of the free man must be one and the same."[17]

True artistic freedom can never be a matter of sheer

willfulness or artistic posturing. It is the outcome of human possibilities, understood and accepted on their own terms. The only valid witness of the artist's creative freedom is his work itself. The artist builds his own freedom and forms his own conscience by the work of his hands. So many myths have grown up about the business of "being an artist," and the special kind of life that artists are reported to live, that Merton thought it would be to the artist's advantage to first of all be free from myths about "art" and, in the West at least, even from myths about the threat which society offers to his "freedom." Merton tried in several of his writings to counter the myth of the artist as a special kind of person, the genius as hero and high priest in a cult of art, exempt from all ethical and aesthetic norms, whose real work is to promote himself.

Some have said that the artist is not a special kind of man, but that every man is a special kind of artist. In the case of a Christian artist, it could be said that the creative Christian is not a special kind of a Christian, but that every Christian has his own creative work to do, his own part in the mystery of the "new creation." The Christian artist should enter deeply into his own vocation and help open men's eyes to the eschatological dimension of Christian creativity as part of the full revelation of God by the restoration of all things in Christ.

On occasion the intellectual will also be drawn into active protest against the forces which threaten to restrict human freedom to love. Merton wrote, "It is the duty of writers to sound the alarm and fight against every form of slavery. That is our job."[18] Since the intellectual lives in a world where politics are decisive, he is indirectly committed to seek some political solutions to problems which endanger the freedom of man. Intellectuals should be in complete solidarity with those who are fighting for rights and freedom against inertia, hypocrisy and coercion. The intellectual should protest as effectively and as vocally as he can against man's present state of alienation in a world that seems to be without meaning for so many because of the moral, cultural and economic crisis of society. This protest certainly can be creative, and there is no doubt that it can bring forth great and living art. Sometimes this protest takes the form of anti-art and nonsymbol as a mode of rejection of the artistic culture of the society in which he lives. For example, Merton's last two volumes of poetry are considered to be anti-poetry, *Cables to the Ace* (1966) and *The Geography of Lograire* (1969). Anti-poetry is, in Merton's description, "an angry protest against contemporary, denatured language. Ironically, it declares that the ordinary modes of communication have broken down into banality and deception. It suggests that violence has gradually come to take the place of other, more polite communications. Where there is such a flood of words that all words are unsure, it becomes necessary to make one's meaning clear with blows."[19] One commentator, Thomas Landess, had this to say about Merton's later poetry: "Merton's loose prosody, his irreverent grammar and his occasional typographical ideosyncrasies are all carefully designed as an ironic reflection on the society he is depicting. . . . He deliberately adopted a debased rhetoric, not merely for ironic contrast, but in order to wring poetry out of bureaucratic prose, company memoes, news broadcasts, advertisements and the inane slang of the marketplace."[20] In painting, it was the abstract expressionist who lodged a deeply spiritual protest against conventional forms and subject matter and the mere formalistic treatment of religious themes. Abstract expressionism is, Merton believed, the natural locus in painting of twentieth-century religious concern.

In some totalitarian countries, the intellectual's response to the restriction of man's freedom is different. For him political activism and open protest are no longer rational options. His response is not anger, bitterness or rebellion, but his resistance finds expression in life-affirming love. He celebrates life itself, not in ideology, but in poetry, work and friendship.

Merton stressed the loyalty and love which intellectuals should have for one another in the face of organized tyranny. In this context Merton was thinking of the Russian novelist Boris Pasternak, with whom he had had some correspondence. Merton, who as an American enjoyed more political freedom than Pasternak, undertook to write in protest to the treatment given Pasternak by the Soviets at the time of the Nobel Prize award to Pasternak in the fall of 1958. He wrote to Aleksei Surkov, head of the Soviet Writer's Union, "I can assure you that this letter has nothing political about it. I am notoriously and conspicuously a non-political writer. . . . I am passionately opposed to every form of violent aggression in war, revolution or police terrorism, no matter who may exercise this aggression, and no matter for what 'good' ends. I am a man dedicated entirely to peace and to justice, and to the rights of man, whether as a citizen, a worker, or, in this case, a writer." He ends by saying, "I had thought momentarily that I might challenge you to publicize this letter in *Pravda* along with your arguments against it. Would such a thing be possible in Russia?"[21]

Another cultural concern of religious man is the general transformation of culture in the entire world. As the modern world enters into the "post-Christian age" in which Christian attitudes and ideas are relegated more and more to the minority, religious man should try to guide and direct cultural change in such a way as to protect man's basic freedom. It is not a matter of resisting social change. Social change is inevitable. But one should also be ready to point out in which respects change is not an improvement. The hope is that the future of civilization can in some way be directed away from mechanical formalization and spiritual disruption. To speak of the breakdown of the present Western culture is taken as an affront by those who think that the technological power of some Western societies represents the highest development of mankind. The very splendor and rapidity of the technological development are factors in the cultural and religious disintegration of the West. The past sixty years have seen violent disruptions in Western society and a radical overthrow of Western Christian culture. The social structures into which Christianity had fitted in the past have all but collapsed. Certain traditional beliefs have been emptied of inner vitality and mask the pseudo-spirituality or outright nihilism of modern man.

Many assume that Western society and Christianity are identical. That is not true. The future of the Church, the Body of Christ, is not subject to the vagaries of political history. There can be no ambiguity and no uncertainty about the Church's fulfillment of her appointed task on earth. For the Church is Christ Himself, present in the world He has redeemed. It is necessary to distinguish the Christian faith from the crisis and collapse of Western culture, and open it to entirely new perspectives. The effect of the previous identification of "God" with "Western civilization," regarded as still implicitly Christian, has been that the crisis of Western civilization has been thought to be also a crisis of Christianity and the Christian faith.

It is a historical fact that the Christian message was largely "Westernized" and it was within the context of Western civilization that the Christian message was brought to the world at large. It is also necessary to realize that Western Christians have largely failed in bringing the message of Christ to the rest of the world, both because of the unilateral imposition of Western culture on others in the process of transmitting the message of Christ and because they were unaware of the way that other cultures were already open to the possibility of God in man.

Western religious man is faced with the challenge of opening his horizons to new cultures and to intercultural exchange. The Christian community, which should never allow the basic Christian message to become too closely identified with any one particular national culture, faces a historic changeover of decisive importance. The unquestioned dominance of Western and European culture is at an end, and a whole new world is in formation. Just what the new civilization that is evolving will ultimately be is still unknown, but Christian religious man can contribute to and guide this evolution toward greater human freedom for men as the images of God. The message of Christ to man must cease being identified as "a white man's religion" and must be truly indigenous to all cultures, a liberating factor for all mankind.

Religious man should be open to the understanding and appreciation of the values of human traditions in all their kaleidoscopic variety.

That which most genuinely glorifies God is a catholicity true enough to respect the manifold variety of races, nations and traditions which seek their fulfillment and their *raison d'etre* in

Christ. Our natures do not manifest Him by being suppressed but by being transfigured by obedience to the Gospel. Just as Christ came to fulfill the Law, not to destroy it, so too He came to fulfill the authentic aspirations of the customs, traditions and philosophies of the Greeks and the "Gentiles" in general. Catholicism should then be English in England, not Italian; Chinese in China, not French; African in Africa, not Belgian.[22]

The cultural values of even small minorities should be protected and appreciated and their perpetuation encouraged to oppose the general cultural leveling and uniformity imposed on peoples by technological society.

Religious man can look forward to a new age for mankind, not an age of eclecticism and syncretism, certainly, but an age of understanding and adaptation that will be able to synthesize and make use of all that is good and noble in all the traditions of the past. If the world is to survive and if civilization is to endure its present crisis and recover the dimension of "wisdom," religious man must hope for a new world culture that takes account of all civilized traditions.

The quest for other "dimensions of wisdom" was one of the major reasons for Merton's trip to the Orient in 1968. "I do not know if I have anything to offer the Asians, but I am convinced that I have an immense amount to learn from Asia. One of the things I would like to share with the Asians is not only Christ but Asia itself."[23]

VI

EVALUATION AND CRITIQUE

The mind of a modern Renaissance figure such as Thomas Merton was too rich and expansive to be encapsulated in any one particular study. Many research studies will have to be made before the contribution of Merton to the self-understanding of modern man can be fully appreciated. The present study has attempted to thematize one basic aspect of his thought, the religious situation of every man before God and the social implications of that relationship for responsible social action. Merton himself did not thematize his own thought as it developed. That is the task of research scholars.

Merton's reflections on religious man were threaded through all his writings as the basic warp of the total fabric of his thought. The social implications of that thought, while of great importance, were strictly secondary to his primary concern, the relationship of man to God, the religious dimension of man. As one of his fellow monks said, "Merton was interested in only one thing, man's search for God."[1]

Merton's thought on this primary relationship has been analyzed and thematized in this study, and the basic principles of responsible social action have been derived.

The present evaluation of Merton's contribution will be based on his developing understanding of the reality of man's situation before God as he saw it. The categories used in this analytical and developmental study have all been taken from Merton's own writings. The other source of information used in this evaluation is the personal recollections of those who knew him best, his fellow monks at Gethsemani. These personal recollections have a unique value. These reflections of his fellow monks are, of course, personal opinions, and have to be weighed as such. They were not by any means consistently laudatory. They knew him best as a person who lived a deeply contemplative life even though he said or wrote very little about his own prayerful awareness of God. It was the prayerful awareness of God in his own life which led to the development of his social consciousness, the foundation on which he built his ideas of religious man's social obligations to his fellowmen in freedom and love. His purpose in writing his social commentaries was to get to the basic realities of man's social condition as he saw it, and to promote the improvement of that condition. This prayerful awareness of God enabled Merton to view the events of the contemporary world in the light of what he considered to be Christian truth, and to give his opinion on the responsible social actions which religious man should take in a contemporary context.

* * *

Merton was convinced that as a man of God he had an obligation to bring the realities of man's situation before God into contemporary focus. Though he often claimed that he was not an expert in politics, sociology, history and other formal disciplines, he felt that he could not remain a silent observer of the world's turmoil in the era of the 1950s and 1960s. He refused to be a guilty bystander and was determined to make his own voice heard, because his sense of commitment to the gospel message of peace and love would not allow him to do otherwise. One of his fellow monks responded to the question "What was Merton's self-image? Did he look upon himself as a social critic?" with "Louis didn't consider himself a great social critic. He wrote as he did because he considered it the Christian thing to say. He was on no great campaign. He was always concerned with man's basic relationship to God."[2] In his own words, he looked upon himself simply as a "self-questioning human person who, like all his brothers, struggles to cope with a turbulent, mysterious, demanding, exacting, frustrating, confused existence."[3] He wanted to hazard a few conjectures that were subjective, provisional, mere intuitions, and which needed to be completed by the thinking of others. As Merton said:

> If they suggest a few useful perspectives to others, then I am satisfied. I am more and more impressed by the fact that it is largely futile to get up and make statements about current problems. At the same time, I know that silent acquiescence in evil is also out of the question.[4]

He was concerned to get into circulation his ideas that might help to improve the quality of life of contemporary man. Merton himself fulfilled his own definition of a true religious writer in that he "tried to point the way to God."[5] He wanted to hold out to the suffering of the world hope in God and in mankind. The perspective from which he wrote was that of one deeply committed to the gospel message. Yet, he did not presume Christian faith in his readers, but he did presuppose at least common human concern, human understanding and good will. He always wrote from a Christian viewpoint. Moreover, he did not write only for Catholic publications but for a great variety of periodicals, both religious and secular. He was of the opinion that a Catholic writer who attempts to reach only Catholic readers proves by that very fact that he is not Catholic enough. Though he attempted to formulate some reflections on many aspects of the modern world and its problems, from the peculiar perspective that his monastic vocation gave him, he never claimed that that perspective was the only true one, or that he had better answers than anyone else.

Merton had a generative mind in that he had the power of presenting his own seminal ideas and reproducing the ideas of others in the light of the Christian Gospel. He was concerned with the search for truth through the process of formulating and refining these ideas, asking pertinent questions, not necessarily producing concrete answers to the world's problems. He was convinced that the quality of a person's interest in the welfare of mankind could be judged by the type of questions he asked. Since he was deeply aware of the problem of communication, his primary concern was the clarity of the presentation of his concept of the truth as he saw it in confrontation with basic human reality and in dialogue with others. He often actively sought criticism of his writings by sending his articles out to a variety of his friends and correspondents before publication to test their reactions. Keenly aware of his deficiencies as a social commentator because of his isolation from the mainstream of American life and the selectivity of the sources he had at his command, he responded gratefully to criticism and improved the presentation of his views through this refining process. Merton was always concerned with presenting his views on the Christian message to the world in a relevant way, in direct, easily understood language. His writings were concrete, existential, intuitive and deeply rooted in the everyday life of modern times. He was not concerned with presenting abstract ideas about God but with the living relationship of man with God in Christ, and this meant a concern for the love of man for man, that love by which one is known as a disciple of Christ. Without this love for his fellowmen, there is, for the Christian, no "Life in Christ" and therefore no true union with God, no true religion, only a religious ideology. Though his writing style was often repetitious, it was the deficiency of one who was basically a speaker, not a refined literary stylist.

Inconsistencies and even contradictions may be found in some of the presentations of his views. Where they occur, they are the results of his dialectical approach to the truth.

> I have become convinced that the very contradictions in my life are in some ways signs of God's mercy to me: if only because someone so complicated and so prone to confusion and self-defeat could hardly survive for long without special mercy. And since this in no way depends on the approval of others, the awareness of it is a kind of liberation.[6]

Speaking in the context of Merton's thought on monastic renewal, Father Tarcisius Conner, a fellow monk who knew Merton well, spoke in terms which apply to Merton in other concerns as well. He said:

> It has been frequently pointed out that [Merton] was a man of apparent contradictions. . . . This is explained by the fact that he was more intuitive than reflexive; more of a mystic or a prophet than a philosopher or a sociologist. . . . It merely indicated that [his] thought was always fragmentary and always "historical" in the sense that it was always centered on that portion of reality which he was confronting. . . . Because his personality was so dynamic and enthusiastic, he tended to give the impression that what he said in each case was an adequate expression of the matter at hand. In actual fact, when this was pointed out to him, he would be the first to say that there were many other elements which had to be considered besides what he said in this particular context.[7]

Merton's consistency was not always apparent on the surface, but an over-all view of the total volume of his literary production shows a consistency on a very deep level. When one of his fellow monks challenged him for some inconsistencies in his stated views, he responded jokingly with a reference to Emerson, "Consistency is the sign of a petty soul."[8] Another fellow monk observed, "Louis was always exploring ideas from a shifting viewpoint and on different levels. He could on occasion tend to be a bulldozer. Events and topics could easily trigger off deep emotions in him."[9]

Some would say he was not consistent because he put forth his views on the contemporary situation of religious man in a great variety of literary genre: poetry and anti-poetry, literary reviews and art criticism, historical studies and theological research papers, forewords, introductions and prefaces to the works of others, essays on topics of immediate social concern, parables, myths, satires, personal manifestoes and freedom songs, conferences and lectures to the Gethsemani community, as well as in a vast personal correspondence, the bulk of which is still unavailable to research scholarship.

Merton realized that he spoke only for himself. He was not in any way an official spokesman, nor did he represent an official position. The result of this was that he had great freedom as a writer, a freedom that was not always popular with others, and could write on topics which appealed to him with a minimum of regard for what those in official positions may have thought. He did not claim to present final answers to contemporary problems, just his own opinions, which were always subject to modification. In the opinion of those who knew him best, Merton was not opinionated but was a very modest man. He did not dominate others. His personal message was presented in such a way that he was not in the foreground. In the words of one of his fellow monks, "Merton didn't reveal himself in any way. He was very reluctant to talk about himself. He had ideas and wanted to write about them. He was interested enough to have his say. He did not look upon himself as any great social critic."[10]

If Thomas Merton developed into a man of Renaissance dimensions it was due to a variety of factors. His artistic temperament and humanistic bent were evident in his early years and were fostered both by family influences and the type of education he received. His conversion to the Christian faith in his early adult years determined the course of his religious development. Entrance into a monastic community channeled his talents and energies into a very specific mode of expression and his religious commitment was the dominant influence in his mature years. His life as a monk and his continuing quest for God enabled him to become a deeply contemplative person with compassionate concern for his fellowman. In his own judgment his priesthood expanded his religious and social horizons considerably.

The continual development and sharpening of his talents as a writer gave him a vehicle of expression which led to his gradual emergence as a commentator of considerable consequence on the problems facing men of all religious faiths. If toward the end of his life Merton's intentional world was truly global, with world-wide horizons of concern, it was because his personal world, that totality of relationships on the intellectual, moral and religious level with which he was consistently concerned, was itself universal and all-embracing. What he had to say was the natural outgrowth of who he was, a man completely committed to God and his fellowmen, a man of constant prayerful awareness of God and man's relationship to God. Thomas Merton, the social commentator, was the externalization of Father Louis, a man of deep religious experience.

This study of Merton's thought on the social dimension of religious man has been developmental because his interpreters must be willing to understand the slowly evolving development of the contexts, questions and categories of Merton's own personal life and intellectual career before they can understand his attitude toward some of the more pressing problems of the contemporary world on which he was writing in his later years.

The external world in which Merton lived changed and developed at an increasingly rapid rate during the course of his lifetime. The relatively quiet years prior to World War II gave place to an era of international conflict and confrontation, atomic and hydrogen bombs, the Cold War, global communications, global responsibilities and concern. Merton's physical isolation in the monastery in no way protected him from the consequences of these international developments. The changing patterns of life in the United States after its emergence as a global power left their mark on him and his emerging social consciousness. The problems of war and peace, racial conflicts and technological and economic development were as much his as of any other American.

The Christian Church, of which he was a devoted Catholic member, rapidly evolved during this period, especially under the influence of Pope John XXIII and Vatican Council II, so that the religious implications of world political, economic and social problems came more and more into the religious consciousness of Church groups. Changing patterns of belief, worship and religious style of life, differing attitudes toward Church leadership and authority, touched all committed Christians, including contemporary monastic communities. This led Merton to become increasingly concerned about the relevance of the Christian message in a world where Christians are becoming a decreasing minority in a "diaspora" situation. The external rigorism of the monastic style of life at his own Abbey of Gethsemani was gradually mitigated under Abbot James Fox, starting long before Vatican Council II, to provide greater personal freedom for the monks to achieve their primary purpose, a deepening of the contemplative spirit.

These external developments all fostered the gradual internal evolution of Merton's social concern and the expansion of his social horizons. As the external contexts of his life changed, so too Merton's own life evolved until he became what he was in his mature years, a committed contemplative person with a finely honed religious and social consciousness. He could say in his later years that he was not the same person who had written *The Seven Storey Mountain*, though he did indicate that much of what was spelled out in detail in his later books and articles had already been implied in his autobiography.

Merton had been trained, according to the custom of the times, in a traditional spirituality which emphasized withdrawal from the world in his earlier monastic years and he had, of necessity, little contact at that time with outside influences. It was the system of training that was in vogue at that time in most religious orders. But his own religious experience, the offices he held in the community, his increasing contacts with fellow intellectuals through correspondence and dialogue, his readings in modern theology and in the philosophy of Christian existentialism and personalism all combined to help him fashion a personal spirituality which was directed to his fellowmen and committed to effecting peaceful social change. Though he continued to write on topics which might be considered by some to be of strictly religious interest until the end of his life, his developing social conscience became more evident, emerging into public view slowly in the 1950s but more rapidly in the 1960s. It led him to write in increasing volume on topics of social concern which evidenced his commitment to the social betterment of all men. When he was surveying all his past literary production in 1962, he confessed, "The books of this fourth period (from 1956 on) seem the most significant to me."[11] He admitted that his perspectives shifted as he became increasingly committed to promoting social change, but he was ready to accept growth and development in his own life as a normal pattern of life.

> All life tends to grow like this, in mystery inscaped with paradox and contradiction, yet centered, in its very heart, on the divine mercy. . . . Without the grace of God, there could be no unity, no simplicity in our lives: only contradiction.[12]

It is true to say that there was no "earlier Merton" or "later Merton." The circumstances and contexts of his life changed: his writings on some topics took on a new emphasis and urgency, but in his mature years he never repudiated the fundamental ideas of his past. He developed the social implications of his fundamentally religious approach to human life. What he had to say on social topics was the mature outgrowth of who he was and what he believed, the externalization of his own religious interiority, achieved through deep contemplation of God and the human situation as he understood it. The increase of compassion for all men and for the world which became more evident in his later years may in itself be taken as external evidence of the deepening of his own contemplation.

* * *

What then is the lasting value of Merton's social commentary? It was the contemplative dimension of Merton's personal life that provided a unique quality to his social writings. Though he wrote very little about his own private contemplative prayer, some inferences can be made about the prayerful awareness of God in his life from his many writings on the ideal of contemplative prayer which he developed. There have been many contemplatives in the history of the Christian Church. There have also been many social commentators who have analyzed specific problems, promoted social programs and provided some tentative answers to social questions. But no social commentator in modern times has combined such a deeply contemplative view of reality with his social commentary on such a broad range of topics over such a long period as has Thomas Merton. His consistent effort was to get to the spiritual and philosophical roots of a social problem and expose them to the light of the Christian Gospel. In that effort he enjoyed a considerable degree of success. It was Merton's contemplative mode of approach to social problems which set him apart from other social commentators. Merton was singular in that his prayerful awareness of the reality of God and of God's purposes for man in the contemporary world provided a rare viewpoint from which to study human relationships. The insights he had into the reality of contemporary man's social situation were derived from his appreciation of man's relationship to God and to his fellowmen in a religious context. As a contemplative, he looked upon all human reality as transfigured and elevated by God's mercy and he brought to light insights based on his deepening sense of social responsibility and awareness. As he became more personally conscious of his union with all men as brothers in Christ, he spoke more insistently of the social implications of that religious belief. It was not that as a contemplative he had deeper practical insights into social, political or economic problems, but that he had the gift of appreciating the values that are permanent and authentically human. He was able to nurture a sense of personal responsibility before God and his own

personal independence from collective irresponsibility.
This gave to his social commentary a root in religious
reality, as he saw it, that is rare in modern times.

He was of the opinion that his contemplative life gave
him a dimension of awareness which could not be authentic without a certain degree of silence and interior solitude. He was cut off from the mass media, which he considered an advantage rather than a hindrance. One of
Merton's fellow monks said, "His sources of information
about the contemporary world were mostly literary, of
highly selected quality. Though his range was cosmopolitan, his selections were invariably weighty and serious."[13] While he did not provide answers to social problems, his work did provide a service to the modern world
through his contemplation, in that he listened in silence.
He raised questions. He was courageous in exposing what
the world tends to forget about itself, both for good and
for evil. Contemplative prayer unified Merton's own life
and led to his desire for unity with all men. His awareness
of God's presence in his life did not blind him to the
world and make him unconcerned about his fellowmen
by selfish withdrawal from the world. Contemplation
helped him to transform his vision of the world, and enabled him to see all men and the history of all mankind,
past and present, in the light of God. No human relationships were excluded by principle from his prayerful concern for human unity. He was convinced that a universal
compassion for all mankind was one of the true fruits of
contemplative prayer.

Merton emphasized that the social dimension of religious man evolves from the very core of his being. Religious man should be in some degree a contemplative
person. His prayerful awareness of the reality of God in
his life leads inevitably to a response in love to his fel-

lowmen. Merton's understanding of divine faith as a commitment to a person, though the doctrine was not uniquely his by any means, was real to him. Commitment to God, through the person of Jesus Christ, leads to direct social implications, based on religious man's true conversion to God and continual awareness of the presence and influence of God in his life.

Merton was convinced, from his personal experience, that it was necessary for religious man to find his true self in God before he could become socially involved. His understanding of the liberating force of human and divine love in the life of religious man, as the image of God in his freedom and social responsibility, was one of his major contributions to the contemporary self-understanding of religious man. He realized that the confusion of the world is in the human heart. It was Merton's firm opinion that if man is to have any influence in changing his social world, he has to change himself first.

In his capacity as social commentator, Merton enjoyed a personal freedom that was singular on the American scene. His freedom helped him to cultivate a certain quality of life, a level of awareness, a depth of consciousness by which he could attain a unique perspective, a critical distance, from which he could make his social commentaries. He developed an authentic understanding of God's presence in the world and of God's intentions for men, because, as a contemplative monk, he had a radically different way of being in the world. His intellectualist position gave him freedom to move about independently in the world of ideas. And his ideas were original in many ways, creative, iconoclastic and independent of the weight of official authority.

This freedom enabled Merton to be a prophetic voice in the Church in the sense that he reflected on the meaning of contemporary events in the light of the gospel message and tried to point out God's purposes for his fellowman. He was uninhibited in expressing his views on some contemporary events, but only after the "event itself had crystallized and he had prayed over it."[14] In the opinion of one of his fellow monks, "Merton realized that it would be folly for him to write about current topics, because of the dearth of information from his relatively restricted sources. After he had prayed over it, he was able to take a longer and deeper view."[15]

Merton was aware that as the reality of an event changed, so did its significance; and for him, the significance of events was intimately tied to the reality of man's position before God. He also exhorted those in authority in the Church, by personal letters and by statements in several of his published articles, to speak out clearly about what he considered to be the attitude Christians should have toward specific public and military policies. Merton was a social commentator by the very type of life which he led, since he looked upon his monastic life as a calculated form of relevant challenge to the world to reassess its basic value system.

The originality of Merton's views and insights was a direct consequence of his contemplative approach to life. Many other modern contemplatives could have written on the same topics from their own personal point of view. Few of them have. He was an original thinker in the sense that his insights were strictly his own, as is evidenced by the intimate journals and some of the books which he published: for example, *No Man Is an Island* (1955) and *Conjectures of a Guilty Bystander* (1966), in which he ruminated on a great variety of topics, many with social implications, in his own personal style. *Raids on the Unspeakable* (1966) is another example of his taking current topics and subjecting them to his own analysis. *Seeds of Contemplation* (1949) and *New Seeds of Contemplation* (1961) were peculiarly his own, reflecting his growth in religious experience. *The New Man* (1961) is an example of his ability to take traditional material and, in the light of his religious experience, produce a book that bears the impress of his character throughout. Much of his poetry was on social topics. *Emblems of a Season of Fury* (1963), *Cables to the Ace* (1968) and *The Geography of Lograire* (1969) contain original ideas that reflect his developing social conscience much more than his earlier volumes of poetry.

Merton admitted that he felt free to depart from current fashions and that he was a nonconformist. He rejoiced in the fact that he had his own tastes and ideas and could express them as they suited him. He was able to maintain his independence from popular movements that came into vogue quickly and faded just as rapidly. The only movement in which he participated was the peace movement in the early 1960s when it was largely unpopular and misunderstood. His function therein was more to provide ideas and general encouragement. His monastic isolation prevented him from playing a more active role.

Though he was concerned about maintaining his independence as a writer, he was not overly concerned with always being original in his social commentaries, as was evident both from his statements and from his mode of composition. Speaking of his attitude as a writer, he said:

> When something has been written, publish it, and go on to something else. You may say the same thing again, someday, on a deeper level. No one need have a compulsion to be utterly and perfectly "original" in every work he writes.

> All that matters is that the old be recovered on a
> new plane and be, by itself, a new reality.[16]

He did not hesitate to take the thoughts of others and
rework them in his own style to fit his purposes. This was
evident in his many book reviews wherein he would present his interpretations in the course of commenting on
the thoughts of others. He readily adopted Karl Rahner's
idea of the Christian in the "diaspora" situation and made
it his own. He popularized Gandhi's principles of nonviolent resistance and made them relevant for the American scene. Merton's ability to adapt the wisdom of the
ancients to modern times was evident from his "free
translations" of the Fathers of the Desert and Chuang
Tzu. Though in actual fact he derived many of his ideas
for his social commentaries from the writings of others,
all that he had to say on social topics bore the imprint of
his own religiously committed approach to human reality.

Since Merton expressed his opinions on such a wide
variety of topics in his published articles and books, it is
not surprising that he was subjected to criticism from
many sources. In 1953 a fellow monk with much experience in religious life, Dom Aelred Graham, O.S.B., wrote
a rather thorough and perceptive review of the books of
Merton to that date in which he characterized Merton as
"a modern man in reverse" and "a young man in a
hurry." Graham mentioned, among other things, a lack of
theological depth, overenthusiasm for "contemplation for
the masses," too much pessimism about "the world," a
poor historical sense, lack of reference to the New Testament in his writings and self-projection of his own experience into his theology.[17] Graham was correct on
many points, of course, but the review did not deter
Merton too much. One of his fellow monks said, "Merton

didn't seem inclined to defend himself on theological positions. He would speak deprecatingly about himself as a theologian. He told me once, 'My theology could be put on the head of a pin.'"[18] In later years, a personal friendship developed between Graham and Merton. They reviewed each other's books with enthusiasm; Graham was able to visit Gethsemani and meet Merton personally. Toward the end of Merton's life, it was Graham who, among others, arranged the invitation for Merton to attend the Far Eastern conference which occasioned his trip to the Orient.

Merton could be characterized as being overenthusiastic on several points, but it was a part of his personality that came through in his writings. He was also pessimistic on many occasions and sometimes painted a dark picture of the evils of the world. Yet he held a basically optimistic attitude toward man. Merton had a tempered optimism, realizing that under the grace of God man could change himself by true love of others. He always held out as a basis of human hope the Christian gospel message of love and reconciliation.

In the opinion of some, such as Dom Aelred Graham, Merton may have lacked theological depth in his earlier works. But he was not interested in theological speculation; rather he was concerned with a theology for life. During his years at Gethsemani he read widely in theology, patristics, medieval and modern thought and wrote several works on monastic theology which may stand the test of time. He was aware of the changes in contemporary theology and was up to date in the "death of God" theology and the movement for a "religionless Christianity." Yet he did make his mark as a theologian. For a compilation of essays in honor of Dr. Albert Schweitzer, which contained articles of many of the leading European theologians, the European editor asked Merton to write on "The Climate of Mercy." He was not timid when it came to the social implications of Christian theology. His first article specifically on war and peace was occasioned by his disagreement with an author on the morality of self-defense in a fallout shelter. In the early 1960s he was constantly urging American theologians to update the "just war theory" that was the basis of much of the theological speculation on war and peace. He started his own writings on this topic because he differed with one of the leading thinkers of American theology at that time, Father John Courtney Murray, S.J. Merton differed with Murray on several points, and subsequently wrote against Murray's position. "My most unpopular opinions have been those in which I have come out against the Bomb, the Vietnam war, and in fact our whole social system. I am supposed to be 'anti-modern' and 'opposed to technology' because I happen to disagree with the myth that technology, all by itself, is solving all man's problems."[19]

Merton could do scholarly work if he wished. Bennett Cerf asked him to do an Introduction to a new edition of Augustine's *The City of God*. He studied Augustine deeply for the first time and it turned out to be one of his best pieces of theological writing. His five articles on St. Anselm, as well as on several prescholastic monastic theologians, were the result of deep theological research. He could produce books with full scholarly apparatus, as evidenced by *Mystics and Zen Masters* (1967). *The Waters of Siloe* (1949), a popularized history of the Cistercian Order, was completely researched. His well-researched writings on the history of hermits in the Cistercian tradition helped bring about several changes in modern Trappist life. These facts, among others, would seem to contradict the statement made by one who recently wrote a book about Merton: "Merton was certainly lacking in a trained historical sense. . . ."[20]

In the minds of some, Merton may have been out of contact with the realities of life and too idealistic. But he did hold out the ideal of Christian love in a largely loveless world of conflict and confrontation. He realized his deficiencies because of his physical isolation from many sources of human experience due to his monastic seclusion, yet he tried as much as possible within the framework of his monastic life and his increasing desire for solitude to remedy that deficiency.

* * * *

Is Merton's thought relevant for today? Merton made many positive contributions to the self-understanding of contemporary man. His own religious attitude toward life was fundamental to him. His understanding of man's basic relationship to God and to his fellowmen in loving freedom was the perspective from which he formulated his opinions. One of his most positive contributions was his religious approach to social evils and to social change. He emphasized the ontological basis for the transformation of human life into the divine life as found in the incarnation of the word of God in Jesus Christ. Merton pointed out the social effects of this transformation of man and of man's union with the whole Christ in the Mystical Body.

His call for a new Christian consciousness which expands the social implications of Christian doctrine was a real contribution to human understanding. Merton publicized the Christian's responsibility to dissent, protest and oppose, by nonviolent resistance, social injustice in every sphere. In his writings on Gandhi he attempted to show that the Gandhian principles of nonviolent resistance to social evils are in conformity with the gospel message of love and reconciliation. In several of his writings he held out the hope of promoting real social change in the United States through nonviolent methods, despite the discouragement of some with that approach. His analysis of the problem of communication and his introduction of Christian elements into the solution of that problem, as well as his emphasis on open dialogue between opposing groups as a mode of deeper mutual understanding, are an advance in the cause of social justice and peace. He set an example for others in religious understanding by his promotion of ecumenical dialogue between Christian groups, and his expansion of the notion of ecumenism to include Jews and Asians furthered the cause of religious understanding. His study of oriental religions and his popularization of Asian modes of self-understanding through their contemplative techniques helped broaden the horizons of Western man. Merton's writings on the Christian liturgy also brought out the social dimensions of Christian community worship. One of his finest contributions was his presentation of the Christian message and its social implications in language that was simple, direct and readily intelligible to contemporary man with a minimum of esoteric terminology.

In the area of politics and the racial question, his analysis of the power structures which inhibit and oppose peaceful social change and the mode of approach to be taken in confrontation with those structures may well stand as one of his unique contributions to the cause of social justice. His writings on suppressed minorities helped call attention to that type of social injustice. His attacks on the myth of American self-righteousness and his analysis of the roots of totalitarianism, as well as his stand against any closed ideologies, helped alert Americans to the realities of their present situation. His understanding of the racial problem was not popular, but his anticipation of increased racial tension, unless the path to social equality is opened by peaceful means, seems to have been well founded.

One of his contributions to the peace movement was to help get the dialogue started. His study of the roots of war and the mode of opposing the military mentality helped to emphasize the religious aspects of the peace movement. By distinguishing the various types of pacifism Merton made it easier for religious man to further the cause of peace. He urged the reformulation of the "just war theory" to make it more relevant in the era of nuclear armaments and contributed to the cause of peace by his efforts to have religious leaders in the United States take a firm stand for world peace and against militarism at a time when their continued silence was a source of confusion to religiously minded men.

Merton contributed to contemporary man's self-understanding by his treatment of alienation in religious terms. He was also beginning to formulate a theology of work, focusing upon the spiritual reality and religious dimensions of everyday employment in the economic sphere. His analysis of the social evils of unrestrained technology and its attendant dehumanization, as well as his early concern for the ecological problems brought on by modern technology, are important contributions to man's understanding of his present situation. Merton also on several occasions urged his fellow intellectuals to take a more active part in promoting social justice.

Thomas Merton had a message for his contemporaries on the importance of a religious viewpoint in confronting social problems and used his literary talents to present that message in a relevant way. Through his writings he was able to identify himself with his contemporaries and bring the light of his own religious experience to bear on the understanding of modern social problems. The lasting influence of his work is, of course, difficult to judge at this time. Though he was relevant to his own times, history itself will judge the relevance and influence of this deeply religious man on future generations.

Notes

CHAPTER I: THOMAS MERTON—THE MAN AND HIS WRITINGS

1. Thomas P. McDonnell, "An Interview with Thomas Merton," *Motive*, XXVIII (October 1967), 31–32.

2. Sister M. Julie, "New Directions Presents a Catholic Poet," *America*, LXXIII (July 21, 1945), 316.

3. Thomas Merton, *The Sign of Jonas* (New York: Harcourt, Brace & Co., 1953). Edition cited: Image Books, Doubleday & Company, 1956, p. 171.

4. Sister M. Thérèse, "Todo y Nada: Writing and Contemplation," unpublished material on *Writing and Contemplation* from the original manuscript of Thomas Merton's *The Seven Storey Mountain*. Introduction by Sister M. Thérèse, *Renascence*, II, No. 2 (Spring 1950), 91.

5. Sister M. Julien Baird, "Blake, Hopkins and Thomas Merton," *Catholic World*, CLXXXIII (April 1956), 48.

6. Howard Gold, "Short Notice on The Behaviour of Titans," *Jubilee*, IX (October 1961), 46.

7. Thomas Merton, *Conjectures of a Guilty Bystander* (New York: Doubleday & Company, 1966). Edition cited: Image Books, Doubleday & Company, 1968, p. 348.

8. Thomas Merton, "The True Legendary Sound: The Poetry and Criticism of Edwin Muir," *The Sewanee Review*, LXXV (Spring 1967), 318.

9. Stefan Baciu, "Latin America and Spain in the

Poetic World of Thomas Merton," *Revue de Littérature Comparée*, XLI (1967), 293.

10. Personal recollection

11. William Robert Miller, "Is the Church Obsolete?: The Crisis of Religion in a Secular Age," *The American Scholar*, XXXVI (Spring 1967), 236.

12. Thomas Merton, *The Seven Storey Mountain* (New York: Harcourt, Brace & Co., 1948). Edition cited: Signet Books, New American Library, 1952, p. 9.

13. *Ibid.*, p. 11.

14. Merton, *Conjectures of a Guilty Bystander*, p. 200.

15. Merton, *The Sign of Jonas*, p. 235.

16. Thomas Merton, "The White Pebble," in *Where I Found Christ*, ed. by John O'Brien (New York: Doubleday & Company, 1950), p. 241.

17. Thomas Merton, "Thomas Merton Replies to a Perceptive Critic," *National Catholic Reporter*, III, No. 12 (January 18, 1967), 4.

18. Thomas Merton, "Theology of Creativity," *The American Benedictine Review*, XI (September-December, 1960), 206.

19. Thomas Merton, *Raids on the Unspeakable* (New York: New Directions, 1966), p. 181.

20. *Ibid.*, p. 179.

21. *Ibid.*, p. 180.

22. John Howard Griffin and Thomas Merton, *A Hidden Wholeness: The Visual World of Thomas Merton*. Photographs by Thomas Merton. Text by John Howard Griffin (Boston: Houghton Mifflin Co., 1970), Merton quoted inside title page.

23. Merton, *Conjectures of a Guilty Bystander*, p. 149.

24. Griffin and Merton, *A Hidden Wholeness*, pp. 3-5.

25. Merton, *The Seven Storey Mountain*, p. 400.

26. *Ibid.*, p. 382.

27. Merton, *The Sign of Jonas*, p. 96.

28. *Ibid.*, p. 96.

29. *Time*, December 20, 1968, p. 65.

30. Merton, *The Sign of Jonas*, p. 58. Thomas Merton, *A Thomas Merton Reader* (New York: Harcourt, Brace & World, 1962), p. ix.

31. Merton, *The Sign of Jonas*, p. 58.

32. Merton, *A Thomas Merton Reader*, p. ix.

33. Naomi Burton Stone, "Thomas Merton's Mountain," *Sign*, XLIV (October 1964), 47.

34. Merton, *The Sign of Jonas*, p. 95.

35. *Ibid.*, p. 247.

36. Thomas P. McDonnell, "An Interview with Thomas Merton," *Motive*, XXVIII (October 1967), 31–32.

37. Thomas Merton, Preface to *The Secular Journal of Thomas Merton* (New York: Farrar, Straus & Cudahy, 1959). Edition cited: Image Books, Doubleday & Company, 1968, p. 10.

38. Personal recollection

39. Merton, *Conjectures of a Guilty Bystander*, p. 189.

40. *Ibid.*, p. 245.

41. *Ibid.*, p. 264, written between 1956–65.

42. Thomas Merton, *Faith and Violence* (Notre Dame, Indiana: University of Notre Dame Press, 1968), p. 205.

43. Merton, *A Thomas Merton Reader*, p. x.

44. Sister Mary Browning, *Kentucky Authors* (Evansville, Indiana: Keller-Crescent Co., 1968), p. 215.

45. Merton, *A Thomas Merton Reader*, pp. ix–x.

46. McDonnell, "An Interview with Thomas Merton," pp. 33–34.

47. Thomas Merton, "Is the World a Problem?"*Commonweal*, LXXXIV, No. 66 (June 3, 1966), 305–6.

48. Merton, Preface to Japanese edition of *The Seven Storey Mountain*, p. 5, 1964.

49. Thomas Merton, "The Monk Today," *Latitudes*, II (Spring 1968), 13.

50. Thomas Merton, "Letter to Lorraine," *Blue Print*, X (Fort Lee, New Jersey: Holy Angels Academy, June 1964), 12–13.

51. Merton, *The Seven Storey Mountain*, pp. 37, 12, 41, 43, 48.

52. *Ibid.*, p. 116.

53. *Ibid.*, pp. 248, 250–51.

54. *Ibid.*, p. 254.

55. Merton, *The Sign of Jonas*, p. 21.

56. Thomas Merton, "In Silentio," in *Seasons of Celebration* (New York: Farrar, Straus & Giroux, 1965), pp. 204–15, originally written, 1955.

57. Thomas Merton, *Silence in Heaven: A Book on the Monastic Life*. Text by Thomas Merton, and ninety photographs. (New York: Studio Publications, in association with Thomas Y. Crowell, 1956), pp. 26–30.

58. Thomas Merton, *Basic Principles of Monastic Spirituality* (Trappist, Kentucky: Abbey of Gethsemani, 1957), p. 34, italics his.

59. Thomas Merton, Introduction to *God Is My Life: The Story of Our Lady of Gethsemani*. Photographs by Shirley Burden. (New York: Reynal & Company, 1960), pp. 1, 3.

60. Merton, *Conjectures of a Guilty Bystander*, pp. 14–15, written between 1956–65, italics his.

61. *Ibid.*, pp. 179–80.

62. *Ibid.*, pp. 291–92.

63. *Ibid.*, pp. 337–38, italics his.

64. Thomas Merton, Preface to *In Search of a Yogi* by Dom Denys Rutledge (New York: Farrar, Straus & Co., 1962), p. x.

65. Thomas Merton, Preface to *No More Strangers* by

Philip Berrigan (New York: The Macmillan Company, 1965), p. 4.

66. Thomas Merton, *Contemplation in a World of Action* (Garden City, N.Y.: Doubleday & Company, 1971), p. 183, citation from Claude Lévi-Strauss, *Tristes Tropiques* (Paris, 1966).

67. Merton, *The Sign of Jonas*, p. 225.

68. *Ibid.*, p. 198.

69. Merton, "The White Pebble," p. 245.

70. *Ibid.*, pp. 248–49.

71. Merton, *The Sign of Jonas*, p. 168.

72. *Ibid.*, p. 168.

73. Personal recollection

74. Browning, *Kentucky Authors*, p. 214.

75. Father John Eudes Bamberger, "Thomas Merton—The Cistercian," *Continuum*, VII, No. 2 (Summer 1969), 232.

76. Father M. Flavian Burns, "Homily at the Mass for Father M. Louis," *Cistercian Studies*, III, No. 4 (1968), 279.

77. Thomas Merton, "My Campaign Platform for non-Abbot and permanent keeper of the present doghouse," *Unicorn Journal*, I (Spring 1968), 95–96.

78. Thomas Merton, quoted from a letter by Dr. James P. Shannon, *New Mexico*, XLIX (May-June 1971), 21.

79. Personal recollection

80. Colman McCarthy, "Renewal Crisis Hits Trappists," *National Catholic Reporter*, IV, No. 8 (December 13, 1967), 5.

81. Thomas Merton, *Disputed Questions* (New York: Farrar, Straus & Cudahy, 1960), p. 154.

82. Thomas Merton, "Community, Politics and Contemplation," *Sisters Today*, XLII, No. 5 (January 1971), 245.

280

83. Merton, *Contemplation in a World of Action*, pp. 132–33, 167–68.

CHAPTER II: THOMAS MERTON AS SOCIAL CRITIC

1. Merton, *Faith and Violence*, p. 147.
2. Thomas Merton, "Letter to Friends, Pre-Lent, 1968," p. 2 (unpublished).
3. Merton, "Is the World a Problem?", pp. 305–6.
4. Merton, *Faith and Violence*, p. 213.
5. Thomas Merton, "Letter to Friends, Spring 1967," p. 1 (unpublished).
6. *Ibid.*, p. 1.
7. Merton, "The Monk Today," p. 13.
8. Thomas Merton, "Letter to Friends, Summer 1968," p. 1 (unpublished).
9. Merton, "Letter to Friends, Pre-Lent, 1968," p. 1 (unpublished).
10. Merton, *Contemplation in a World of Action*, Introduction by Jean Leclercq, pp. xiv, xviii.
11. Merton, *Faith and Violence*, p. 68.
12. Thomas Merton, "A Buyer's Market for Love?" *Ave Maria*, CIV, No. 26 (December 24, 1966), 27.
13. Merton, *Contemplation in a World of Action*, p. 23.
14. Thomas Merton, *The Behaviour of Titans* (New York: New Directions, 1961), pp. 65–71.
15. Merton, Preface to Japanese Edition of *The Seven Storey Mountain*, 1964, p. 4.
16. Personal recollection
17. Personal recollection
18. Personal recollection
19. Personal recollection

CHAPTER III: RELIGIOUS MAN IN THE WRITINGS OF THOMAS MERTON

1. Merton, *Conjectures of a Guilty Bystander*, p. 334.

2. Thomas Merton, "Creative Silence," *Baptist Student*, XLVIII (February 1969), 21.

3. Merton, *Faith and Violence*, p. 111.

4. Thomas Merton, *New Seeds of Contemplation* (New York: New Directions, 1961), pp. 32–33.

5. Thomas Merton, "Letter to T. L. Dickson," *Religious Book Guide* (July-August 1970), 10.

6. Thomas Merton, Introduction to *The Monastic Theology of Aelred of Rievaulx* by Amedee Hallier (Spencer, Mass.: Cistercian Publications, 1969), p. ix.

7. Seely Beggiani, "A Case for Logocentric Theology," *Theological Studies*, XXXII, No. 3 (September 1971), 406.

8. Merton, *Conjectures of a Guilty Bystander*, p. 178.

9. *Ibid.*, p. 154.

10. Merton, *New Seeds of Contemplation*, p. 154.

11. *Ibid.*, p. 268.

12. Thomas Merton, *The New Man* (New York: Farrar, Straus & Cudahy, 1961), p. 188.

13. Thomas Merton, *Thoughts in Solitude* (New York: Farrar, Straus & Cudahy, 1958), p. 123.

14. Thomas Merton, *Contemplative Prayer* (New York: Herder and Herder, 1969), p. 39.

15. Merton, *Disputed Questions*, "The Power and Meaning of Love," pp. 123–25.

16. Quotation from Vatican Council II, "Pastoral Constitution on the Church in the Modern World," No. 19, in William Abbott, ed., *The Documents of Vatican II* (New York: America Press, 1966), p. 217.

17. Thomas Merton, "Letter to Friends, Christmas Morning, 1966" (unpublished).

18. Thomas Merton, "Easter Letter to Friends, 1967" (unpublished).

19. Merton, *The New Man,* pp. 125–26.

20. Thomas Merton, "On Prayer: Conference at Darjeeling, India," Thomas Merton Room, Gethsemani, 1968 (unpublished).

21. Merton, *Seasons of Celebration,* p. 217.

22. Quoted by David Steindl-Rast, "Recollections of Thomas Merton's Last Days in the West," *Monastic Studies,* VII (1969), 2.

23. Thomas Merton, Foreword to *The Mysticism of the Cloud of Unknowing: A Modern Interpretation* by William Johnston (New York: Desclée and Company, 1967), p. x.

24. Thomas Merton, "Symbolism: Communication or Communion?" *Mountain Path* (India), III, No. 4 (October 1966), 345.

25. Thomas Merton, *Bread in the Wilderness* (New York: New Directions, 1953), pp. 37–38, 136.

26. Merton, *Seasons of Celebration,* pp. 22–23.

27. *Ibid.,* pp. 10, 55.

28. Thomas Merton, "First and Last Thoughts: An Author's Preface," in *A Thomas Merton Reader,* pp. x–xi.

29. Thomas Merton, "Christian Humanism," *Spiritual Life,* XIII (1967), 226.

30. Merton, Introduction to *God Is My Life,* p. 2.

31. Personal recollection

32. Merton, "A Buyer's Market for Love?" p. 7.

33. Thomas Merton, *The Living Bread* (Farrar, Straus & Cudahy, 1956), p. xii.

34. Thomas Merton, *Seeds of Destruction* (New York: Farrar, Straus & Giroux, 1964), p. 233.

35. *Ibid.*, p. 254.

36. Merton, "A Buyer's Market for Love?" pp. 8, 10.

37. Patrick Hart, "Thomas Merton," *The Lamp*, LXIX, No. 1 (January 1971), 2.

38. Merton, *New Seeds of Contemplation*, p. 36.

39. *Ibid.*, pp. 32–33.

40. Merton, *Contemplative Prayer*, p. 84.

41. Thomas Merton, "The Prison Meditations of Father Delp," in *Faith and Violence*, p. 55.

42. Merton, *New Seeds of Contemplation*, p. 21; Merton, Preface to *A Thomas Merton Reader*, p. xi.

43. Thomas Merton, Introduction to *The Plague* by Albert Camus (New York: The Seabury Press, 1968), pp. 4–5.

44. Merton, *Conjectures of a Guilty Bystander*, p. 265.

45. Thomas Merton, from private notes of one who heard a homily given by Merton in a small chapel at Gethsemani, May 29, 1968 (unpublished).

46. Merton, *Conjectures of a Guilty Bystander*, pp. 143–44.

47. Thomas Merton, "The Climate of Mercy," in *L'Evangile de la Misericordé*, Hommage du Dr. A. Schweitzer, presenté par Alphonse Goettmann (Paris: Les Éditions du Cerf, 1964), p. 9.

48. Thomas Merton, Prologue to *No Man Is an Island* (New York: Harcourt, Brace & Co., 1955), pp. 16–17.

49. Thomas Merton, "Merton View on Monasticism," the Washington *Post* (January 18, 1969), p. C9.

50. Merton, *The New Man*, pp. 168–69. Citation from F. Prat, *The Theology of St. Paul* (Westminster, Maryland, 1952), Vol. I, p. 300.

51. Merton, *The New Man*, pp. 189–90.

52. Thomas Merton, "Concerning the Collection in the Bellarmine College Library," in *Thomas Merton Study Center*, November 10, 1963, pp. 14–15.

53. Merton, *The Living Bread,* pp. 150–51.

54. Thomas Merton, *Life and Holiness* (New York: Herder and Herder, 1963), pp. 24, 31.

55. Merton, *The New Man,* pp. 67–78.

CHAPTER IV: THE SOCIAL DIMENSION OF RELIGIOUS MAN

1. Merton, *Conjectures of a Guilty Bystander,* pp. 81–82.

2. Merton, "Is the World a Problem?" p. 306.

3. Thomas Merton, *Opening the Bible* (Collegeville, Minnesota: The Liturgical Press, 1970), pp. 3–4.

4. "Pastoral Constitution on the Church in the Modern World," in *The Documents of Vatican II,* ed. by W. M. Abbott (New York: America Press, 1966), 38, p. 236.

5. Thomas Merton, "Where the Religious Dimension Enters In," *Center Letter,* No. 3 (1968), General Correspondence, unpaged, published by The Deerfield Foundation, Lakeville, Connecticut.

6. Merton, *Faith and Violence,* p. 208.

7. Merton, *Conjectures of a Guilty Bystander,* p. 317.

8. Merton, *Faith and Violence,* p. 263.

9. Leslie Dewart, "A Post-Christian Age?" (Dialogue with Merton.) *Continuum,* I (Winter 1964), 564.

10. Thomas Merton, "Letter to Friends, Septuagesima Sunday, 1967," (unpublished).

11. McDonnell, "An Interview with Thomas Merton," p. 41.

CHAPTER V: SPECIFIC SOCIAL CONCERNS OF RELIGIOUS MAN

1. *Pacem in Terris,* quoted on the flyleaf of *Gandhi on Nonviolence,* ed. with an Introduction by Thomas Merton, 1965.

2. *Breakthrough to Peace,* ed. by Thomas Merton, with an Introduction and a Contribution, "Peace: A Religious Responsibility" (New York: New Directions, 1962), p. 10.

3. Thomas Merton, "Nonviolence Does Not—Cannot—Mean Passivity," *Ave Maria,* CVIII (September 7, 1968), 9.

4. Thomas Merton, "Neither Caliban nor Uncle Tom," *Liberation,* VIII (June 1963), 21–22.

5. *Ibid.,* p. 20.

6. Thomas Merton, "A Catch of Anti-Letters," *Voyages,* II (Summer 1968), 47.

7. *Ibid.,* p. 50.

8. Thomas Merton, "Lenten Letter to Friends, 1967," p. 1 (unpublished).

9. Merton, *The Secular Journal of Thomas Merton,* p. 26.

10. Thomas Merton, "The Wild Places," *The Catholic Worker,* XXXV (June 1968), 6.

11. *Ibid.,* p. 6.

12. Thomas Merton, "Letter to Editor," *Center Magazine,* a publication of The Center for the Study of Democratic Institutions, Santa Barbara, California, IV (1968), 7.

13. Thomas Merton, *Zen and the Birds of Appetite* (New York: New Directions, 1968), p. 21.

14. Michael Zeik, "Zen Catholicism," *Commonweal,* LXXVIII (June 14, 1963), 324.

15. Thomas Merton, "Asian Letter No. 1," New Delhi, India, November 9, 1968, *Cistercian Studies,* III, p. 275.

16. *Ibid.*

17. Thomas Merton, "Camus: Journals of the Plague Years," *The Sewanee Review,* LXXV (October-December, 1967), 727.

18. Thomas Merton, "Albert Camus and the Church," in *A Penny a Copy,* ed. by Thomas C. Cornell and James

H. Forest (New York: The Macmillan Company, 1968), p. 265.

19. Thomas Merton, "War and the Crisis of Language," in *Thomas Merton on Peace*. With an Introduction by Gordon C. Zahn. (New York: The McCall Publishing Company, 1971), p. 235.

20. Thomas Landess, "Monastic Life and the Secular City," *The Sewanee Review*, LXXVII (Summer 1969), 534.

21. Thomas Merton, "Letter to Surkov," in *A Penny a Copy*, pp. 285, 287.

22. Thomas Merton, "The English Mystics," in *Mystics and Zen Masters* (New York: Farrar, Straus & Giroux, 1967), p. 130.

23. Merton, "Letter to a Chinese Priest in California," in *Seeds of Destruction*, p. 287, 1962.

CHAPTER VI: EVALUATION AND CRITIQUE

1. Personal recollection
2. Personal recollection
3. Merton, "Is the World a Problem?" p. 305.
4. Thomas Merton, "Events and Pseudo-Events: Letter to a Southern Churchman," in *Faith and Violence*, p. 147, 1966.
5. Albert Fowler, "A Visit with Thomas Merton," *Friends Journal*, VII (December 1, 1966), 491.
6. Merton, "First and Last Thoughts: An Author's Preface," in *A Thomas Merton Reader*, p. x.
7. Tarcisius Conner, "Merton, Monastic Exchange and Renewal," *Monastic Exchange* (Summer 1969), 2.
8. Personal recollection
9. Personal recollection

10. Personal recollection

11. Merton, "First and Last Thoughts: An Author's Preface," in *A Thomas Merton Reader*, p. ix.

12. *Ibid.*, pp. vii, x–xi.

13. Personal recollection

14. Personal recollection

15. Personal recollection

16. Merton, "First and Last Thoughts: An Author's Preface," in *A Thomas Merton Reader*, pp. ix–x.

17. Aelred Graham, "Thomas Merton: A Modern Man in Reverse," *The Atlantic Monthly*, CXCI (January 1953), 70–74.

18. Personal recollection

19. McDonnell, "An Interview with Thomas Merton," p. 34.

20. James T. Baker, *Thomas Merton: Social Critic* (Lexington, Kentucky: The University Press of Kentucky, 1971), p. 113.